Infrastructure as Code (IAC) Cookbook

Over 90 practical, actionable recipes to automate, test, and manage your infrastructure quickly and effectively

Stephane Jourdan

Pierre Pomès

BIRMINGHAM - MUMBAI

Infrastructure as Code (IAC) Cookbook

First published: February 2017

Production reference: 1150217

Published by Packt Publishing Ltd.
Livery Place
35 Livery Street
Birmingham B3 2PB, UK.

ISBN 978-1-78646-491-0

www.packtpub.com

Credits

Authors
Stephane Jourdan
Pierre Pomès

Reviewer
Pierre Mavro

Commissioning Editor
Kartikey Pandey

Acquisition Editor
Prachi Bisht

Content Development Editors
Sanjeet Rao
Monika Sangwan

Technical Editor
Devesh Chugh

Copy Editor
Tom Jacob

Project Coordinator
Kinjal Bari

Proofreader
Safis Editing

Indexer
Mariammal Chettiyar

Graphics
Kirk D'Penha

Production Coordinator
Shantanu N. Zagade

Cover Work
Shantanu N. Zagade

About the Authors

Stephane Jourdan is a passionate infrastructure engineer, enthusiastic entrepreneur, zealous trainer, and continuous learner, working on innovative infrastructures since the early 2000s. He focuses equally on tools and culture, in environments as different as startups, online audio/video media, e-commerce, and semi-conductors. The common point between all these experiences is that success comes with rigor, technical repeatability, communication, and a shared team culture. He co-founded an infrastructure automation consultancy (`https://www.linkedin.com/company/green-alto`), a web radio (`http://phauneradio.com/`), a container/serverless platform for developers (`https://www.squarescale.com/`), and a sound design studio (`http://www.tarabust.com/`).

When Stephane isn't starting or contributing to new open source projects, he's usually found hiking in remote places with his camera.

Pierre Pomès is a senior enthusiastic engineer of open source technologies and a Linux adept since 1994. He has been working in the IT industry for the last twenty years mostly in C development, system administration, and security including PCI-DSS. He is currently an architect and a DevOps team leader for Reservit, an online hotel booking engine. He has also contributed to the pfSense project.

About the Reviewer

Pierre Mavro lives in a suburb of Paris. He's an open source software lover and has been working with Linux for more than 10 years now. Today, he works as a Lead SRE at Criteo, where he manages distributed systems and NoSQL technologies. During the last few years, he has been designing distributed and high-available infrastructures on public/private cloud infrastructures. He also worked for financial software companies on high-frequency trading technologies. He also wrote a book on MariaDB named *MariaDB High Performance* by *Packt Publishing*. He is also one of the co-founders of Nousmotards, an application for bike riders.

www.PacktPub.com

Customer Feedback

Thanks for purchasing this Packt book. At Packt, quality is at the heart of our editorial process. To help us improve, please leave us an honest review on this book's Amazon page at `https://www.amazon.com/dp/1786464918`.

If you'd like to join our team of regular reviewers, you can email us at `customerreviews@packtpub.com`. We award our regular reviewers with free eBooks and videos in exchange for their valuable feedback. Help us be relentless in improving our products!

Table of Contents

Preface

In continuously evolving environments, operations and development teams are increasingly working together, using tools and techniques and sharing a common culture popularized as part of the DevOps movement. From development to production, a common tooling and approach emerged—often borrowed from developers and the agile techniques.

Now that APIs are everywhere in the datacenter, automation took over every aspect and every step of what used to be a sysadmin or IT job—infrastructure is now basically code, and should be considered as such while working alone in development or in production within a distributed team.

Learning the most important tools, techniques, and workflows that fit in an infrastructure-as-code description can be a daunting task, and many teams can either be misled or discouraged by the amount of information, change, and knowledge required to switch to infrastructure-as-code.

This book has been written keeping in mind all those teams that we have met in the past few years through our respective jobs—teams interested in DevOps, automation, and code, sometimes already doing part of it quite well, but willing to discover other tools and techniques, discovering how they could do better by improving the quality of their code, the stability of their infrastructure, the scalability of their services, the speed of their deployments, the efficiency of team work, and the feedback loop.

This book is a humble attempt to cover everything related to infrastructure-as-code, based on our real-life experience, from development workflows with Vagrant to complex production infrastructure deployments with Terraform or Ansible, from configuration management essentials using Chef and Puppet to advanced Test-Driven Development (TDD) techniques, and thorough infrastructure code coverage testing. It will also give insights and advanced Docker techniques, and much more. Whenever it was possible or relevant, we tried to show alternative ways of doing the same thing with another tool or approach, so that everyone with any prior knowledge of the subject can still find something to learn in any section of the book.

We hope you'll get much out of this book, and that automating and testing using infrastructure-as-code will be as fun for you as it's been for us to write about.

What this book covers

Chapter 1, *Vagrant Development Environments*, is all about automated development environments using Vagrant. Launch simple or complex environments, simulate various virtual networking configurations, combine Vagrant and Docker or the Amazon cloud, and hand over the provisioning of virtual machines to Chef and Ansible. All examples are self-contained real-life little projects.

Chapter 2, *Provisioning IaaS with Terraform*, is everything needed to get started with Terraform on Amazon Web Services, from managed database servers to log handling, storage, credentials, Docker registries, and EC2 instances.

Chapter 3, *Going Further with Terraform*, sheds light on some more advanced techniques of using Terraform code, such as dynamic data sources, separate environments, Docker, GitHub or StatusCake integration, team work, and how the code linter works.

Chapter 4, *Automating Complete Infrastructures with Terraform*, will show and describe complete, real-life Terraform code for infrastructures on Amazon Web Services, Digital Ocean, OpenStack, Heroku, Packet, and Google Cloud. We'll deploy a Docker Swarm cluster on a bare metal CoreOS cluster for containers, an n-tier web infrastructure, or a GitLab + CI combo.

Chapter 5, *Provisioning the Last Mile with Cloud-Init*, explores everything we can do with cloud-init code—file management, server configuration, adding users and keys, repositories and packages, or examples of extensions such as Chef, CoreOS, and Docker.

Chapter 6, *Fundamentals of Managing Servers with Chef and Puppet*, shows the essentials of using Chef code to automate an infrastructure. From the workstation setup to writing our own recipes to managing external cookbooks, this chapter contains it all—we'll manage packages, services, files, dynamic templates, dependencies, relationships, shared data, and more, all using code. Alternative ways of doing similar actions using Puppet code are also shown for you to have a better view of the ecosystem.

Chapter 7, *Testing and Writing Better Infrastructure Code with Chef and Puppet*, is all about advanced techniques of testing code for quality and sustainability. It also covers unit and integration testing, linters, and tools for Chef and Puppet, so that you'll produce the best infrastructure code possible.

Chapter 8, *Maintaining Systems Using Chef and Puppet*, shows advanced features made possible by Chef or Puppet code, such as scheduled convergence, encrypted secrets, environments, live system information retrieval, application deployments, and workflows or practices to be safe.

Chapter 9, Working with Docker, is about using Docker containers from a developer point of view—choosing a base image, optimizations, tags, versioning, deploying Ruby-on-Rails or Go applications, networking, security, linting, and using our own durable private registry—all using simple Docker instructions—as code.

Chapter 10, Maintaining Docker Containers, is showing more advanced Docker usage for developers and engineers, such as code testing, automated build pipelines and Continuous Integration, automated vulnerability scanning, monitoring, and debugging.

What you need for this book

The essential requirement is a computer capable of running a Linux virtual machine and an Internet connection. The author's computers are laptops running Mac OS 10.11 and Fedora 25, with VirtualBox 5, but any other Linux distribution will work as well. Vagrant, Terraform, the Chef Development Kit, and Docker also work on the Windows platform, although this is untested by the authors.

As we're dealing with Infrastructure-as-a-Service (IaaS) here, also required are valid accounts with Amazon Web Services (AWS), Google Cloud, Digital Ocean, Packet, Heroku, or an OpenStack deployment.

Through the various chapters of this book, we'll also use free Software-as-a-Service (SaaS) accounts such as GitHub, Travis CI, Docker Hub, Quay.io, Hosted Chef, and StatusCake.

Who this book is for

This book is for DevOps engineers and developers working in cross-functional teams or operations and would like to switch to IAC to manage complex infrastructures.

Sections

In this book, you will find several headings that appear frequently (Getting ready, How to do it..., How it works..., There's more..., and See also).

To give clear instructions on how to complete a recipe, we use these sections as follows:

Getting ready

This section tells you what to expect in the recipe, and describes how to set up any software or any preliminary settings required for the recipe.

How to do it...

This section contains the steps required to follow the recipe.

How it works...

This section usually consists of a detailed explanation of what happened in the previous section.

There's more...

This section consists of additional information about the recipe in order to make the reader more knowledgeable about the recipe.

See also

This section provides helpful links to other useful information for the recipe.

Conventions

In this book, you will find a number of text styles that distinguish between different kinds of information. Here are some examples of these styles and an explanation of their meaning.

Code words in text, database table names, folder names, filenames, file extensions, pathnames, dummy URLs, user input, and Twitter handles are shown as follows: "Include both the NGINX configuration and docker-compose.yml files from the previous recipe and you're good to go."

A block of code is set as follows:

```
Vagrant.configure("2") do |config|
  # all your Vagrant configuration here
end
```

When we wish to draw your attention to a particular part of a code block, the relevant lines or items are set in bold:

```
config.vm.provision "ansible_local" do |ansible|
  ansible.version = "1.9.6"
  ansible.install_mode = :pip
  ansible.playbook = "playbook.yml"
end
```

Any command-line input or output is written as follows:

```
$ vagrant plugin list
vagrant-vbguest (0.13.0)
```

New terms and **important words** are shown in bold. Words that you see on the screen, for example, in menus or dialog boxes, appear in the text like this: "You can see your newly created security group by logging into the AWS Console and navigating to **EC2 Dashboard** | **Network & Security** | **Security Groups**."

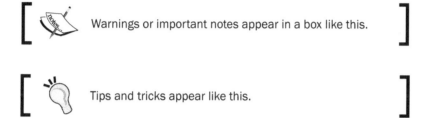

> Warnings or important notes appear in a box like this.

> Tips and tricks appear like this.

Reader feedback

Feedback from our readers is always welcome. Let us know what you think about this book—what you liked or disliked. Reader feedback is important for us as it helps us develop titles that you will really get the most out of.

To send us general feedback, simply e-mail feedback@packtpub.com, and mention the book's title in the subject of your message.

If there is a topic that you have expertise in and you are interested in either writing or contributing to a book, see our author guide at www.packtpub.com/authors.

Customer support

Now that you are the proud owner of a Packt book, we have a number of things to help you to get the most from your purchase.

Downloading the example code

You can download the example code files for this book from your account at http://www.packtpub.com. If you purchased this book elsewhere, you can visit http://www.packtpub.com/support and register to have the files e-mailed directly to you.

You can download the code files by following these steps:

1. Log in or register to our website using your e-mail address and password.
2. Hover the mouse pointer on the **SUPPORT** tab at the top.
3. Click on **Code Downloads & Errata**.
4. Enter the name of the book in the **Search** box.
5. Select the book for which you're looking to download the code files.
6. Choose from the drop-down menu where you purchased this book from.
7. Click on **Code Download**.

Once the file is downloaded, please make sure that you unzip or extract the folder using the latest version of:

- WinRAR / 7-Zip for Windows
- Zipeg / iZip / UnRarX for Mac
- 7-Zip / PeaZip for Linux

The code bundle for the book is also hosted on GitHub at `https://github.com/PacktPublishing/Infrastructure-as-Code-IAC-Cookbook`. We also have other code bundles from our rich catalog of books and videos available at `https://github.com/PacktPublishing/`. Check them out!

Downloading the color images of this book

We also provide you with a PDF file that has color images of the screenshots/diagrams used in this book. The color images will help you better understand the changes in the output. You can download this file from `https://www.packtpub.com/sites/default/files/downloads/InfrastructureasCode_IAC_Cookbook_ColorImages.pdf`

Errata

Although we have taken every care to ensure the accuracy of our content, mistakes do happen. If you find a mistake in one of our books—maybe a mistake in the text or the code—we would be grateful if you could report this to us. By doing so, you can save other readers from frustration and help us improve subsequent versions of this book. If you find any errata, please report them by visiting `http://www.packtpub.com/submit-errata`, selecting your book, clicking on the **Errata Submission Form** link, and entering the details of your errata. Once your errata are verified, your submission will be accepted and the errata will be uploaded to our website or added to any list of existing errata under the Errata section of that title.

To view the previously submitted errata, go to `https://www.packtpub.com/books/content/support` and enter the name of the book in the search field. The required information will appear under the **Errata** section.

Piracy

Piracy of copyrighted material on the Internet is an ongoing problem across all media. At Packt, we take the protection of our copyright and licenses very seriously. If you come across any illegal copies of our works in any form on the Internet, please provide us with the location address or website name immediately so that we can pursue a remedy.

Please contact us at `copyright@packtpub.com` with a link to the suspected pirated material.

We appreciate your help in protecting our authors and our ability to bring you valuable content.

Questions

If you have a problem with any aspect of this book, you can contact us at `questions@packtpub.com`, and we will do our best to address the problem.

1
Vagrant Development Environments

In this chapter, we will cover the following recipes:

- Adding an Ubuntu Xenial (16.04 LTS) Vagrant box
- Using a disposable Ubuntu Xenial (16.04) in seconds
- Enabling VirtualBox Guest Additions in Vagrant
- Using a disposable CentOS 7.x with VMware in seconds
- Extending the VMware VM capabilities
- Enabling multiprovider Vagrant environments
- Customizing a Vagrant VM
- Using Docker with Vagrant
- Using Docker in Vagrant for a Ghost blog behind NGINX
- Using Vagrant remotely with AWS EC2 and Docker
- Simulating dynamic multiple host networking
- Simulating a networked three-tier architecture app with Vagrant
- Showing your work on the LAN while working with Laravel
- Sharing access to your Vagrant environment with the world
- Simulating Chef upgrades using Vagrant
- Using Ansible with Vagrant to create a Docker host
- Using Docker containers on CoreOS with Vagrant

Introduction

Vagrant is a free and open source tool by Hashicorp aimed at building a repeatable development environment inside a virtual machine, using simple Ruby code. You can then distribute this simple file with other people, team members, and external contributors, so that they immediately have a working running environment as long as they have virtualization on their laptop. It also means that you can use a Mac laptop, and with a simple command, launch a fully configured Linux environment for you to use locally. Everyone can work using the same environment, regardless of their own local machine. Vagrant is also very useful to simulate full production environments, with multiple machines and specific operating system versions. Vagrant is compatible with most hypervisors, such as VMware, VirtualBox, or Parallels, and can be largely extended using plugins.

Vagrant uses *boxes* to run. These boxes are just packaged virtual machines images that are available, for example, from `https://atlas.hashicorp.com/boxes/search`, or you can alternatively build your own using various tools.

Vagrant can be greatly extended using plugins. There're plugins for almost anything you can think about, and most of them are community supported. From specific guest operating systems to remote IaaS providers, features around sharing, caching or snapshotting, networking, testing or specifics to Chef/Puppet, a lot can be done through plugins in Vagrant.

A list of all available plugins, including all Vagrant providers is available on the Vagrant wiki here: `https://github.com/mitchellh/vagrant/wiki/Available-Vagrant-Plugins`.

More information about all integrated providers can be found on Vagrant's website: `https://www.vagrantup.com/docs/providers/`.

You can download a Vagrant installer for your platform from `https://www.vagrantup.com/downloads.html`.

 The Vagrant version in use for this book is Vagrant 1.8.4

Adding an Ubuntu Xenial (16.04 LTS) Vagrant box

Vagrant boxes are referred to by their names, usually following the *username/boxname* naming scheme. A 64-bits *Precise* box released by *Ubuntu* will be named *ubuntu/precise64* while the *centos/7* box will always be the latest CentOS 7 official box.

Getting ready

To step through this recipe, you will need the following:

- A working Vagrant installation using the free and open source Virtualbox hypervisor
- An Internet connection

How to do it...

Open a terminal and type the following code:

```
$ vagrant box add ubuntu/xenial64
==> box: Loading metadata for box 'ubuntu/xenial64'
    box: URL: https://atlas.hashicorp.com/ubuntu/xenial64
==> box: Adding box 'ubuntu/xenial64' (v20160815.0.0) for provider:
virtualbox
    box: Downloading: https://atlas.hashicorp.com/ubuntu/boxes/xenial64/
versions/20160815.0.0/providers/virtualbox.box
==> box: Successfully added box 'ubuntu/xenial64' (v20160815.0.0) for
'virtualbox'!
```

How it works...

Vagrant knows where to look for the latest version for the requested box on the Atlas service and automatically downloads it over the Internet. All boxes are stored by default in `~/.vagrant.d/boxes`.

There's more...

If you're interested in creating your own base Vagrant boxes, refer to Packer (`https://www.packer.io/`) and the Chef Bento project (`http://chef.github.io/bento/`).

Using a disposable Ubuntu Xenial (16.04) in seconds

We want to access and use an Ubuntu Xenial system (16.04 LTS) as quickly as possible.

To do that, Vagrant uses a file named `Vagrantfile` to describe the Vagrant infrastructure. This file is in fact pure Ruby that Vagrant reads to manage your environment. Everything related to Vagrant is done inside a block such as the following:

```
Vagrant.configure("2") do |config|
  # all your Vagrant configuration here
end
```

Getting ready

To step through this recipe, you will need the following:

- A working Vagrant installation
- A working VirtualBox installation
- An Internet connection

How to do it...

1. Create a folder for the project:

   ```
   $ mkdir vagrant_ubuntu_xenial_1 && cd $_
   ```

2. Using your favorite editor, create this very minimal Vagrantfile to launch an ubuntu/xenial64 box:

   ```
   Vagrant.configure("2") do |config|
     config.vm.box = "ubuntu/xenial64"
   end
   ```

3. Now you can execute Vagrant, by explicitly using the Virtualbox hypervisor:

   ```
   $ vagrant up --provider=virtualbox
   ```

4. Within seconds, you'll have a running Ubuntu 16.04 Vagrant box on your host and you can do whatever you want with it. For example, start by logging into it via **Secure Shell** (**SSH**) by issuing the following vagrant command and use the system normally:

   ```
   $ vagrant ssh
   Welcome to Ubuntu 16.04.1 LTS (GNU/Linux 4.4.0-34-generic x86_64)
   [...]
   ubuntu@ubuntu-xenial:~$ hostname
   ubuntu-xenial
   ubuntu@ubuntu-xenial:~$ free -m
   ubuntu@ubuntu-xenial:~$ cat /proc/cpuinfo
   ```

5. When you're done with your Vagrant VM, you can simply destroy it:

   ```
   $ vagrant destroy
   ==> default: Forcing shutdown of VM...
   ==> default: Destroying VM and associated drives...
   ```

   Alternatively, we can just stop the Vagrant VM with the goal of restarting it later in its current state using vagrant halt:

   ```
   $ vagrant halt
   ```

How it works...

When you started Vagrant, it read the Vagrantfile, asking for a specific box to run (Ubuntu Xenial). If you previously added it, it will launch it right away through the default hypervisor (in this case, VirtualBox), or if it's a new box, download it for you automatically. It created the required virtual network interfaces, then the Ubuntu VM got a private IP address. Vagrant took care of configuring **SSH** by exposing an available port and inserting a default key, so you can log into it via SSH without problems.

Enabling VirtualBox Guest Additions in Vagrant

The VirtualBox Guest Additions are a set of drivers and applications to be deployed on a virtual machine to have better performance and enable features such as folder sharing. While it's possible to include the **Guest Additions** directly in the box, not all the boxes you'll find have it, and even when they do, they can be outdated very quickly.

The solution is to automatically deploy the VirtualBox Guest Additions on demand, through a plugin.

 The downside to using this plugin is that the Vagrant box may now take longer to boot, as it may need to download and install the right guest additions for the box.

Getting ready

To step through this recipe, you will need the following:

- A working Vagrant installation
- A working VirtualBox installation
- An internet connection
- The Vagrantfile from the previous recipe

How to do it...

Follow these steps to enable VirtualBox Guest Additions in Vagrant:

1. Install the `vagrant-vbguest` plugin:

    ```
    $ vagrant plugin install vagrant-vbguest
    Installing the 'vagrant-vbguest' plugin. This can take a few
    minutes...
    Installed the plugin 'vagrant-vbguest (0.13.0)'!
    ```

2. Confirm that the plugin is installed:

    ```
    $ vagrant plugin list
    vagrant-vbguest (0.13.0)
    ```

3. Start Vagrant and see that the VirtualBox Guest Additions are installed:

    ```
    $ vagrant up
    [...]
    Installing Virtualbox Guest Additions 5.0.26
    [...]
    Building the VirtualBox Guest Additions kernel modules
     ...done.
    Doing non-kernel setup of the Guest Additions ...done.
    ```

4. Now, maybe you don't want to do this every time you start you Vagrant box, because it takes time and bandwidth or because the minor difference between your host VirtualBox version and the one already installed in the Vagrant box isn't a problem for you. In this case, you can simply tell Vagrant to disable the auto-update feature right from the Vagrantfile:

    ```
    config.vbguest.auto_update = false
    ```

5. An even better way to keep your code compatible with people without this plugin is to use this plugin configuration only if the plugin is found by Vagrant itself:

    ```
    if Vagrant.has_plugin?("vagrant-vbguest") then
        config.vbguest.auto_update = false
    end
    ```

6. The full Vagrantfile now looks like this:

    ```
    Vagrant.configure("2") do |config|
        config.vm.box = "ubuntu/xenial64"
        if Vagrant.has_plugin?("vagrant-vbguest") then
            config.vbguest.auto_update = false
        end
    end
    ```

How it works...

Vagrant plugins are automatically installed from the vendor's website, and made available globally on your system for all other Vagrant environments you'll run. Once the virtual machine is ready, the plugin will detect the operating system, decide if the Guest Additions need to be installed or not, and if they do, install the necessary tools to do that (compilers, kernel headers, and libraries), and finally download and install the corresponding Guest Additions.

There's more...

Using Vagrant plugins also extends what you can do with the Vagrant CLI. In the case of the VirtualBox Guest Addition plugin, you can do a lot of things such as status checks, manage the installation, and much more:

```
$ vagrant vbguest --status
[default] GuestAdditions 5.0.26 running --- OK.
```

The plugin can later be called through Vagrant directly; here it's triggering the Guest Additions installation in the virtual machine:

```
$ vagrant vbguest --do install
```

Using a disposable CentOS 7.x with VMware in seconds

Vagrant supports both VMware Workstation and VMware Fusion through official plugins available on the Vagrant store (https://www.vagrantup.com/vmware). Follow the indications from the official website to install the plugins.

Vagrant boxes depend on the hypervisor—a VirtualBox image won't run on VMware. You need to use dedicated images for each supervisor you choose to use. For example, Ubuntu official releases only provide VirtualBox images. If you try to create a Vagrant box with a provider while using an image built for another provider, you'll get an error.

Getting ready

To step through this recipe, you will need the following:

▸ A working Vagrant installation

▸ A working VMware Workstation (PC) or Fusion (Mac) installation

▸ A working Vagrant VMware plugin installation

▸ An Internet connection

How to do it...

The Chef Bento project provides various multiprovider images we can use. For example, let's use a CentOS 7.2 with Vagrant (bento/centos-7.2) with this simplest Vagrantfile:

```
Vagrant.configure("2") do |config|
  config.vm.box = "bento/centos-7.2"
end
```

Start your CentOS 7.2 virtual environment and specify the hypervisor you want to run:

```
$ vagrant up --provider=vmware_fusion
$ vagrant ssh
```

You're now running a CentOS 7.2 Vagrant box using VMware!

How it works...

Vagrant is powered by plugins extending its usage and capabilities. In this case, the Vagrant plugin for VMware delegates all the virtualization features to the VMware installation, removing the need for VirtualBox.

There's more...

If VMware is your primary hypervisor, you'll soon be tired to always specify the provider in the command line. By setting the `VAGRANT_DEFAULT_PROVIDER` environment variable to the corresponding plugin, you will never have to specify the provider again, VMware will be the default:

```
$ export VAGRANT_DEFAULT_PROVIDER=vmware_fusion
$ vagrant up
```

See also

- The Chef Bento Project at `http://chef.github.io/bento/`
- A community VMware vSphere plugin at `https://github.com/nsidc/vagrant-vsphere`
- A community VMware vCloud Director plugin at `https://github.com/frapposelli/vagrant-vcloud`
- A community VMware vCenter plugin at `https://github.com/frapposelli/vagrant-vcenter`
- A community VMware vCloud Air plugin at `https://github.com/frapposelli/vagrant-vcloudair`

Extending the VMware VM capabilities

The hardware specifications of the Vagrant box vary from image to image as they're specified at the creation time. However, it's not fixed forever: it's just the default behavior. You can set the requirements right in the Vagrantfile, so you can keep a daily small Vagrant box and on-demand.

Getting ready

To step through this recipe, you will need the following:

- ▸ A working Vagrant installation
- ▸ A working VMware Workstation (PC) or Fusion (Mac) installation
- ▸ A working Vagrant VMware plugin installation
- ▸ An internet connection
- ▸ The Vagrantfile from the previous recipe using a bento/centos72 box

How to do it...

The VMware provider can be configured inside the following configuration blocks:

```
# VMware Fusion configuration
config.vm.provider "vmware_fusion" do |vmware|
  # enter all the vmware configuration here
end

# VMware Workstation configuration
config.vm.provider "vmware_workstation" do |vmware|
  # enter all the vmware configuration here
end
```

If the configuration is the same, you'll end up with a lot of duplicated code. Take advantage of the Ruby nature of the Vagrantfile and use a simple loop to iterate through both values:

```
["vmware_fusion", "vmware_workstation"].each do |vmware|
  config.vm.provider vmware do |v|
    # enter all the vmware configuration here
  end
end
```

Our default Bento CentOS 7.2 image has only 512 MB of RAM and one CPU. Let's double that for better performance using the `vmx["numvcpus"]` and `vmx["memsize"]` keys:

```
["vmware_fusion", "vmware_workstation"].each do |vmware|
  config.vm.provider vmware do |v|
    v.vmx["numvcpus"] = "2"
    v.vmx["memsize"] = "1024"
  end
end
```

Start or restart your Vagrant machine to apply the changes:

```
$ vagrant up
[...]
```

Your box is now using two CPUs and 1 GB of RAM.

How it works...

Virtual machine configuration is the last thing done by Vagrant before starting up. Here, it just tells VMware to allocate two CPUs and 1 GB of RAM to the virtual machine it's launching the way you would have done manually from inside the software.

There's more...

Vagrant's authors may merge both plugins into one at some point in the future. The current 4.x version of the plugins is still split.

The VMX format is not very well documented by VMware. The possible keys and values can be found on most VMware Inc. documentation about VMX configuration.

Enabling multiprovider Vagrant environments

You might be running VMware on your laptop, but your coworker might not. Alternatively, you want people to have the choice, or you simply want both environments to work! We'll see how to build a single Vagrantfile to support them all.

Getting ready

To step through this recipe, you will need the following:

- A working Vagrant installation
- A working VirtualBox installation
- A working VMware Workstation (PC) or Fusion (Mac) installation
- A working Vagrant VMware plugin installation
- An internet connection
- The Vagrantfile from the previous recipe using a bento/centos72 box

How to do it...

Some Vagrant boxes are available for multiple hypervisors, such as the CentOS 7 Bento box we previously used. This way, we can simply choose which one to use.

Let's start with our previous Vagrantfile including customizations for VMware:

```
Vagrant.configure("2") do |config|
  config.vm.box = "bento/centos-7.2"
  ["vmware_fusion", "vmware_workstation"].each do |vmware|
    config.vm.provider vmware do |v|
      v.vmx["numvcpus"] = "2"
      v.vmx["memsize"] = "1024"
    end
  end
end
```

How would we add the same configuration on VirtualBox as we have on VMware? Here's how to customize VirtualBox similarly in the Vagrantfile:

```
config.vm.provider :virtualbox do |vb|
  vb.memory = "1024"
  vb.cpus = "2"
end
```

Add this to your current Vagrantfile, reload and you'll get the requested resources from your hypervisor, be it VMware or VirtualBox.

It's nice, but we're still repeating ourselves with the values, leading to possible errors, omissions, or mistakes in the future. Let's take advantage once again of the Ruby nature of our Vagrantfile and declare some meaningful variables at the top of our file:

```
vm_memory = 1024
vm_cpus = 2
```

Now replace the four values by their variable names and you're done: you're centrally managing characteristics of the Vagrant environment you're using and distributing, whatever hypervisor you're using.

How it works...

The simple fact that the Vagrantfile is a pure Ruby file helps creating powerful and dynamic configuration, by simply setting variables that we use later for all the providers.

Customizing a Vagrant VM

Vagrant supports many configuration options through the Vagrantfile. Here are the most useful ones for daily use.

Getting ready

To step through this recipe, you will need the following:

- ▶ A working Vagrant installation (with a hypervisor)
- ▶ An Internet connection
- ▶ The Vagrantfile from the previous recipe using a bento/centos72 box

How to do it...

Here are some possible customizations for your Vagrant Virtual Machine.

Set the hostname

If you want to specify the VM name right from Vagrant, just add the following:

```
config.vm.hostname = "vagrant-lab-1"
```

This will also add an entry with the hostname to the `/etc/host` file.

Disable new box version check at startup

You may be using a slow internet connection, or you know you do want to use your current installed box, or maybe you're in a hurry and just want to get the job done; you can just remove the option to check for a new version of the box at startup by adding the following:

```
config.vm.box_check_update = false
```

Use a specific box version

If you know you want to use a specific version of the box (maybe for debugging purposes or compliance) and not the latest, you can simply declare it as follows:

```
config.vm.box_version = "2.2.9"
```

Display an informational message to the user

A useful feature is to display some basic but relevant information to the user launching the Vagrant box, such as usage or connection information. Don't forget to escape the special characters. As it's Ruby, you can access all available variables, so the message can be even more dynamic and useful to the user:

```
config.vm.post_up_message = "Use \"vagrant ssh\" to log into the
box. This VM uses #{vm_cpus} CPUs and #{vm_memory}MB of RAM."
```

Specify a minimum Vagrant version

Vagrant is updated quite often, and new features are added regularly. A good practice, if you use a feature that is known to work only after a specific version, is to declare it in the Vagrantfile, so people with an older version know they have to update:

```
Vagrant.require_version ">= 1.8.0"
```

Using Docker with Vagrant

Development environments can often be mixed, using both virtual machines and Docker containers. While virtual machines include everything needed to run a full operating system like memory, CPU, a kernel and all required libraries, a container is much more lightweight and can share all this with its host, while keeping a good isolation through special kernel features named cgroups. Docker containers helps developers use, share and ship a *bundle* including everything needed to run their application. Here, we'll show how to use Vagrant to start containers. Since Docker usage is a little different between Linux hosts and other platforms, the reference used here is the native Docker platform—Linux.

Getting ready

To step through this recipe, you will need the following:

- ▸ A working Vagrant installation (no hypervisor needed)
- ▸ A working Docker installation and basic Docker knowledge
- ▸ An Internet connection

How to do it...

We'll see how to use, access, and manipulate an NGINX container in Vagrant using Docker as a provider.

Using NGINX Docker container through Vagrant

Let's start with the simplest Vagrantfile possible, using the `nginx:stable` container with the Docker Vagrant provider:

```
Vagrant.configure("2") do |config|
  config.vm.hostname = "vagrant-docker-1"
  config.vm.post_up_message = "HTTP access: http://localhost/"
  config.vm.provider "docker" do |docker|
      docker.image = "nginx:stable"
  end
end
```

Simply start it up with the following code:

```
$ vagrant up --provider=docker
Bringing machine 'default' up with 'docker' provider...
==> default: Creating the container...
[...]
==> default: HTTP access: http://localhost/
```

Let's remove the need to specify the provider on the command line by setting a simple Ruby environment access code at the top of the Vagrantfile:

```
ENV['VAGRANT_DEFAULT_PROVIDER'] = 'docker'
```

Now you can distribute your Vagrantfile and not worry about people forgetting to explicitly specify the Docker provider.

Exposing Docker ports in Vagrant

Okay, the previous example wasn't terribly useful as we didn't expose any ports. Let's tell Vagrant to expose the Docker container HTTP (TCP/80) port to our host's HTTP (TCP/80) port:

```
config.vm.provider "docker" do |docker|
    docker.image = "nginx:stable"
    docker.ports = ['80:80']
end
```

Restart the Vagrant and verify you can access your NGINX container:

```
$ curl http://localhost/
```

Sharing folders with Docker through Vagrant

What about sharing a local folder so you can code on your laptop and see the result processed by the Vagrant environment? The default NGINX configuration reads files from `/usr/share/nginx/html`. Let's put our own `index.html` in there.

Create a simple `src/index.html` file, containing some text:

```
$ mkdir src; echo "<h1>Hello from Docker via Vagrant<h1>" > src/index.
html
```

Add the Docker volume configuration to our Docker provider block in Vagrant:

```
config.vm.provider "docker" do |docker|
    docker.image = "nginx:stable"
    docker.ports = ['80:80']
    docker.volumes = ["#{Dir.pwd}/src:/usr/share/nginx/html"]
end
```

 `#{Dir.pwd}` is the Ruby for finding the current directory, so you don't hardcode paths, making it highly distributable.

Restart the Vagrant environment and see the result:

```
$ curl http://localhost
<h1>Hello from Docker via Vagrant<h1>
```

 On SELinux-enabled systems you may need to do some configuration that's beyond the scope of this book. We encourage you to secure your Docker systems using SELinux, but to disable SELinux just type the following:

```
$ sudo setenforce 0
```

There's more...

You can choose not to use your local or default Docker installation, but instead use a dedicated VM, maybe to reflect production or a specific OS (such as CoreOS). In this case, you can specify a dedicated Vagrantfile as follows:

```
config.vm.provider "docker" do |docker|
docker.vagrant_vagrantfile = "docker_host/Vagrantfile"
end
```

Using Docker in Vagrant for a Ghost blog behind NGINX

Vagrant in Docker can be used more usefully to simulate traditional setups such as an application behind a load balancer or a reverse proxy. We've already set up NGINX, so what about using it as a front reverse proxy with a blog engine such as Ghost behind it? We'll end up by showing how to do something similar with docker-compose.

Getting ready

To step through this recipe, you will need the following:

- A working Vagrant installation (no hypervisor needed)
- A working Docker installation and basic Docker knowledge
- An Internet connection

How to do it...

The previous example allows only one container to be launched simultaneously, which is sad considering the power of Docker. Let's define multiple containers and start by creating a `front` container (our previous NGINX):

```
config.vm.define "front" do |front|
  front.vm.provider "docker" do |docker|
    docker.image = "nginx:stable"
    docker.ports = ['80:80']
    docker.volumes = ["#{Dir.pwd}/src:/usr/share/nginx/html"]
  end
end
```

Now how about creating an application container, maybe a blog engine such as Ghost? Ghost publishes a ready-to-use container on the Docker Hub, so let's use that (version 0.9.0 at the time of writing) and expose on TCP/8080 the application container listening on TCP/2368:

```
config.vm.define "app" do |app|
  app.vm.provider "docker" do |docker|
    docker.image = "ghost:0.9.0"
    docker.ports = ['8080:2368']
  end
end
```

Check if you can access the blog on `http://localhost:8080` and NGINX on `http://localhost`:

```
$ curl -IL http://localhost:8080
HTTP/1.1 200 OK
X-Powered-By: Express
[...]


$ curl -IL http://localhost
HTTP/1.1 200 OK
Server: nginx/1.10.1
```

Now let's use NGINX for what it's for—serving the application. Configuring NGINX as a reverse proxy is beyond the scope of this book, so just use the following simple configuration for the `nginx.conf` file at the root of your working folder:

```
server {
  listen 80;
  location / {
    proxy_set_header    X-Real-IP $remote_addr;
    proxy_set_header    Host        $http_host;
    proxy_pass          http://app:2368;
  }
}
```

Change the configuration of the `front` container in Vagrant to use this configuration, remove the old `index.html` as we're not using it anymore, and link this container to the `app` container:

```
config.vm.define "front" do |front|
  front.vm.provider "docker" do |docker|
    docker.image = "nginx:stable"
    docker.ports = ['80:80']
    docker.volumes = ["#{Dir.pwd}/nginx.conf:/etc/nginx/conf.d/
default.conf"]
    docker.link("app:app")
  end
end
```

Linking the app container makes it available to the front container, so now there's no need to expose the Ghost blog container directly, let's make it simpler and more secure behind the reverse proxy:

```
config.vm.define "app" do |app|
  app.vm.provider "docker" do |docker|
    docker.name = "app"
    docker.image = "ghost:0.9.0"
  end
end
```

We're close! But this setup will eventually fail for a simple reason: our systems are too fast, and Vagrant parallelizes the startup of virtual machines by default, and also does this for containers. Containers start so fast that the app container may not be ready for NGINX when it's started. To ensure sequential startup, use the VAGRANT_NO_PARALLEL environment variable at the top of the Vagrantfile:

```
ENV['VAGRANT_NO_PARALLEL'] = 'true'
```

Now you can browse to http://localhost/admin and start using your Ghost blog in a container, behind a NGINX reverse proxy container, with the whole thing managed by Vagrant!

There's more...

You can access the containers logs directly using Vagrant:

```
$ vagrant docker-logs --follow
==> app: > ghost@0.9.0 start /usr/src/ghost
==> app: > node index
==> app: Migrations: Creating tables...
[...]
==> front: 172.17.0.1 - - [21/Aug/2016:10:55:08 +0000] "GET /
HTTP/1.1" 200 1547 "-" "Mozilla/5.0 (X11; Fedora; Linux x86_64;
rv:48.0) Gecko/20100101 Firefox/48.0" "-"
==> app: GET / 200 113.120 ms - -
[...]
```

A Docker Compose equivalent

Docker Compose is a tool to orchestrate multiple containers and manage Docker features from a single YAML file. So if you're more familiar with Docker Compose, or if you'd like to do something similar with this tool, here's what the code would look like in the docker-compose.yml file:

```
version: '2'
services:
```

```
front:
  image: nginx:stable
  volumes:
    - "./nginx.conf:/etc/nginx/conf.d/default.conf"
  restart: always
  ports:
    - "80:80"
  depends_on:
    - app
  links:
    - app
app:
  image: ghost:0.9.0
  restart: always
```

 Remember that with Vagrant, you can mix virtual machines and Docker containers, while you can't with docker-compose.

Using Vagrant remotely with AWS EC2 and Docker

Another powerful usage of Vagrant can be with remote IaaS resources such as Amazon EC2. Amazon Web Services Elastic Compute Cloud (EC2) and similar Infrastructure-as-a-Service providers like Google Cloud, Azure or Digital Ocean, to name a few, are selling virtual machines with varying compute power and network bandwidth for a fee. You don't always have all the necessary CPU and memory you need on your laptop, or you need to have some specific computing power for a task, or you just want to replicate part of an existing production environment: here's how you can leverage the power of Vagrant using Amazon EC2.

Here, we'll deploy a Ghost blog with an NGINX reverse proxy, all on Docker, using an Ubuntu Xenial 16.04 on AWS EC2! This is to simulate a real deployment of an application, so you can see if it is working in real conditions.

Getting ready

To step through this recipe, you will need the following:

- ▸ A working Vagrant installation (no hypervisor needed)
- ▸ An Amazon EC2 account (or create one for free at `https://aws.amazon.com/` if you don't have one already), with valid Access Keys, a keypair named *iac-lab*, a security group named *iac-lab* allowing at least HTTP ports, and SSH access.
- ▸ An Internet connection

How to do it...

Begin by installing the plugin:

```
$ vagrant plugin install vagrant-aws
```

A requirement of this plugin is the presence of a dummy Vagrant box that does nothing:

```
$ vagrant box add dummy https://github.com/mitchellh/vagrant-
aws/raw/master/dummy.box
```

Remember how we configured the Docker provider in the previous recipes? This is no different:

```
config.vm.provider :aws do |aws, override|
  # AWS Configuration
  override.vm.box = "dummy"
end
```

Then, defining an application VM will consist of specifying which provider it's using (AWS in our case), the **Amazon Machine Image** (**AMI**) (Ubuntu 16.04 LTS in our case), and a provisioning script that we creatively named `script.sh`.

You can find other AMI IDs at `http://cloud-images.ubuntu.com/locator/ec2/`:

```
config.vm.define "srv-1" do |config|
    config.vm.provider :aws do |aws|
      aws.ami = "ami-c06b1eb3"
    end
    config.vm.provision :shell, :path => "script.sh"
end
```

So what is the AWS-related information we need to fill in so Vagrant can launch servers on AWS?

We need the AWS Access Keys, preferably from environment variables so you don't hardcode them in your Vagrantfile:

```
aws.access_key_id = ENV['AWS_ACCESS_KEY_ID']
aws.secret_access_key = ENV['AWS_SECRET_ACCESS_KEY']
```

Indicate the region and availability zone where you want the instance to start:

```
aws.region = "eu-west-1"
aws.availability_zone = "eu-west-1a"
```

Include the instance type; here, we've chosen the one included in the AWS free tier plan so it won't cost you a dime with a new account:

```
aws.instance_type = "t2.micro"
```

Indicate in which security group this instance will live (it's up to you to adapt the requirements to your needs):

```
aws.security_groups = ['iac-lab']
```

Specify the AWS keypair name, and override the default SSH username and keys:

```
aws.keypair_name = "iac-lab"
override.ssh.username = "ubuntu"
override.ssh.private_key_path = "./keys/iac-lab.pem"
```

Under some circumstances, you can experience a bug with NFS while using Vagrant and AWS EC2, so I choose to disable this feature:

```
override.nfs.functional = false
```

Finally, it's a good practice to tag the instances, so you can later find out where they come from:

```
aws.tags = {
  'Name'   => 'Vagrant'
}
```

Add a simple shell script that will install Docker and `docker-compose`, then execute the docker-compose file:

```
#!/bin/sh
# install Docker
curl -sSL https://get.docker.com/ | sh
# add ubuntu user to docker group
sudo usermod -aG docker ubuntu
# install docker-compose
curl -L https://github.com/docker/compose/releases/download/1.8.0/docker-
compose-`uname -s`-`uname -m` > /usr/local/bin/docker-compose
```

```
sudo chmod +x /usr/local/bin/docker-compose
# execute the docker compose file
cd /vagrant
docker-compose up -d
```

Include both NGINX configuration and `docker-compose.yml` files from the previous recipe and you're good to go:

```
$ vagrant up
Bringing machine 'srv-1' up with 'aws' provider...
[...]
==> srv-1: Launching an instance with the following settings...
==> srv-1:   -- Type: t2.micro
==> srv-1:   -- AMI: ami-c06b1eb3
==> srv-1:   -- Region: eu-west-1
[...]
==> srv-1: Waiting for SSH to become available...
==> srv-1: Machine is booted and ready for use!
[...]
==> srv-1:   docker version
[...]
==> srv-1: Server:
==> srv-1:  Version:       1.12.1
[...]
==> srv-1: Creating vagrant_app_1
==> srv-1: Creating vagrant_front_1
```

Open your browser at `http://a.b.c.d/` (using the EC2 instance public IP) and you'll see your Ghost blog behind an NGINX reverse proxy, using Docker containers, using Vagrant on Amazon EC2.

A common usage for such a setup is for the developer to test the application in close to real production conditions, maybe to show a new feature to a remote product owner, replicate a bug seen only in this setup, or at some point in the CI. Once Docker containers have been built, smoke test them on EC2 before going any further.

Simulating dynamic multiple host networking

Vagrant is also very useful when used to simulate multiple hosts in a network. This way you can have full systems able to talk to each other in the same private network and easily test connectivity between systems.

Getting ready

To step through this recipe, you will need the following:

- ▶ A working Vagrant installation
- ▶ A working VirtualBox installation
- ▶ An Internet connection

How to do it...

Here's how we would create one CentOS 7.2 machine with 512 MB of RAM and one CPU, in a private network with a fixed IP 192.168.50.11, and a simple shell output:

```
vm_memory = 512
vm_cpus = 1

Vagrant.configure("2") do |config|

  config.vm.box = "bento/centos-7.2"

  config.vm.provider :virtualbox do |vb|
    vb.memory = vm_memory
    vb.cpus = vm_cpus
  end

  config.vm.define "srv-1" do |config|
    config.vm.provision :shell, :inline => "ip addr | grep \"inet\" |
awk '{print $2}'"
    config.vm.network "private_network", ip: "192.168.50.11",
virtualbox__intnet: "true"
  end
end
```

To add a new machine to this network, we could simply duplicate the `srv-1` machine definition, as in the following code:

```
config.vm.define "srv-2" do |config|
    config.vm.provision :shell, :inline => "ip addr | grep
\"inet\" | awk '{print $2}'"
    config.vm.network "private_network", ip: "192.168.50.12",
virtualbox__intnet: "true"
end
```

That's not very DRY, so let's take advantage of the Ruby nature of the Vagrantfile to create a loop that will dynamically and simply create as many virtual machines as we want.

First, declare a variable with the amount of virtual machines we want (2):

```
vm_num = 2
```

Then iterate through that value, so it can generate values for an IP and for a hostname:

```
(1..vm_num).each do |n|
    # a lan lab in the 192.168.50.0/24 range
    lan_ip = "192.168.50.#{n+10}"
    config.vm.define "srv-#{n}" do |config|
        config.vm.provision :shell, :inline => "ip addr | grep \"inet\"
| awk '{print $2}'"
        config.vm.network "private_network", ip: lan_ip, virtualbox__
intnet: "true"
    end
  end
```

This will create two virtual machines (srv-1 at 192.168.50.11 and srv-2 at 192.168.50.12) on the same internal network, so they can talk to each other.

Now you can simply change the value of vm_num and you'll easily spawn new virtual machines in seconds.

There's more...

We can optionally go even further, using the following cloning and networking features.

Speed up deployments with linked clones

Linked clones is a feature that enables new VMs to be created based on an initial existing disk image, without the need to duplicate everything. Each VM stores only its delta state, allowing very fast virtual machines boot times.

As we're launching many machines, you can optionally enable linked clones to speed things up:

```
config.vm.provider :virtualbox do |vb|
    vb.memory = vm_memory
    vb.cpus = vm_cpus
    vb.linked_clone = true
end
```

Using named NAT networks

VirtualBox has the option to let you define your own networks for further reference or reuse. Configure them under **Preferences | Network | NAT Networks**. Luckily, Vagrant can work with those named NAT networks too. To test the feature, you can create in VirtualBox a network (like iac-lab) and assign it the network `192.168.50.0/24`.

Just change the network configuration from the preceding Vagrantfile to launch the VMs in this specific network:

```
config.vm.network "private_network", ip: lan_ip,
virtualbox__intnet: "iac-lab"
```

Simulating a networked three-tier architecture app with Vagrant

Vagrant is a great tool to help simulate systems in isolated networks, allowing us to easily mock architectures found in production. The idea behind the multiple tiers is to separate the logic and execution of the various elements of the application, and not centralize everything in one place. A common pattern is to get a first layer that gets the common user requests, a second layer that does the application job, and a third layer that stores and retrieves data, usually from a database.

In this simulation, we'll have the traditional three tiers, each running CentOS 7 virtual machines on their own isolated network:

- **Front**: NGINX reverse proxy
- **App**: a Node.js app running on two nodes
- **Database**: Redis

Virtual Machine Name	front_lan IP	app_lan IP	db_lan IP
front-1	10.10.0.11/24	10.20.0.101/24	N/A
app-1	N/A	10.20.0.11/24	10.30.0.101/24
app-2	N/A	10.20.0.12/24	10/30.0.102/24
db-1	N/A	N/A	10.30.0.11/24

You will access the reverse proxy (NGINX), which alone can contact the application server (Node.js), which is the only one to be able to connect to the database.

To step through this recipe, you will need the following:

- A working Vagrant installation
- A working VirtualBox installation
- An Internet connection

Follow these steps for simulating a networked three-tier architecture app with Vagrant.

Tier 3 – the database

The database lives in a db_lan private network with the IP 10.30.0.11/24.

This application will use a simple Redis installation. Installing and configuring Redis is beyond the scope of this book, so we'll keep it as simple as possible (install it, configure it to listen on the LAN port instead of 127.0.0.1, and start it):

```
config.vm.define "db-1" do |config|
    config.vm.hostname = "db-1"
    config.vm.network "private_network", ip: "10.30.0.11",
virtualbox__intnet: "db_lan"
    config.vm.provision :shell, :inline => "sudo yum install -q -y
epel-release"
    config.vm.provision :shell, :inline => "sudo yum install -q -y
redis"
    config.vm.provision :shell, :inline => "sudo sed -i 's/bind
127.0.0.1/bind 127.0.0.1 10.30.0.11/' /etc/redis.conf"
    config.vm.provision :shell, :inline => "sudo systemctl enable
redis"
    config.vm.provision :shell, :inline => "sudo systemctl start
redis"
  end
```

Tier 2: the application servers

This tier is where our application lives, backed by an application (web) server. The application can connect to the database tier, and will be available to the end user through tier 1 proxy servers. This is usually where all the logic is done (by the application).

The Node.js application

This will be simulated with the simplest Node.js code I could produce to demonstrate the usage, displaying the server hostname (the filename is app.js).

First, it creates a connection to the Redis server on the db_lan network:

```
#!/usr/bin/env node
var os = require("os");
var redis = require('redis');
var client = redis.createClient(6379, '10.30.0.11');
client.on('connect', function() {
    console.log('connected to redis on '+os.hostname()+'
10.30.0.11:6379');
});
```

Then if it goes well, it creates an HTTP server listening on :8080, displaying the server's hostname:

```
var http = require('http');
http.createServer(function (req, res) {
  res.writeHead(200, {'Content-Type': 'text/plain'});
  res.end('Running on '+os.hostname()+'\n');
}).listen(8080);
console.log('HTTP server listening on :8080');
```

Start the app, the simplest of the systemd service file (systemd unit files are out of the scope of this book):

```
[Unit]
Description=Node App
After=network.target

[Service]
ExecStart=/srv/nodeapp/app.js
Restart=always
User=vagrant
Group=vagrant
Environment=PATH=/usr/bin
Environment=NODE_ENV=production
WorkingDirectory=/srv/nodeapp
[Install]
WantedBy=multi-user.target
```

Let's iterate through the deployment of a number of application servers (in this case: two) to serve the app. Once again, deploying Node.js applications is out of the scope of this book, so I kept it as simple as possible—simple directories and permissions creation and systemd unit deployment. In production, this would probably be done through a configuration management tool such as Chef or Ansible and maybe coupled with a proper deployment tool:

```
# Tier 2: a scalable number of application servers
vm_app_num = 2
  (1..vm_app_num).each do |n|
    app_lan_ip = "10.20.0.#{n+10}"
    db_lan_ip = "10.30.0.#{n+100}"
    config.vm.define "app-#{n}" do |config|
      config.vm.hostname = "app-#{n}"
      config.vm.network "private_network", ip: app_lan_ip,
virtualbox__intnet: "app_lan"
      config.vm.network "private_network", ip: db_lan_ip,
virtualbox__intnet: "db_lan"
      config.vm.provision :shell, :inline => "sudo yum install -q
-y epel-release"
      config.vm.provision :shell, :inline => "sudo yum install -q
-y nodejs npm"
      config.vm.provision :shell, :inline => "sudo mkdir
/srv/nodeapp"
      config.vm.provision :shell, :inline => "sudo cp
/vagrant/app.js /src/nodeapp"
      config.vm.provision :shell, :inline => "sudo chown -R
vagrant.vagrant /srv/"
      config.vm.provision :shell, :inline => "sudo chmod +x
/srv/nodeapp/app.js"
      config.vm.provision :shell, :inline => "cd /srv/nodeapp; npm
install redis"
      config.vm.provision :shell, :inline => "sudo cp
/vagrant/nodeapp.service /etc/systemd/system"
      config.vm.provision :shell, :inline => "sudo systemctl
daemon-reload"
      config.vm.provision :shell, :inline => "sudo systemctl start
nodeapp"
    end
  end
```

Tier 1: the NGINX reverse proxy

Tier 1 is represented here by an NGINX reverse proxy configuration on CentOS 7, as simple as it could be for this demo. Configuring an NGINX reverse proxy with a pool of servers is out of the scope of this book:

```
events {
```

```
  worker_connections 1024;
}
http {
  upstream app {
    server 10.20.0.11:8080 max_fails=1 fail_timeout=1s;
    server 10.20.0.12:8080 max_fails=1 fail_timeout=1s;
  }
  server {
    listen 80;
    server_name  _;
    location / {
      proxy_set_header   X-Real-IP $remote_addr;
      proxy_set_header   Host      $http_host;
      proxy_pass         http://app;
    }
  }
}
```

Now let's create the reverse proxy VM that will serve `http://localhost:8080` through the pool of application servers. This VM listens on 10.10.0.11/24 on its own LAN (`front_lan`), and on `10.20.0.101/24` on the application servers' LAN (`app_lan`):

```
# Tier 1: an NGINX reverse proxy VM, available on http://
localhost:8080
  config.vm.define "front-1" do |config|
    config.vm.hostname = "front-1"
    config.vm.network "private_network", ip: "10.10.0.11",
virtualbox__intnet: "front_lan"
    config.vm.network "private_network", ip: "10.20.0.101",
virtualbox__intnet: "app_lan"
    config.vm.network "forwarded_port", guest: 80, host: 8080
    config.vm.provision :shell, :inline => "sudo yum install -q -y
epel-release"
    config.vm.provision :shell, :inline => "sudo yum install -q -y
nginx"
    config.vm.provision :shell, :inline => "sudo cp
/vagrant/nginx.conf /etc/nginx/nginx.conf"
    config.vm.provision :shell, :inline => "sudo systemctl enable
nginx"
    config.vm.provision :shell, :inline => "sudo systemctl start
nginx"
  end
```

Start this up (`vagrant up`) and navigate to `http://localhost:8080`, where the app displays the application server hostname so you can confirm that the load balancing across networks is working (while application servers can talk to the Redis backend).

Showing your work on the LAN while working with Laravel

You're working on your application using Laravel, the free and open source PHP framework (https://laravel.com/), and you'd like to showcase your work to your colleagues. Using a Vagrant development environment can help keep your work machine clean and allow you to use your usual tools and editors while using an infrastructure close to production.

In this example, we'll deploy a CentOS 7 server, with NGINX, PHP-FPM, and MariaDB, all the PHP dependencies, and install Composer. You can build from this example and others in this book to create an environment that mimics production (three-tier, multiple machines, and other characteristics).

This environment will be available for access to all your coworkers on your network, and the code will be accessible to you locally.

Getting ready

To step through this recipe, you will need the following:

- ▶ A working Vagrant installation
- ▶ A working VirtualBox or VMware installation
- ▶ An Internet connection

How to do it...

Let's start with the simplest Vagrant environment we know:

```
Vagrant.configure("2") do |config|
  config.vm.box = "bento/centos-7.2"
  config.vm.define "srv-1" do |config|
    config.vm.hostname = "srv-1"
  end
end
```

A sample NGINX configuration for Laravel

Configuring NGINX for Laravel is out of the scope for this book, but for reference, here's a simple NGINX configuration that will work well for us, listening on HTTP, serving files located on /srv/app/public, and using PHP-FPM (the file name is nginx.conf):

```
events {
  worker_connections 1024;
}
```

```
http {
  sendfile off;
  server {
    listen 80;
    server_name  _;
    root /srv/app/public ;
    try_files $uri $uri/ /index.php?q=$uri&$args;
    index index.php;
    location / {
      try_files $uri $uri/ /index.php?$query_string;
    }
    location ~ \.php$ {
      try_files $uri /index.php =404;
      fastcgi_split_path_info ^(.+\.php)(/.+)$;
      fastcgi_pass 127.0.0.1:9000;
      fastcgi_param SCRIPT_FILENAME $document_root$fastcgi_script_
name;
      fastcgi_param PATH_INFO $fastcgi_script_name;
      include fastcgi_params;
    }
  }
}
```

Simple shell provisioning

We'll create a provisioning script that we'll name as `provision.sh`, which contains all the steps we need to have a fully working Laravel environment. The details are out of the scope of this book, but here are the steps:

1. We want **Extra Packages for Enterprise Linux** (**EPEL**):

   ```
   sudo yum install -q -y epel-release
   ```

2. We want PHP-FPM:

   ```
   sudo yum install -q -y php-fpm
   ```

3. We want PHP-FPM to run as the Vagrant user so we have the rights:

   ```
   sudo sed -i 's/user = apache/user = vagrant/' /etc/php-
   fpm.d/www.conf
   ```

4. Install a bunch of PHP dependencies:

   ```
   sudo yum install -q -y php-pdo php-mcrypt php-mysql php-cli
   php-mbstring php-dom
   ```

5. Install Composer:

   ```
   curl -sS https://getcomposer.org/installer | php

   sudo mv composer.phar /usr/local/bin/composer

   sudo chmod +x /usr/local/bin/composer
   ```

6. Install and ship a good enough NGINX configuration:

```
sudo yum install -q -y nginx
sudo cp /vagrant/nginx.conf /etc/nginx/nginx.conf
```

7. Install MariaDB Server:

```
sudo yum install -q -y mariadb-server
```

8. Start all the services:

```
sudo systemctl enable php-fpm
sudo systemctl start php-fpm
sudo systemctl enable nginx
sudo systemctl start nginx
sudo systemctl enable mariadb
sudo systemctl start mariadb
```

Enable provisioning

To enable provisioning using our script, add the following code in the VM definition block:

```
config.vm.provision :shell, :path => "provision.sh"
```

Shared folder

To share the `src` folder between your host and the Vagrant VM under `/srv/app`, you can add the following code:

```
config.vm.synced_folder "src/", "/srv/app"
```

Public LAN Networking

The last thing we need to do now is to add a network interface to our Vagrant virtual machine, that will be on the real LAN, so our coworkers will access it easily through the network:

```
config.vm.network "public_network", bridge: "en0: Wi-Fi (AirPort)"
```

Adapt the name of your network adapter to use (this was on a Mac, as you can guess) to your needs. Another solution is not to specify any adapter name, so you will be presented a list of possible adapters to bridge:

```
==> srv-1: Available bridged network interfaces:
1) en0: Wi-Fi (AirPort)
[...]
```

Start the Vagrant environment (`vagrant up`), and when it's available, you can execute commands such as finding out the network information: `vagrant ssh -c "ip addr"`. Your mileage will vary, but in this network, the public IP of this Vagrant box is `192.168.1.106`, so our work is available.

Now you can start coding in the `./src/` folder. This is not a Laravel book, but a way to create a new project in a clean directory is as follows:

```
cd /srv/app
composer create-project --prefer-dist laravel/laravel.
```

Don't forget to remove all files from the folder beforehand. Navigate to `http://local-ip/` and you'll see the default Laravel welcome screen.

To verify the file sharing sync is working correctly, edit the `./resources/views/welcome.blade.php` file and reload your browser to see the change reflected.

There's more...

If you include the Vagrantfile directly with your project's code, coworkers or contributors will only have to run `vagrant up` to see it running.

Other Vagrantfile sharing options include Windows Sharing (smb), rsync (useful with remote virtual machines such as on AWS EC2), and even NFS.

A noticeable bug in the sharing feature using VirtualBox leads to corrupted or non-updating files. The workaround is to deactivate in the web server configuration `sendfile`, using NGINX:

```
sendfile off;
```

Using Apache, it is as follows:

```
EnableSendfile Off
```

Sharing access to your Vagrant environment with the world

You're working on your project with your local Vagrant environment, and you'd like to show the status of the job to your customer who's located in another city. Maybe you have an issue configuring something and you'd like some remote help from your coworker on the other side of the planet. Alternatively, maybe you'd like to access your work Vagrant box from home, hotel, or coworking space? There's a neat Vagrant sharing feature we'll use here, working with a Ghost blog on CentOS 7.2.

Getting ready

To step through this recipe, you will need the following:

- A working Vagrant installation
- A working VirtualBox installation
- A free HashiCorp Atlas account (`https://atlas.hashicorp.com/account/new`)
- An Internet connection

How to do it...

Let's start with this simple Vagrantfile:

```
Vagrant.configure("2") do |config|
  config.vm.box = "bento/centos-7.2"
  config.vm.define "blog" do |config|
    config.vm.hostname = "blog"
  end
end
```

We know we'll have to install some packages, so let's add a provisioning script to be executed:

```
config.vm.provision :shell, :path => "provision.sh"
```

We'll want to hack locally on our Ghost blog, such as adding themes and more, so let's sync our `src/` folder to the remote `/srv/blog` folder:

```
config.vm.synced_folder "src/", "/srv/blog"
```

We want a local private network so we can access the virtual machine, with the `2368` TCP port (Ghost default) redirected to our host `8080` HTTP port:

```
config.vm.network "private_network", type: "dhcp"
config.vm.network "forwarded_port", guest: 2368, host: 8080
```

Provisioning

1. To configure our new box, we'll first need to enable EPEL:

   ```
   sudo yum install -q -y epel-release
   ```

2. Then install the requirements, `node`, `npm`, and `unzip`:

   ```
   sudo yum install -q -y node npm unzip
   ```

3. Download the latest Ghost version:

   ```
   curl -L https://ghost.org/zip/ghost-latest.zip -o ghost.zip
   ```

4. Uncompress it in the `/srv/blog` folder:

```
sudo unzip -uo ghost.zip -d /srv/blog/
```

5. Install the Ghost dependencies:

```
cd /srv/blog && sudo npm install --production
```

Put all those commands in the `provisioning.sh` script and we're good to go: `vagrant up`.

Starting Ghost engine

As you would do normally, log in to your Vagrant box to launch the node server:

```
vagrant ssh
cd /srv/blog && sudo npm start --production
[...]
Ghost is running in production...
Your blog is now available on http://my-ghost-blog.com
Ctrl+C to shut down
```

Change the host IP from `127.0.0.1` to `0.0.0.0` in the generated `config.js` file so the server listens on all interfaces:

```
server: {
        host: '0.0.0.0',
        port: '2368'
    }
```

Restart the node server:

```
cd /srv/blog && sudo npm start --production
```

You now have a direct access to the blog through your box LAN IP (adapt the IP to your case): `http://172.28.128.3:2368/`.

Sharing access

Now you can access your application locally through your Vagrant box, let's give access to it to others through the Internet using `vagrant share`:

HTTP

The default is to share through HTTP, so your work is available through a web browser:

```
$ vagrant share
==> srv-1: Detecting network information for machine...
[...]
```

```
==> srv-1: Your Vagrant Share is running! Name: anxious-cougar-6317
==> srv-1: URL: http://anxious-cougar-6317.vagrantshare.com
```

This URL is the one you can give to anyone to access publicly your work: Vagrant servers being used as proxy.

SSH

Another possible sharing option is by SSH (deactivated by default). The program will ask you for a password you'll need to connect to the box remotely:

```
$ vagrant share --ssh
==> srv-1: Detecting network information for machine...
[...]
srv-1: Please enter a password to encrypt the key:
    srv-1: Repeat the password to confirm:
[...]
==> srv-1: You're sharing with SSH access. This means that another user
==> srv-1: simply has to run `vagrant connect --ssh subtle-platypus-4976`
==> srv-1: to SSH to your Vagrant machine.
[...]
```

Now, at home or at the coworking space, you can simply connect to your work Vagrant box (if needed, the default Vagrant password is vagrant):

```
$ vagrant connect --ssh subtle-platypus-4976
Loading share 'subtle-platypus-4976'...
[...]
[vagrant@srv-1 ~]$ head -n1 /srv/blog/config.js
// # Ghost Configuration
```

You or your coworker are now remotely logged into your own Vagrant box over the Internet!

Simulating Chef upgrades using Vagrant

Wouldn't it be awesome to simulate production changes quickly? Chances are you're using Chef in production. We'll see how to use both Chef cookbooks with Vagrant, as well as how to simulate Chef version upgrades between environments. This kind of setup is the beginning of a good combination of infrastructure as code.

Getting ready

To step through this recipe, you will need the following:

- A working Vagrant installation
- A working VirtualBox installation
- An Internet connection

How to do it...

Let's start with a minimal virtual machine named `prod` that simply boots a CentOS 7.2, like we have in our production environment:

```
Vagrant.configure("2") do |config|
  config.vm.box = "bento/centos-7.2"
  config.vm.define "prod" do |config|
    config.vm.hostname = "prod"
    config.vm.network "private_network", type: "dhcp"
  end

end
```

Vagrant Omnibus Chef plugin

Now, if we want to use Chef code, if we want to use Chef code (Ruby files organized in directories that form a unit called a 'cookbook' that configure and maintain a specific area of a system), we first need to install Chef on the Vagrant box. There're many ways to do this, from provisioning shell scripts to using boxes with Chef already installed. A clean, reliable, and repeatable way is to use a Vagrant plugin to do just that—vagrant-omnibus. Omnibus is a packaged Chef. Install it like any other Vagrant plugin:

```
$ vagrant plugin install vagrant-omnibus
Installing the 'vagrant-omnibus' plugin. This can take a few minutes...
Installed the plugin 'vagrant-omnibus (1.4.1)'!
```

Then, just add the following configuration in your VM definition of the Vagrantfile and you'll always have the latest Chef version installed on this box:

```
config.omnibus.chef_version = :latest
```

However, our goal is to mimic production, maybe we're still using the latest in v11.x series of Chef instead of the latest 12.x, so instead let's specify exactly which version we want:

```
config.omnibus.chef_version = "11.18.12"
```

Now that we're using a new plugin, our Vagrantfile won't work out of the box for everybody. Users will have to install this vagrant-omnibus plugin. If you care about consistency and repeatability, an option is to add the following Ruby check at the beginning of your Vagrantfile:

```
%w(vagrant-vbguest vagrant-omnibus).each do |plugin|
  unless Vagrant.has_plugin?(plugin)
    raise "#{plugin} plugin is not installed! Please install it using
`vagrant plugin install #{plugin}`"
  end
end
```

This code snippet will simply iterate over each plugin name to verify that Vagrant returns them as *installed*. If not, stop there and return a helpful exit message on how to install the required plugins.

A sample Chef recipe

This part of the book isn't about writing Chef recipes (read more about it later in the book!), so we'll keep that part simple. Our objective is to install the Apache 2 web server on CentOS 7 (httpd package), and start it. Here's what our sample recipe looks like (cookbooks/apache2/recipes/default.rb); it does exactly what it says in plain English:

```
package "httpd"

service "httpd" do
  action [ :enable, :start ]
end
```

Vagrant and Chef integration

Here's how, in our VM definition block, we'll tell Vagrant to work with Chef Solo (a way of running Chef in standalone mode, without the need of a Chef server) to provision our box:

```
config.vm.provision :chef_solo do |chef|
  chef.add_recipe 'apache2'
end
```

As simple as that. Vagrant this up (vagrant up), and you'll end up with a fully provisioned VM, using the old 11.18.12 version, and a running Apache 2 web server.

Our manual tests can include checking that the chef-solo version is the one we requested:

```
$ chef-solo --version
Chef: 11.18.12
```

They can also check if we have httpd installed:

```
$ httpd -v
Server version: Apache/2.4.6 (CentOS)
```

Also, we can check if `httpd` is running:

```
$ pidof httpd
13029 13028 13027 13026 13025 13024
```

 Various other options than chef-solo exist, such as chef-client and chef-zero.

Testing the Chef version update

So we simulated our production environment locally, with the same CentOS version, the apache2 cookbook used in production, and the old Chef version 11. Our next task is to test if everything is still running smoothly after an upgrade to the new version 12. Let's create a second "staging" VM, very similar to our production setup, except we want to install the current latest Chef version (12.13.37 at the time of writing, feel free to use `:latest` instead):

```
config.vm.define "staging" do |config|
  config.vm.hostname = "staging"
  config.omnibus.chef_version = "12.13.37"
  config.vm.network "private_network", type: "dhcp"
  config.vm.provision :chef_solo do |chef|
    chef.add_recipe 'apache2'
  end
end
```

Launch this new machine (`vagrant up staging`) and we'll see if our setup still works with the new major Chef version:

```
$ vagrant ssh staging
$ chef-solo --version
Chef: 12.13.37
$ httpd -v
Server version: Apache/2.4.6 (CentOS)
$ pidof httpd
13029 13028 13027 13026 13025 13024
```

So we can safely assume, as far as our testing goes, that the newest Chef version still works correctly with our production Chef code.

There's more...

Here are more ways of controlling a Vagrant environment, and use even better Chef tooling inside it.

Controlling default Vagrant VMs

You may not always want to boot both production and staging vagrant virtual machines, especially when you just want to work on the default production setup. To specify a default VM:

```
config.vm.define "prod", primary: true do |config|
  [...]
end
```

To not start automatically a VM when issuing the `vagrant up` command:

```
config.vm.define "staging", autostart: false do |config|
  [...]
end
```

Berkshelf and Vagrant

Chances are, if your production environment is using Chef, you're also using Berkshelf for dependency management and not 100% local cookbooks (if you aren't, you should!).

Vagrant work pretty well with a Berkshelf enabled Chef environment, using the `vagrant-berkshelf` plugin.

 Your workstation will need the Chef Development Kit (Chef DK: `https://downloads.chef.io/chef-dk/`) for this to work correctly.

Testing with Test Kitchen

This setup is in fact so close to what's used to make infrastructure code testing that you'll see a lot of similarities in the dedicated section of this book.

Using Ansible with Vagrant to create a Docker host

Ansible (`https://www.ansible.com/`) is a very simple and powerful open source automation tool. While using and creating Ansible *playbooks* is off-topic for this book, we'll use a very simple *playbook* to install and configure Docker on a CentOS 7 box. Starting from here, you'll be able to iterate through more complex Ansible playbooks.

Getting ready

To step through this recipe, you will need the following:

▸ A working Vagrant installation

▸ A working hypervisor

▸ A working Ansible installation on your machine (an easy way is to `$ pip install ansible` or to pick your usual package manager like APT or YUM/DNF)

▸ An Internet connection

How to do it...

Because writing complex Ansible playbooks is out of the scope of this book, we'll use a very simple one, so you can learn more about Ansible later and still reuse this recipe.

A simple Ansible Docker playbook for Vagrant

Our playbook file (`playbook.yml`) is a plain YAML file, and we'll do the following in this order:

1. Install EPEL.
2. Create a Docker Unix group.
3. Add the default Vagrant user to the new Docker group.
4. Install Docker from CentOS repositories.
5. Enable and start Docker Engine.

Here's how the `playbook.yml` file looks:

```
---
- hosts: all
  become: yes
  tasks:
    - name: Enable EPEL
      yum: name=epel-release state=present
    - name: Create a Docker group
      group: name=docker state=present
    - name: Add the vagrant user to Docker group
      user: name=vagrant groups=docker append=yes
    - name: Install Docker
      yum: name=docker state=present
    - name: Enable and Start Docker Daemon
      service: name=docker state=started enabled=yes
```

Apply Ansible from Vagrant

To use our Ansible playbook, let's start with a simple Vagrantfile starting a CentOS 7 box:

```
Vagrant.configure("2") do |config|
  config.vm.box = "bento/centos-7.2"
  config.vm.define "srv-1" do |config|
    config.vm.hostname = "srv-1"
    config.vm.network "private_network", type: "dhcp"
  end
end
```

Simply add Ansible provisioning like this to the VM definition so it will load and apply your `playbook.yml` file:

```
config.vm.provision "ansible" do |ansible|
  ansible.playbook = "playbook.yml"
end
```

You can now run `vagrant up` and use CentOS 7 Docker Engine version right away:

```
$ vagrant ssh
[vagrant@srv-1 ~]$ systemctl status docker
[vagrant@srv-1 ~]$ docker --version
Docker version 1.10.3, build d381c64-unsupported
[vagrant@srv-1 ~]$ docker run -it --rm alpine /bin/hostname
0f44a4d7afcd
```

There's more...

What if for some reason you don't or can't have Ansible installed on your host machine? Alternatively, maybe you need a specific Ansible version on your Vagrant box to mimic production and you don't want to mess with your local Ansible installation. There's an interesting variant Ansible provider you can use: it will either use Ansible directly from the guest VM, and if it's not installed, it will install it from official repositories or PIP. You can use this very simple default configuration:

```
config.vm.provision "ansible_local" do |ansible|
  ansible.playbook = "playbook.yml"
end
```

You can also use the following command:

```
$ vagrant up
[...]
==> srv-1: Running provisioner: ansible_local...
```

```
    srv-1: Installing Ansible...
    srv-1: Running ansible-playbook...
[...]
```

Log in to the box via SSH and check that Ansible is locally installed with the latest version:

```
$ vagrant ssh
$ ansible --version
ansible 2.1.1.0
```

If your use case is different, you can use more precise deployment options, to be able to fix an Ansible version number using PIP (here, version 1.9.6 instead of the latest 2.x series):

 It will take noticeably longer to start, as it needs to install many packages on the guest system.

```
    config.vm.provision "ansible_local" do |ansible|
      ansible.version = "1.9.6"
      ansible.install_mode = :pip
      ansible.playbook = "playbook.yml"
    end
```

You can also use the following command:

```
$ vagrant up
[...]
==> srv-1: Running provisioner: ansible_local...
    srv-1: Installing Ansible...
    srv-1: Installing pip... (for Ansible installation)
    srv-1: Running ansible-playbook...
```

Inside the Vagrant guest, you can now check for the PIP and Ansible versions:

```
$ pip --version
pip 8.1.2 from /usr/lib/python2.7/site-packages (python 2.7)
$ ansible --version
ansible 1.9.6
```

You can also check if our playbook has been installed correctly with the old 1.x Ansible version:

```
$ docker version
```

Also check if Docker is installed, and verify now it's working as the Vagrant user:

```
$ docker run -it --rm alpine ping -c2 google.com
PING google.com (216.58.211.78): 56 data bytes
64 bytes from 216.58.211.78: seq=0 ttl=61 time=22.078 ms
64 bytes from 216.58.211.78: seq=1 ttl=61 time=21.061 ms
```

Using Docker containers on CoreOS with Vagrant

Vagrant can help in simulating environments, and Docker containers are not forgotten with Vagrant. We'll use one of the best platforms to run containers, the free and open source lightweight operating system CoreOS. Based on Linux, targeting easy container and clustered deployments, it also provides official Vagrant boxes. We'll deploy the official WordPress container with MariaDB on another container using the Vagrant Docker provisioner (and not the Vagrant Docker provider).

Getting ready

To step through this recipe, you will need the following:

- A working Vagrant installation
- A working hypervisor
- An Internet connection

How to do it...

CoreOS doesn't host its official images at the default location on Atlas, it hosts it itself. So, we have to specify the full URL to the Vagrant box in our Vagrantfile:

```
Vagrant.configure("2") do |config|
  config.vm.box = https://stable.release.core-os.net/amd64-usr/
current/coreos_production_vagrant.box
end
```

As CoreOS is a minimal OS, it doesn't support any of the VirtualBox guest addition tools, so we'll disable them, and don't try anything if we (most likely) have the `vagrant-vbguest` plugin:

```
config.vm.provider :virtualbox do |vb|
    vb.check_guest_additions = false
    vb.functional_vboxsf    = false
```

```
    end

    if Vagrant.has_plugin?("vagrant-vbguest") then
      config.vbguest.auto_update = false
    end
```

Let's create a new VM definition, using the CoreOS Vagrant box:

```
config.vm.define "core-1" do |config|
  config.vm.hostname = "core-1"
  config.vm.network "private_network", type: "dhcp"
end
```

We now need to run the `mariadb` and `wordpress` official containers from the Docker Hub. Using Docker directly, we would have run the following:

```
$ docker run -d --name mariadb -e MYSQL_ROOT_PASSWORD=h4ckm3 mariadb
$ docker run -d -e WORDPRESS_DB_HOST=mariadb -e
'WORDPRESS_DB_PASSWORD=h4ckm3 --link mariadb:mariadb -p 80:80
wordpress
```

Let's translate this into our Vagrantfile:

```
db_root_password = "h4ckm3"

config.vm.provision "docker" do |docker|

    docker.run "mariadb",

      args: "--name 'mariadb' -e
'MYSQL_ROOT_PASSWORD=#{db_root_password}'"

    docker.run "wordpress",

      args: "-e 'WORDPRESS_DB_HOST=mariadb' -e
'WORDPRESS_DB_PASSWORD=#{db_root_password}' --link 'mariadb:mariadb'
-p '80:80'"

  end
```

Vagrant this up (`$ vagrant up`), and you'll access a ready-to-use WordPress installation running on CoreOS:

```
$ curl -IL http://172.28.128.3/wp-admin/install.php
HTTP/1.1 200 OK
Date: Thu, 25 Aug 2016 10:54:17 GMT
Server: Apache/2.4.10 (Debian)
X-Powered-By: PHP/5.6.25
Expires: Wed, 11 Jan 1984 05:00:00 GMT
Cache-Control: no-cache, must-revalidate, max-age=0
Content-Type: text/html; charset=utf-8
```

There's more...

The CoreOS team proposes a full Vagrant environment to try and manipulate a CoreOS cluster `https://github.com/coreos/coreos-vagrant`. You'll then be able to try all CoreOS features and configuration options for all release channels (alpha, beta, or stable).

Other operating systems such as Ubuntu or CentOS are fully supported to provision Docker containers, even if Docker isn't installed at first on the base image. Vagrant will install Docker for you, so it will work transparently and run the containers as soon as it's installed.

2
Provisioning IaaS with Terraform

In this chapter, we will cover the following recipes:

- ► Configuring the Terraform AWS provider
- ► Creating and using an SSH key pair to use on AWS
- ► Using AWS security groups with Terraform
- ► Creating an Ubuntu EC2 instance with Terraform
- ► Generating meaningful outputs with Terraform
- ► Using contextual defaults with Terraform
- ► Managing S3 storage with Terraform
- ► Creating private Docker repositories with Terraform
- ► Creating a PostgreSQL RDS database with Terraform
- ► Enabling CloudWatch Logs for Docker with Terraform
- ► Managing IAM users with Terraform

Introduction

A modern infrastructure often uses multiple providers **Amazon Web Services (AWS)**, OpenStack, Google Cloud, Digital Ocean, and many others), combined with multiple external services (DNS, mail, monitoring, and others). Many providers propose their own automation tool, but the power of Terraform is that it allows you to manage it all from one place, all using code. With it, you can dynamically create machines at two IaaS providers depending on the environment, register their names at another DNS provider, enable monitoring at a third-party monitoring company, while configuring the company GitHub account and sending the application logs to an appropriate service. On top of that, it can delegate configuration to those who do it well (configuration management tools such as Chef, Puppet, and so on), all with the same tool. The state of your infrastructure is described, stored, versioned, and shared.

In this chapter, we'll discover how to use Terraform to bootstrap a fully capable infrastructure on AWS. You'll know everything from launching fine-tuned EC2 instances and optimized RDS databases dynamically in different regions, to creating tight security groups, deploying SSH key pairs and securing IAM access keys, enabling log storage with CloudWatch, generating useful outputs, handling infinite **Simple Storage Service (S3)** storage, and using private Docker repositories.

 The Terraform version in use for this book is 0.7.2.

Configuring the Terraform AWS provider

We can use Terraform with many IaaS providers, such as Google Cloud or Digital Ocean. Here, we'll configure Terraform to be used with AWS and stick with this provider for the rest of the chapter.

For Terraform to interact with an IaaS, it needs to have a *provider* configured.

Getting ready

To step through this recipe, you will need the following:

- An AWS account with keys
- A working Terraform installation
- An empty directory to store your infrastructure code
- An Internet connection

How to do it...

To configure the AWS provider in Terraform, we'll need the following three files:

- ▶ A file declaring our variables, an optional description, and an optional default for each (`variables.tf`)
- ▶ A file setting the variables for the whole project (`terraform.tfvars`)
- ▶ A provider file (`provider.tf`)

Lets declare our variables in the `variables.tf` file. We can start by declaring what's usually known as the `AWS_DEFAULT_REGION`, `AWS_ACCESS_KEY_ID`, and `AWS_SECRET_ACCESS_KEY` environment variables:

```
variable "aws_access_key" {
  description = "AWS Access Key"
}

variable "aws_secret_key" {
  description = "AWS Secret Key"
}

variable "aws_region" {
  default     = "eu-west-1"
  description = "AWS Region"
}
```

Set the two variables matching the AWS account in the `terraform.tfvars` file. It's not recommended to check this file into source control: it's better to use an example file instead (that is: `terraform.tfvars.example`). It's also recommended to use a dedicated Terraform user for AWS, not the root account keys:

```
aws_access_key = "< your AWS_ACCESS_KEY >"
aws_secret_key = "< your AWS_SECRET_KEY >"
```

Now, let's tie all this together into a single file, `provider.tf`:

```
provider "aws" {
  access_key = "${var.aws_access_key}"
  secret_key = "${var.aws_secret_key}"
  region     = "${var.aws_region}"
}
```

Apply the following Terraform code:

```
$ terraform apply
```

```
Apply complete! Resources: 0 added, 0 changed, 0 destroyed.
```

It only means the code is valid, not that it can really authenticate with AWS (try with a bad pair of keys). For this, we'll need to create a resource on AWS.

 You now have a new file named `terraform.tfstate` that has been created at the root of your repository. This file is critical: it's the stored state of your infrastructure. Don't hesitate to look at it, it's a text file.

How it works...

This first encounter with **HashiCorp Configuration Language** (**HCL**), the language used by Terraform, and other Hashicorp products looks pretty familiar: it's a structured language fully compatible with JSON. We can find more information about HCL here: `https://github.com/hashicorp/hcl`. In this case, we've declared variables with an optional description for reference. We could have declared them simply with the following:

```
variable "aws_access_key" { }
```

All variables are referenced to use the following structure:

```
${var.variable_name}
```

If the variable has been declared with a default, as our `aws_region` has been declared with a default of `eu-west-1`; this value will be used if there's no override in the `terraform.tfvars` file.

What would have happened if we didn't provide a safe default for our variable? Terraform would have asked us for a value when executed:

```
$ terraform apply
var.aws_region
  AWS Region

  Enter a value:
```

There's more...

We've used values directly inside the Terraform code to configure our AWS credentials. If you're already using AWS on the command line, chances are you already have a set of standard environment variables:

```
$ echo ${AWS_ACCESS_KEY_ID}
<your AWS_ACCESS_KEY_ID>
$ echo ${AWS_SECRET_ACCESS_KEY}
<your AWS_SECRET_ACCESS_KEY>
```

```
$ echo ${AWS_DEFAULT_REGION}

eu-west-1
```

If not, you can simply set them as follows:

```
$ export AWS_ACCESS_KEY_ID="123"

$ export AWS_SECRET_ACCESS_KEY="456"

$ export AWS_DEFAULT_REGION="eu-west-1"
```

Then Terraform can use them directly, and the only code you have to type would be to declare your provider! That's handy when working with different tools.

The `provider.tf` will then look as simple as this:

```
provider "aws" { }
```

Creating and using an SSH key pair to use on AWS

Now we have our AWS provider configured in Terraform, let's add a SSH key pair to use on a default account of the virtual machines we intend to launch soon.

Getting ready

To step through this recipe, you will need the following:

- A working Terraform installation
- An AWS provider configured in Terraform
- Generate a pair of SSH keys somewhere you remember, for example, in the `keys` folder at the root of your repo:

  ```
  $ mkdir keys

  $ ssh-keygen -q -f keys/aws_terraform -C
  aws_terraform_ssh_key -N ''
  ```

- An Internet connection

How to do it...

The resource we want for this is named `aws_key_pair`. Let's use it inside a `keys.tf` file, and paste the public key content:

```
resource "aws_key_pair" "admin_key" {
  key_name   = "admin_key"
```

```
    public_key = "ssh-rsa AAAAB3 […] "
  }
```

This will simply upload your public key to your AWS account under the name `admin_key`:

```
$ terraform apply
aws_key_pair.admin_key: Creating...
  fingerprint: "" => "<computed>"
  key_name:    "" => "admin_key"
  public_key:  "" => "ssh-rsa AAAAB3 […] "
aws_key_pair.admin_key: Creation complete

Apply complete! Resources: 1 added, 0 changed, 0 destroyed.
```

If you manually navigate to your AWS account, in **EC2 | Network & Security | Key Pairs**, you'll now find your key:

Another way to use our key with Terraform and AWS would be to read it directly from the file, and that would show us how to use file interpolation with Terraform.

To do this, let's declare a new empty variable to store our public key in `variables.tf`:

```
variable "aws_ssh_admin_key_file" { }
```

Initialize the variable to the path of the key in `terraform.tfvars`:

```
aws_ssh_admin_key_file = "keys/aws_terraform"
```

Now let's use it in place of our previous `keys.tf` code, using the `file()` interpolation:

```
resource "aws_key_pair" "admin_key" {
  key_name   = "admin_key"
  public_key = "${file("${var.aws_ssh_admin_key_file}.pub")}"
}
```

This is a much clearer and more concise way of accessing the content of the public key from the Terraform resource. It's also easier to maintain, as changing the key will only require to replace the file and nothing more.

How it works...

Our first resource, `aws_key_pair` takes two arguments (a key name and the public key content). That's how all resources in Terraform work.

We used our first *file* interpolation, using a variable, to show how to use a more dynamic code for our infrastructure.

There's more...

Using Ansible, we can create a *role* to do the same job. Here's how we can manage our EC2 key pair using a variable, with the name `admin_key`. For simplification, we're using the three usual environment variables—`AWS_ACCESS_KEY_ID`, `AWS_SECRET_ACCESS_KEY`, and `AWS_DEFAULT_REGION`:

Here's a typical Ansible file hierarchy:

```
├── keys
│   ├── aws_terraform
│   └── aws_terraform.pub
├── main.yml
└── roles
    └── ec2_keys
        └── tasks
            └── main.yml
```

In the main file (`main.yml`), let's declare that our host (`localhost`) will apply the role dedicated to manage our keys:

```
---
- hosts: localhost
  roles:
  - ec2_keys
```

In the ec2_keys main task file, create the EC2 key (`roles/ec2_keys/tasks/main.yml`):

```
---
    - name: ec2 admin key
```

```
      ec2_key:
        name: admin_key
        key_material: "{{ item }}"
    with_file: './keys/aws_terraform.pub'
```

Execute the code with the following command:

```
$ ansible-playbook -i localhost main.yml

TASK [ec2_keys : ec2 admin key]
**************************************************

ok: [localhost] => (item=ssh-rsa AAAA[...] aws_terraform_ssh)


PLAY RECAP ************************************************************
*******

localhost                    : ok=2    changed=0    unreachable=0
failed=0
```

Using AWS security groups with Terraform

Amazon's security groups are similar to traditional firewalls, with ingress (incoming traffic) and egress (outgoing traffic) rules applied to EC2 instances. Those rules can be updated on-demand. We'll create an initial security group allowing ingress **Secure Shell** (**SSH**) traffic only for our own IP address, while allowing all outgoing traffic.

Getting ready

To step through this recipe, you will need the following:

▸ A working Terraform installation

▸ An AWS provider configured in Terraform (refer to the previous recipe)

▸ An Internet connection

How to do it...

The resource we're using is called `aws_security_group`. Here's the basic structure:

```
resource "aws_security_group" "base_security_group" {
  name        = "base_security_group"
  description = "Base Security Group"
```

```
    ingress { }

    egress { }

}
```

We know we want to allow inbound TCP/22 for SSH only for our own IP (replace 1.2.3.4/32 with yours!), and allow everything outbound. Here's how it looks:

```
ingress {
  from_port   = 22
  to_port     = 22
  protocol    = "tcp"
  cidr_blocks = ["1.2.3.4/32"]
}

egress {
  from_port   = 0
  to_port     = 0
  protocol    = "-1"
  cidr_blocks = ["0.0.0.0/0"]
}
```

You can add a name tag for easier reference later:

```
tags {
  Name = "base_security_group"
}
```

Apply this and you're good to go:

```
$ terraform apply
aws_security_group.base_security_group: Creating...
[...]
aws_security_group.base_security_group: Creation complete

Apply complete! Resources: 1 added, 0 changed, 0 destroyed.
```

You can see your newly created security group by logging into the AWS Console and navigating to **EC2 Dashboard | Network & Security | Security Groups**:

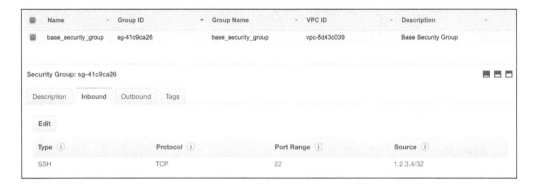

Another way of accessing the same AWS Console information is through the AWS command line:

```
$ aws ec2 describe-security-groups --group-names base_security_group
{...}
```

There's more...

We can achieve the same result using Ansible. Here's the equivalent of what we just did with Terraform in this recipe:

```
---
- name: base security group
  ec2_group:
    name: base_security_group
    description: Base Security Group
    rules:
      - proto: tcp
        from_port: 22
        to_port: 22
        cidr_ip: 1.2.3.4/32
```

Creating an Ubuntu EC2 instance with Terraform

We have previously created the requirements to launch a standard virtual machine on AWS EC2 (an SSH key pair and a security group). Let's now launch this virtual machine on EC2, using the specified SSH key pair to log into it and placed inside the security group, so (in our case) SSH is only available from a specific IP address.

This example uses the `t2.micro` instance available for free in the AWS Free Tier.

Getting ready

To step through this recipe, you will need the following:

- A working Terraform installation
- An AWS provider, a SSH key pair, and a Security Group configured in Terraform (refer to the previous recipes)
- An Internet connection

How to do it...

First, you need to find the correct AMI for your machine. An AMI is like a system disk image for AWS, and is referred to by its ID (that is: ami-df3bceb0 or ami-f2fc9d81). In the Ubuntu case, you can find the AMI you want by going to their Amazon EC2 AMI Locator page (`https://cloud-images.ubuntu.com/locator/ec2/`). In this case, I selected a Xenial release (16.04 LTS), on the eu-west-1 zone (Ireland), running on HVM virtualization and backed by SSD disks. This leaves us with one result—`ami-ee6b189d`:

Zone	Name	Version	Arch	Instance Type	Release	AMI-ID	AKI-ID
eu-west-1	xenial	16.04 LTS	amd64	hvm:ebs-ssd	20160830	ami-ee6b189d	hvm
eu-west-1	xenial	Any	Any	hvm:ebs-ssd	Any	Any	Any
Showing 1 to 1 of 1 entries (filtered from 1,017 total entries)							

Start by declaring this variable in the `variables.tf` file started in the first recipe, using a default value corresponding to the AMI ID we found previously:

```
variable "ami" {
  default = "ami-ee6b189d"
}
```

Now let's declare the instance type, specifying it as a default:

```
variable "aws_instance_type" {
  default = "t2.micro"
}
```

Let's use those variables to create the Terraform `aws_instance` resource. Locally declared variables are available using the `${var.variable_name}` structure, and internal resource attributes are accessed using the `${resource_type.resource_name.attribute}` structure:

```
resource "aws_instance" "dev" {
```

```
  ami                          = "${var.ami}"
  instance_type                = "${var.aws_instance_type}"
  key_name                     = "${aws_key_pair.admin_key.key_name}"
  security_groups              = ["${aws_security_group.base_security_
group.name}"]
  associate_public_ip_address = true

  tags {
    Name = "Ubuntu launched by Terraform"
  }
}
```

Apply the following code:

```
$ terraform apply
aws_key_pair.admin_key: Creating...
[...]
aws_security_group.base_security_group: Creating...
[...]
aws_instance.dev: Creating...
[...]
```

Navigate to the AWS EC2 dashboard under **Instances | Instances**, select your instance and note the public IP:

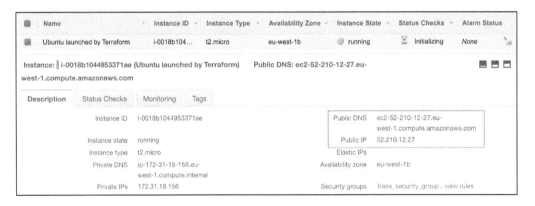

Try to log into it:

```
$ ssh -i keys/aws_terraform ubuntu@52.210.12.27
Welcome to Ubuntu 16.04.1 LTS (GNU/Linux 4.4.0-36-generic x86_64)
ubuntu@ip-172-31-18-156:~$
```

You can apply and apply by refreshing its state against Amazon's as Terraform knows remote and local states are the same, and therefore it doesn't recreate endlessly new VMs each time.

You've successfully launched your first AWS EC2 instance using repeatable Terraform code!

Scaling the number of instances

What if you want to launch two similar instances, maybe for debugging purposes, or for instant action behind a load balancer? It's very easy with Terraform, just use the `count` option inside the `aws_instance` resource, and that will launch the required amount of instances:

```
count = 2
```

Next, `terraform apply` this and observe Terraform automatically creating a new machine according to the counter:

```
$ terraform apply
aws_key_pair.admin_key: Refreshing state... (ID: admin_key)
aws_security_group.base_security_group: Refreshing state... (ID: sg-
d3dbd8b4)
aws_instance.dev.0: Refreshing state... (ID: i-0018b1044953371ae)
aws_instance.dev.1: Creating...
[...]
aws_instance.dev.1: Creation complete

Apply complete! Resources: 1 added, 0 changed, 0 destroyed.
```

The second server shows up in the AWS Console:

 Remember, the command to destroy a Terraform infrastructure is `terraform destroy`.

There's more...

We can achieve similar results using Ansible. Here's how it looks, using `admin_key` and `base_security_group` created in the previous recipes:

```
---
  - name: dev instance
    ec2:
      key_name: admin_key
      group: base_security_group
      instance_type: t2.micro
      image: ami-ee6b189d
      wait: yes
```

Generating meaningful outputs with Terraform

Wouldn't it be great if Terraform could show us useful, informational output after a successful run? Following what we've done so far, it would be helpful to know how to connect to the instance, what are the local and public IP addresses, or see the security groups used. That's what Terraform's outputs are for.

Getting ready

To step through this recipe, you will need the following:

▶ A working Terraform installation

▶ An AWS provider and an EC2 instance (using a SSH keypair and a Security Group), all configured in Terraform (refer to the previous recipes)

▶ An Internet connection

How to do it...

Thankfully, we can use the same syntax we're already using to access variables and attributes of references, but this time in an `output` resource.

Let's start by simply adding a line in `outputs.tf` that would show us how to connect to our virtual machine, using the `public_ip` attribute of our `dev` EC2 instance:

```
output "login" {
  value = "ssh ubuntu@${aws_instance.dev.public_ip} -i
${var.aws_ssh_admin_key_file}"
}
```

When applying terraform next time, it will display the following:

```
login = ssh ubuntu@52.51.242.17 -i keys/aws_terraform
```

No doubt it's much quicker than having to log into the AWS dashboard, find the instance, and copy and paste the IP in the terminal.

What if it's important for us to know at a glimpse under what security groups our EC2 instance is running? We know security groups can be multiple, so it's an array. We can access the content of this array using the `formatlist` interpolation syntax as follows:

```
output "security_groups" {
  value = "${formatlist("%v", aws_instance.dev.security_groups)}"
}
```

So now, at the next `terraform apply`, we'll instantly know our security groups:

```
security_groups = [
    base_security_group
]
```

Also, if we have a lot of information to display from multiple sources, we can use the same syntax:

```
output "instance_information" {
    value = "${formatlist("instance: %v public: %v private: %v",
    aws_instance.dev.*.id, aws_instance.dev.*.public_ip,
    aws_instance.dev.*.private_ip)}"
}
```

This will display the instance ID and its local and public IP addresses.

There's more...

Note that we used `${aws_instance.dev.public_ip}` in the first output and `aws_instance.dev.*.public_ip` in our last output. If you use the latter, the output will iterate through all available machines. It's very useful if you launch more than one instance using the `count=n` parameter in the `aws_instance` Terraform resource.

Using contextual defaults with Terraform

We've seen how to declare and use default values in our Terraform code, such as the Ubuntu AMI for our region or our VM size. An interesting feature in Terraform is the ability to declare and use *maps* of values, so, depending on a key, the variable can have a different value. We'll see how it applies to the correct AMI of the corresponding AWS.

Getting ready

To step through this recipe, you will need the following:

- A working Terraform installation
- An AWS provider and an EC2 instance (using a SSH key pair and a security group), all configured in Terraform (refer to the previous recipes)
- An Internet connection

How to do it...

Here's how we simply declared the AMI we wanted for the `eu-west-1` region in the `variables.tf` file:

```
variable "ami" {
  default = "ami-ee6b189d"
}
```

We accessed it easily like this in the `instances.tf` file:

```
ami = "${var.ami}"
```

A similar, but more explicit way would be to use a map, so we know which region the value refers to:

```
variable "ami" {
  default = {
    eu-west-1 = "ami-ee6b189d"
  }
}
```

Here's how we access the same value in a map:

```
ami = "${var.ami["eu-west-1"]}"
```

Now let's add more valid AMI IDs for other regions:

```
variable "ami" {
  default = {
    eu-west-1 = "ami-ee6b189d"
    us-east-1 = "ami-4f680658"
    us-west-1 = "ami-68a9e408"
  }
}
```

The `ami` variable can now be valid for either of the three regions if accessed correctly in the `instances.tf` file:

```
ami = "${var.ami["us-east-1"]}"
```

Now is a good time to start managing the AWS region directly in the code, for better portability. Add the following to `variables.tf` to use `eu-west-1` as a default region:

```
variable "aws_region" {
  default = "eu-west-1"
}
```

You can now use this variable in the `provider.tf` file to set the region:

```
provider "aws" {
  region = "${var.aws_region}"
}
```

Now the region variable is globally available, let's use it to access our map in `instances.tf`:

```
ami = "${var.ami["${var.aws_region}"]}"
```

We now have an easily geographically deployable infrastructure that anyone in your team can launch close to him or her without the need to change code.

There's more...

We can perform the same dynamic access to a map using the `lookup()` function in Terraform:

```
ami = "${lookup(var.ami, var.aws_region)}"
```

Managing S3 storage with Terraform

Storing and accessing files easily and in a scalable way is an essential part of a modern infrastructure. Amazon S3 is Amazon's answer to this need. S3 stores "objects" in "buckets" and has no storage limit (one exception is the bucket name: it has to be unique on Amazon's S3, the namespace being shared). We'll see how to make the best use of S3 with Terraform.

Getting ready

To step through this recipe, you will need the following:

- A working Terraform installation
- An AWS provider configured in Terraform (refer to the previous recipes)
- An Internet connection

How to do it...

We'll start by creating a simple and explicitly public bucket on S3 named `iac-book`, using the `aws_s3_bucket` resource (and a tag for the sake of it):

```
resource "aws_s3_bucket" "iac_book" {
  bucket = "iac-book"
  acl    = "public-read"

  tags {
    Name = "IAC Book Bucket in ${var.aws_region}"
  }
}
```

After a `terraform apply`, your bucket is immediately available for storing objects. You can see it on the AWS S3 Console (`https://console.aws.amazon.com/s3/`):

Let's store a first object right now, a very simple file containing a simple string (`"Hello Infrastructure-as-Code Cookbook!"`). The resource is named `aws_s3_bucket_object`, and you need to reference the bucket previously created, the destination name (`index.html`), and its content. The ACL is here again explicitly public:

```
resource "aws_s3_bucket_object" "index" {
  bucket = "${aws_s3_bucket.iac_book.bucket}"
  key = "index.html"
  content = "<h1>Hello Infrastructure-as-Code Cookbook!</h1>"
  content_type = "text/html"
  acl     = "public-read"
}
```

You can alternatively provide a file directly instead of its content:

```
source = "index.html"
```

If you navigate to the AWS S3 Console, you can see it available with some extended information:

It would be awesome if we could know easily the URL of our file right from Terraform, so we could give it to others. Unfortunately, there's no easy function for that. However, we know how URLs are constructed: `http://s3-<region>.amazonaws.com/bucket_name/object_name`. Let's create an output containing this information:

```
output "S3" {
  value = "http://s3-${aws_s3_bucket.iac_book.region}.amazonaws.
com/${aws_s3_bucket.iac
_book.id}/${aws_s3_bucket_object.index.key}"
}
```

Paste the link in a web browser and you'll be able to access your file.

A workaround is to use the *static website hosting* feature of S3 by simply adding the following to your `aws_s3_bucket` resource:

```
website {
  index_document = "index.html"
}
```

An optional output will give you its static hosting URL (in our case, `iac-book.s3-website-eu-west-1.amazonaws.com` instead of `http://s3-eu-west-1.amazonaws.com/iac-book/index.html`):

```
output "S3 Endpoint" {
  value = "${aws_s3_bucket.iac_book.website_endpoint}"
}
```

There's more...

Using Ansible, there are many ways to create a bucket. Here's a simple bucket with public read permissions, using the classic `s3` module:

```
---
- name: create iac-book bucket
  s3:
    bucket: iac-book
    mode: create
    permission: public-read
```

 Note that Ansible 2.2 also comes with an `s3_website` module for specifically handling S3 websites.

Here's how we would simply upload our previous `index.html` file using the same `s3` module:

```
- name: create index.html file
  s3:
    bucket: iac-book
    object: index.html
    src: index.html
    mode: put
    permission: public-read
```

Creating private Docker repositories with Terraform

To host your Docker images, you need what's called a **registry**. This registry is either run by you or as a service. It stores your images for you and sometimes builds them too. The Docker Hub and Quay.io from CoreOS are the main Docker-managed registries you can subscribe to. Both are interesting in terms of features or pricing. However, an interesting alternative is AWS **Elastic Container Registry** (**ECR**): pricing is different and fully integrated in the AWS ecosystem. Let's create countless repositories simply with Terraform!

Getting ready

To step through this recipe, you will need the following:

▸ A working Terraform installation

▸ An AWS provider configured in Terraform (refer to the previous recipes)

- ▶ A configured AWS CLI (`http://docs.aws.amazon.com/cli/latest/userguide/installing.html`)

- ▶ An Internet connection

How to do it...

Let's say you want to store your application container in a repository named `myapp`, so you can deploy it easily. It's very simple with Terraform. Add the following code to a file named `ecr.tf`:

```
resource "aws_ecr_repository" "myapp" {
  name = "myapp"
}
```

If you want to know the URL to access your new repository, you can create an output using the corresponding exported attribute:

```
output "ECR" {
  value = "${aws_ecr_repository.myapp.repository_url}"
}
```

If you're used to the other Docker registries, the first step is to authenticate so you create private repositories. Here, no login or password are provided by AWS. We need to use the official AWS command line to authenticate, and that will give us temporary Docker credentials. The output of this command is the Docker command to type:

```
$ aws ecr get-login --region eu-west-1
docker login -u AWS -p AQECAHh... -e none
https://<account_number>.dkr.ecr.eu-west-1.amazonaws.com
```

Now we can `docker build`, `tag`, and `push` images at will! (See more about using Docker images in the dedicated chapter of this book.)

A nice advanced feature is the ability to use fine-grained policies for each repository created.

Creating a PostgreSQL RDS database with Terraform

Amazon Relational Database Service (**RDS**) is an on-demand, ready-to-use, and resizable EC2 instance specifically tailored and configured to run the requested database server. You can launch many different relational database servers on RDS, and we'll focus on PostgreSQL for this recipe.

Getting ready

To step through this recipe, you will need the following:

- ▸ A working Terraform installation
- ▸ An AWS provider configured in Terraform (refer to the previous recipes)
- ▸ An Internet connection

How to do it...

There are many parameters at play in a database deployment, even a simple one. To be certain of what we'll deploy, we'll start by filling a simple table with the database requirements, and build on it:

Parameter	Variable name	Value
RDS Database Engine	`rds_engine`	`postgresql`
RDS Database Engine Version	`rds_engine_version`	`9.5.2`
RDS Instance Name	`rds_identifier`	`db`
RDS Instance Type	`rds_instance_type`	`db.t2.micro`
RDS Storage Size (GB)	`rds_storage_size`	`5`
RDS First Database Name	`rds_db_name`	`iac_book_db`
RDS Administrator Username	`rds_admin_user`	`dbadmin`
RDS Administrator Password	`rds_admin_password`	`super_secret_password`
RDS Publicly Accessible	`rds_publicly_ accessible`	`true`

Let's set all those variables in our `variables.tf` file:

```
variable "rds_identifier" {
  default = "db"
}

variable "rds_instance_type" {
  default = "db.t2.micro"
}
variable "rds_storage_size" {
  default = "5"
}

variable "rds_engine" {
  default = "postgres"
```

```
}

variable "rds_engine_version" {
  default = "9.5.2"
}

variable "rds_db_name" {
  default = "iac_book_db"
}

variable "rds_admin_user" {
  default = "dbadmin"
}

variable "rds_admin_password" {
  default = "super_secret_password"
}

variable "rds_publicly_accessible" {
  default = "true"
}
```

As we're running PostgreSQL and we want it to be available on the Internet (though generally not a good idea for production), we'll need a security group allowing just the default PgSQL port (TCP/5432) for our IP address (refer to the *Using AWS security groups with Terraform* recipe), in `securitygroups.tf`:

```
resource "aws_security_group" "rds_security_group" {
  name        = "rds_security_group"
  description = "RDS Security Group"

  ingress {
    from_port   = 5432
    to_port     = 5432
    protocol    = "tcp"
    cidr_blocks = ["1.2.3.4/32"]
  }

  egress {
    from_port   = 0
    to_port     = 0
    protocol    = "-1"
    cidr_blocks = ["0.0.0.0/0"]
  }
```

```
    tags {
      Name = "rds_security_group"
    }
  }
}
```

Now we have everything in place to construct the `aws_db_instance` resource:

```
resource "aws_db_instance" "db" {
  engine            = "${var.rds_engine}"
  engine_version    = "${var.rds_engine_version}"
  identifier        = "${var.rds_identifier}"
  instance_class    = "${var.rds_instance_type}"
  allocated_storage = "${var.rds_storage_size}"
  name              = "${var.rds_db_name}"
  username          = "${var.rds_admin_user}"
  password          = "${var.rds_admin_password}"
  publicly_accessible   = "${var.rds_publicly_accessible}"
  vpc_security_group_ids = ["${aws_security_group.rds_security_group.
id}"]
  tags {
    Name = "IAC Database in ${var.aws_region}"
  }
}
```

As we did previously, a quick output giving us the FQDN of our new database will help us to use it quickly, in `outputs.tf`:

```
output "RDS" {
  value = "address: ${aws_db_instance.db.address}"
}
```

Let's `terraform apply` now and try the result:

```
# psql -h <your_db_address> -d iac_book_db -U dbadmin
Password for user dbadmin:
psql (9.5.4, server 9.5.2)
[...]


iac_book_db=> \l
                            List of databases
    Name     |  Owner   | Encoding  |   Collate     |    Ctype     |
Access privileges
-------------+----------+-----------+---------------+--------------+---------
---------------
```

```
iac_book_db  | dbadmin   | UTF8    | en_US.UTF-8 | en_US.UTF-8 |
postgres     | dbadmin   | UTF8    | en_US.UTF-8 | en_US.UTF-8 |
rdsadmin     | rdsadmin  | UTF8    | en_US.UTF-8 | en_US.UTF-8 |
rdsadmin=CTc/rdsadmin
template0    | rdsadmin  | UTF8    | en_US.UTF-8 | en_US.UTF-8 |
=c/rdsadmin        +

             |           |         |             |             |
rdsadmin=CTc/rdsadmin
template1    | dbadmin   | UTF8    | en_US.UTF-8 | en_US.UTF-8 |
=c/dbadmin         +

             |           |         |             |             |
dbadmin=CTc/dbadmin
(5 rows)
```

There are many more useful options you can use or set, such as maintenance windows, backup retention periods, dedicated database subnets, storage encryption, and master/slave configuration.

There's more...

How would that work when using Ansible to do a similar job with the same values? Just as easy as usual:

```
---
- name: create RDS PgSQL
  rds:
    command: create
    instance_name: db
    db_engine: postgres
    engine_version: 9.5.2
    db_name: iac_book_db
    size: 5
    instance_type: db.t2.micro
    username: dbadmin
    password: super_secure_password
    publicly_accessible: yes
    tags:
      Name: IAC Database
```

After executing this playbook, a similar PostgreSQL server will run on RDS as we just did with Terraform.

Enabling CloudWatch Logs for Docker with Terraform

CloudWatch Logs is a log aggregation service by Amazon you can use to send your logs to. It's very useful to keep some logs centralized, share access to them, receive alarms when errors happen, or simply store them safely. We'll see how to create a CloudWatch Log group and use it to stream logs from a Docker container logs inside it.

Getting ready

To step through this recipe, you will need the following:

▶ A working Terraform installation

▶ An AWS provider configured in Terraform (refer to the previous recipes)

▶ An Internet connection

▶ A Docker Engine running on Linux for the optional usage demonstration

How to do it...

Let's say we want the log group to be named `docker_logs`, and that we want to keep those logs for seven days. In the `variables.tf` file, that would look like this:

```
variable "log_group_name" {
  default = "docker_logs"
}

variable "log_retention_days" {
  default = "7"
}
```

Also, in a new `cloudwatch.tf` file, we can use the simple `aws_cloudwatch_log_group` resource:

```
resource "aws_cloudwatch_log_group" "docker_logs" {
  name             = "${var.log_group_name}"
  retention_in_days = "${var.log_retention_days}"
}
```

After a `terraform apply`, if you navigate to the AWS CloudWatch page, you'll see the newly created group under the **Log Groups** entry on the left (`https://eu-west-1.console.aws.amazon.com/cloudwatch/`).

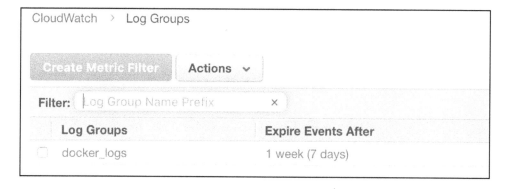

Amazon CloudWatch Logs Docker logging driver

You can now use this group to create a log stream from an application or a container. Using it as recommended by AWS is well documented, so let's use it with Docker instead. It only requires to give the Docker daemon access to the `AWS_ACCESS_KEY_ID` and `AWS_SECRET_ACCESS_KEY` environment variables (configuring the Docker daemon is out of the scope of this chapter, but that's under `/etc/sysconfig/docker` for Red Hat-based systems such as Fedora or CentOS, and `/etc/default/docker` for Debian/Ubuntu systems). Restart the daemon and start logging your containers output using a new Docker logging driver, using the log group name specified in Terraform earlier (`docker_logs`):

```
$ docker run -it --rm -p 80:80 --log-driver=awslogs --log-opt
awslogs-region=eu-west-1 --log-opt awslogs-group=docker_logs --log-
opt awslogs-stream=nginx nginx:stable
```

Generate some activity on the container:

```
$ curl -IL http://localhost
HTTP/1.1 200 OK
```

Refresh the AWS CloudWatch page and you'll see a new entry named `nginx` with the container logs. You can run all your containers in your infrastructure like this and get centralized logging very easily!

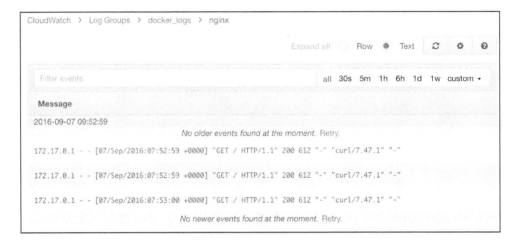

Managing IAM users with Terraform

An essential part of using AWS is controlling access to the resources. We've seen with all the previous recipes how often we need to use the AWS Access Keys, and it's surely not a good idea to use a single key for all your activities. Imagine what would happen if a single one of your services was hacked—the intruder would get the main AWS key and would be able to do everything on your behalf.

A good secure setup would be dedicated keys with a dedicated scope of access rights for every person in your team and every service in your infrastructure.

Thankfully, **Identity and Access Management** (**IAM**) is there just for that. We'll see how to use it with Terraform.

Getting ready

To step through this recipe, you will need the following:

- A working Terraform installation
- An AWS provider configured in Terraform (refer to the previous recipes)
- An Internet connection

How to do it...

Let's start with a simple case: two members of a team (Mary and Joe) need to access resources on AWS. They currently all share the same main key, which is a disaster if a leakage happens. So let's ask them what exactly they need to access in the AWS space:

Mary	S3 in read and write
Joe	EC2 in read only

As expected, neither user really needs full access!

Amazon helps by offering prebuilt security policies for IAM. If those aren't enough, you can tailor the ones you need:

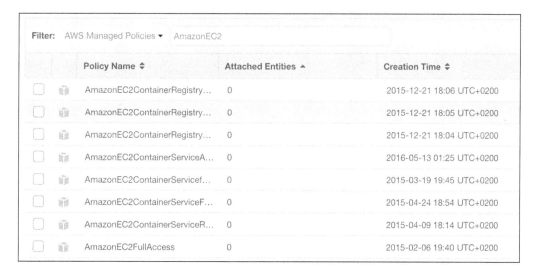

 You can find all AWS Managed IAM Policies at `https://console.aws.amazon.com/iam/home#policies`.

An IAM user for S3 access

Let's create a first IAM user for Mary in a new `iam.tf` file using the `aws_iam_user` resource:

```
resource "aws_iam_user" "mary" {
  name = "mary"
  path = "/team/"
}
```

The `path` is purely optional and informative, I'm simply suggesting structured paths. So we'll have `/apps/` as well later.

We can now create an AWS Access Key for our user Mary, using the `aws_iam_access_key` resource with reference to our user:

```
resource "aws_iam_access_key" "mary" {
  user = "${aws_iam_user.mary.name}"
}
```

And finally, as we know, we want to attach to this user the `AmazonS3FullAccess` managed policy, let's use the dedicated resource:

```
resource "aws_iam_user_policy_attachment" "mary_s3full" {
  user = "${aws_iam_user.mary.name}"
  policy_arn = "arn:aws:iam::aws:policy/AmazonS3FullAccess"
}
```

Let's write an `output` so we know both parts of the key in `outputs.tf`:

```
output "mary" {
  value = "ACCESS_KEY: ${aws_iam_access_key.mary.id}, SECRET:
${aws_iam_access_key.mary.secret}"
}
```

Also, `terraform apply` this to create the `mary` user:

```
[...]
Outputs:
mary = ACCESS_KEY: AKIAJPQB7HBK2KLAARRQ, SECRET: wB+Trao2R8qTJ36IEE64G
NIGTqeWrpMwid69Etna
```

Testing the restrictions

Now, `terraform apply` this, and confirm using an S3 browser that you can access S3! Here's an example of creating a simple S3 bucket with `s3cmd`:

```
$ s3cmd --access_key=<mary_access_key> --secret_key=<mary_secret_key>
mb s3://iacbook-iam-bucket

Bucket 's3://iacbook-iam-bucket/' created
```

Is this account really limited to S3, as it pretends to be? Let's try to list EC2 hosts with Mary's account using the `aws` command line (provided you configured the `aws` tool accordingly):

```
$ aws --profile iacbook-mary ec2 describe-hosts

An error occurred (UnauthorizedOperation) when calling the
DescribeHosts operation: You are not authorized to perform this
operation.
```

So it all looks good and secure! Mary can do her job on S3 safely.

An IAM user for EC2 in read-only

Is there a similar managed policy for Joe, with a read-only scope on EC2? Fortunately, there is! It's creatively named `AmazonEC2ReadOnlyAccess`.

Let's create our second user, with this IAM policy in the `iam.tf` file:

```
resource "aws_iam_user" "joe" {
  name = "joe"
  path = "/team/"
}

resource "aws_iam_access_key" "joe" {
  user = "${aws_iam_user.joe.name}"
}

resource "aws_iam_user_policy_attachment" "joe_ec2ro" {
  user = "${aws_iam_user.joe.name}"
  policy_arn = "arn:aws:iam::aws:policy/AmazonEC2ReadOnlyAccess"
}
```

Don't forget the useful output that comes with it:

```
output "joe" {
  value = "ACCESS_KEY: ${aws_iam_access_key.joe.id}, SECRET: ${aws_
iam_access_key.joe.secret}"
}
```

Next, `terraform apply` this once again, and can the Joe user see what's on S3? No, he can't:

```
$ s3cmd --access_key=<joe_access_key> --secret_key=<joe_secret_key>
ls

ERROR: S3 error: 403 (AccessDenied): Access Denied
```

But can the Joe user simply list the EC2 VMs as he needs to, with the same command that was forbidden to Mary? Yes, he can:

```
$ aws --profile iacbook-joe ec2 describe-hosts
{
  "Hosts": []
}
```

We're on track to securely manage our infrastructure access using code!

An application user IAM – CloudWatch Logs

We've used the CloudWatch Logs service in a previous recipe. If you remember, you had to enter once again your keys in the Docker Engine configuration. If you had 100 servers, your master keys would be on each of them. This is rather unnecessary, if you consider that the scope of this configuration in Docker is just to send logs. Fortunately, there's a managed IAM policy for that named `CloudWatchLogsFullAccess`.

So let's create another user, exactly as before for Mary and Joe, except this one will be for our Docker Engines and not for a real user in `iam.tf`. I suggest using a different path, just to separate real users and application users. However, that's totally optional and opinionated:

```
resource "aws_iam_user" "logs" {
  name = "logs"
  path = "/apps/"
}

resource "aws_iam_access_key" "logs" {
  user = "${aws_iam_user.logs.name}"
}

resource "aws_iam_user_policy_attachment" "logs_cloudwatch_full" {
  user = "${aws_iam_user.logs.name}"
  policy_arn = "arn:aws:iam::aws:policy/CloudWatchLogsFullAccess"
}
```

The relevant `output` in `outputs.tf` is as follows:

```
output "logs" {
  value = "ACCESS_KEY: ${aws_iam_access_key.logs.id}, SECRET:
${aws_iam_access_key.logs.secret}"
}
```

Now, `terraform apply` this and try the *Enabling CloudWatch Logs for Docker with Terraform* recipe again with those credentials instead of the master keys: it will still work on the CloudWatch scope, but if something goes wrong, it will never put the rest of your infrastructure in danger. The worst that can happen in this area is the total waste of the logs.

```
[...]
Outputs:

joe = ACCESS_KEY: AKIAJQPSXBKSD3DY47BQ, SECRET:
VQgtQ7D8I+mxRX28/x5qbFk6cdyxZajhhSsh7Rha
logs = ACCESS_KEY: AKIAISIUXTG5RIJZAEYA, SECRET:
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
mary = ACCESS_KEY: AKIAJPQB7HBK2KLAARRQ, SECRET:
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
```

	User Name ⬍	Groups	Password	Password Last Used ⬍	Access Keys	Creation Time ⬍
Filter						Showing 3 results
☐	joe	0		N/A	1 active	2016-09-07 10:04 U...
☐	logs	0		N/A	1 active	2016-09-07 10:04 U...
☐	mary	0		N/A	1 active	2016-09-07 10:04 U...

There's more...

If you'd prefer to see how this would work using Ansible, it's a bit different. IAM support is not equivalent, as there's no IAM Managed Policies support. However, you can simply create users like this:

```
---
- name: create mary user
  iam:
      iam_type: user
      name: mary
      state: present
      access_key_state: create
      path: /team/
```

As there's currently no IAM Managed Policy support, a workaround is to use the JSON from the IAM Policy we want, such as `AmazonS3FullAccess` for our user Mary. It's easy to find in the AWS Console in the **Policies** section (`https://console.aws.amazon.com/iam/home#policies`). Paste the following JSON content in `AmazonS3FullAccess.json` at the root of the `Ansible` folder:

```
{
    "Version": "2012-10-17",
    "Statement": [
      {
        "Effect": "Allow",
        "Action": "s3:*",
        "Resource": "*"
      }
    ]
}
```

Use this local policy in the `iam_policy` module:

```
- name: Assign a AmazonS3FullAccess policy to mary
  iam_policy:
    iam_type: user
    iam_name: mary
    policy_name: AmazonS3FullAccess
    state: present
    policy_document: AmazonS3FullAccess.json
```

3
Going Further with Terraform

In this chapter, we will cover the following recipes:

- ▸ Handling different environments with Terraform
- ▸ Provisioning a CentOS 7 EC2 instance with Chef using Terraform
- ▸ Using data sources, templates, and local execution
- ▸ Executing remote commands at bootstrap using Terraform
- ▸ Using Docker with Terraform
- ▸ Simulating infrastructure changes using Terraform
- ▸ Teamwork – sharing Terraform infrastructure state
- ▸ Maintaining a clean and standardized Terraform code
- ▸ One Makefile to rule them all
- ▸ Team workflow example
- ▸ Managing GitHub with Terraform
- ▸ External monitoring integration with StatusCake

Introduction

In this chapter, we'll go beyond the essentials of using Terraform we covered in *Chapter 2, Provisioning IaaS with Terraform*. We'll discover many important techniques to use Terraform in conjunction with other players in the field such as Docker and Chef, how it can be used in multiple environments (such as development/staging/production), how powerful it can be to manage not only infrastructure but many SaaS as well, and how to integrate the tool within a team workflow (sharing, synchronizing, maintaining, harmonizing, and so on). These topics are all equally important, as they will define the quality of our daily work and our ability to interact with other people, services, and systems.

 The Terraform version in use for this book is 0.7.3.

Handling different environments with Terraform

It's a common and recommended setup to have different infrastructure environments, with some level of parity. Those environments can vary greatly between companies and projects in both names and focus, but here are commonly found environments:

- Development: where developers can implement and quickly test new features
- Staging: where the new features are tested in a more consistent environment than the development one, sometimes very similar to a preproduction environment
- Preproduction: this environment is the most similar possible to production
- Production: the full-featured live production environment

We'll see how using infrastructure-as-code and especially how Terraform fundamentally helps to build strong and replicated environments. This time we'll use a CoreOS AMI for a change.

Getting ready

To step through this recipe, you will need the following:

- A working Terraform installation
- An AWS account with an SSH key configured in Terraform (refer to the *Chapter 2, Provisioning IaaS with Terraform,* recipes)
- An Internet connection

How to do it...

Using infrastructure-as-code, the easiest thing is to simply duplicate the code to create as many environments as needed. However, there's a much more powerful way to leverage the full capabilities of Terraform.

Let's define the requirements of simple target environments that we'll translate into dynamic Terraform code:

Parameter	Staging	Production
Number of instances	1	3
Type of instance	`t2.micro`	`t2.medium`
Operating system	CoreOS Stable	CoreOS Stable
AMI in eu-west-1	`ami-85097ff6`	`ami-85097ff6`
AMI in us-east-1	`ami-0aef8e1d`	`ami-0aef8e1d`
S3 bucket naming	iacbook-staging	iacbook-production
Default environment	Yes	No

Let's start by declaring those variables in the `variables.tf` file, exactly as we' saw in *Chapter 2, Provisioning IaaS with Terraform*, except we'll describe environments such as *staging* and *production* instead of the AWS regions for the cluster size and instance types.

Define the CoreOS AMI variable:

```
variable "aws_coreos_ami" {
  type = "map"

  default = {
    eu-west-1 = "ami-85097ff6"
    us-east-1 = "ami-0aef8e1d"
  }
}
```

Define a cluster size variable with different values according to the environment:

```
variable "cluster_size" {
  type = "map"

  default = {
    staging    = "1"
    production = "3"
  }

  description = "Number of nodes in the cluster"
}
```

Finally, define the different AWS instance types:

```
variable "aws_instance_type" {
  type = "map"

  default = {
    staging    = "t2.micro"
    production = "t2.medium"
  }

  description = "Instance type"
}
```

Now let's use those in a highly dynamic infrastructure code (`instances.tf`), using the `aws_instance` resource and by choosing automatically the correct cluster size and instance type according to the environment, while choosing the right AMI according to the execution region:

```
resource "aws_instance" "coreos" {
  count                       = "${lookup(var.cluster_size,
var.environment)}"
  ami                         = "${lookup(var.aws_coreos_ami,
var.aws_region)}"
  instance_type               = "${lookup(var.aws_instance_type,
var.environment)}"
  key_name                    = "${aws_key_pair.admin_key.key_name}"
  associate_public_ip_address = true

  tags {
    Name        = "coreos_${var.environment}_${count.index+1}"
    Environment = "${var.environment}"
  }
}
```

 We constructed each instance `Name` tag according to its environment and its numerical value in the count (that is, `coreos_production_2`).

Our specification table indicates we need two different S3 buckets as well. Let's reuse in `s3.tf` something close to what we did in *Chapter 2, Provisioning IaaS with Terraform*:

```
resource "aws_s3_bucket" "bucket" {
  bucket = "iacbook-${var.environment}"

  tags {
    Name        = "IAC Book ${var.environment} Bucket"
    Environment = "${var.environment}"
  }
}
```

It's the same construction here, each environment will get its bucket dynamically named after it.

Keeping the tfstate isolated

It's strongly recommended to **not mix** Terraform state files between environments. One elegant solution to keep them well separated is to use the following option when executing the `terraform` command:

```
$ terraform apply -state=staging.tfstate
```

Your default environment (set to staging) will now reside in the `staging.tfstate` file.

Setting the production flag

Now we have our staging infrastructure running smoothly, it's time to launch the real thing—the production environment. As we're already using a dedicated terraform state file, let's do the same for production, and set the `environment` variable directly through the command line:

```
$ terraform plan -state=production.tfstate -var
environment=production
```

You now have two clearly separated environments using the very same code, but living independently from each other. Concise and elegant!

Provisioning a CentOS 7 EC2 instance with Chef using Terraform

Once the underlying infrastructure is generated by Terraform, chances are the job isn't already finished. That's the moment a configuration management tool such as Chef, Ansible, or Puppet enters the game, to provision the virtual machine. Thankfully, Chef is a first class provisioning tool in Terraform. We'll see here how to fully bootstrap a CentOS 7.2 instance on AWS with Terraform, from nothing to a fully configured node, by gracefully handing over the configuration to Chef after having it automatically deployed and registered on Hosted Chef.

If it's the first time you've launched CentOS 7 servers on AWS, you have to agree their terms and conditions at `https://aws.amazon.com/marketplace/pp/B00O7WM7QW`.

Getting ready

To step through this recipe, you will need the following:

▸   A working Terraform installation
▸   An AWS account with an SSH key configured in Terraform and a security group allowing SSH connections from outside (refer to the *Chapter 2, Provisioning IaaS with Terraform,* recipes)

▸ An account on a Chef server (we recommend using a free hosted Chef account. Please refer to the *Creating a free hosted server Chef account and a Puppet server* recipe of *Chapter 6, Fundamentals of Managing Servers with Chef and Puppet*), with the default cookbook uploaded

▸ An Internet connection

How to do it...

As there're a lot of sources involved, let's put all the required information in a table (the Chef information is taken from the Chef Starter Kit, or your own Chef server, fill in your own values):

Hostname	`centos-1`
Instance type	`t2.micro`
AMI in eu-west-1	ami-7abd0209
AMI in us-east-1	ami-6d1c2007
SSH username	centos
SSH key	`keys/aws_terraform`
TCP ports needed	22
Cookbook(s) to apply	starter
Chef server URL	`https://api.chef.io/organizations/iacbook`
Validation key	`iacbook.pem`
Validation client name	iacbook
Chef client version	12.13.37

1. Let's start by declaring our AMIs as a map in the `variables.tf` file:

```
variable "aws_centos_ami" {
  type = "map"

  default = {
    eu-west-1 = "ami-7abd0209"
    us-east-1 = "ami-6d1c2007"
  }
}
```

2. Now add the instance type in the same file:

```
variable "aws_instance_type" {
  default     = "t2.micro"
  description = "Instance Type"
}
```

3. Declare the Chef version we're currently using in production, so it's stable and stays the same:

```
variable "chef_version" {
   default = "12.13.37"
}
```

4. Declare the Chef server URL. If you're using the book example with hosted Chef, you'll find the correct address in the `knife.rb` file: it's simply `https://api.chef.io/organizations/<your_organization_name>`, otherwise, use your own Chef server):

```
variable "chef_server_url" {
   default = "https://api.chef.io/organizations/iacbook"
}
```

5. Finally, add the *validation client* name for the Chef server:

```
variable "chef_validation_client_name" {
   default = "iacbook"
}
```

6. To connect to the instance, we know the default username is `centos`, but as it can evolve or you may use your own images, it's better to fix it in a variable as well:

```
variable "ssh_user" {
   default = "centos"
}
```

Creating the EC2 instance

We know from previous recipes that a basic instance running CentOS looks like this in Terraform's `instances.tf` using a security group named `base_security_group`:

```
resource "aws_instance" "centos" {
  ami                         = "${lookup(var.aws_centos_ami,
var.aws_region)}"
  instance_type               = "${var.aws_instance_type}"
  key_name                    = "${aws_key_pair.admin_key.key_name}"
  security_groups             = ["${aws_security_group.base_security_
group.name}"]
  associate_public_ip_address = true

  tags {
    Name = "CentOS-${count.index+1} by Terraform"
  }
}
```

Now we need to provide two kinds of information to our Terraform file: what to do with Chef on the server and how to connect to it.

Passing connection information

To tell Terraform how to connect itself to the new EC2 instance, we use a `connection {}` block inside the `aws_instance` resource to tell it which user and key to use through SSH:

```
connection {
    type     = "ssh"
    user     = "${var.ssh_user}"
    key_file = "${var.aws_ssh_admin_key_file}"
}
```

Giving Chef information

We need to give some information to Terraform to pass it on to Chef. This will all happen inside a `provisioner "chef" {}` block inside the `aws_instance` resource.

Using all the variables we declared, here's how it looks:

```
resource "aws_instance" "centos" {
[...]
  provisioner "chef" {
    node_name               = "centos-${count.index+1}"
    run_list                = ["starter"]
    server_url              = "${var.chef_server_url}"
    validation_client_name  = "${var.chef_validation_client_name}"
    validation_key          = "${file("chef/validator.pem")}"
    version                 = "${var.chef_version}"
  }
}
```

 Don't forget to use a valid path for the validation key!

Now you can `terraform apply` this and see everything happen, from instance creation to Chef Client deployment and cookbook installation.

How it works...

First, Terraform creates the required AWS environment (keys, security groups, and instances), and once the instance is running, it connects to it with the right credentials by SSH, then deploys the specified Chef client version from the official source, and finally executes an initial chef-client run that registers the node on the Chef server and applies the requested cookbooks.

There's more...

A lot more configuration options are possible for the Chef provisioner inside Terraform. For example, all available chef-client options can be passed as an array using `client_options`, and the Chef environment (usually very important) is passed using `environment` as a string. If you use a custom built image with the Chef client already baked in, you will be interested in setting `skip_install` to `true` so it doesn't get reinstalled.

Using data sources, templates, and local execution

When we deploy or update an infrastructure with Terraform, it's sometimes enjoyable to have some local content dynamically generated. For example, if you want to provision with Ansible the new virtual machine launched by Terraform, chances are you'll need to populate a `hosts` file with the public IP address of this host locally on your laptop.

Ansible can use some dynamic inventories with AWS by itself, but we'll see here how to use a template in Terraform and dynamically fill in the required information so we end up with a working Ansible setup, thanks to Terraform.

Getting ready

To step through this recipe, you will need the following:

- A working Terraform installation
- An AWS account with an SSH key configured in Terraform and a security group allowing SSH connections from outside (refer to the *Chapter 2, Provisioning IaaS with Terraform* recipes)
- An Internet connection

How to do it...

Let's start by launching a standard CentOS 7.2 on AWS with a standard set of variables in `variables.tf`:

```
variable "aws_centos_ami" {
  type = "map"

  default = {
    eu-west-1 = "ami-7abd0209"
    us-east-1 = "ami-6d1c2007"
  }
}
```

```
variable "aws_instance_type" {
  default     = "t2.micro"
  description = "Instance Type"
}
```

Here's the simplest `instances.tf` file to launch the instance:

```
resource "aws_instance" "centos" {
  ami                         = "${lookup(var.aws_centos_ami,
var.aws_region)}"
  instance_type               = "${var.aws_instance_type}"
  key_name                    = "${aws_key_pair.admin_key.key_name}"
  security_groups             = ["${aws_security_group.base_security_
group.name}"]
  associate_public_ip_address = true

  tags {
    Name = "CentOS"
  }
}
```

Data and templates

Now, how does a typical `hosts` file look for Ansible? It looks like this:

```
[section_name_1]
1.2.3.4
[section_name_2]
5.6.7.8
a.server.fqdn
```

So, later, Ansible will apply whatever role is needed for each server of each section.

In our case, we want a simple section named `centos7_hosts` and the servers IP as follows:

```
[centos7_hosts]
1.2.3.4
```

Let's construct our first template named `hosts.tpl` with a variable named `host_public_ipv4` that will ultimately be replaced by the real future IP of the host we'll later launch:

```
[centos7_hosts]
${host_public_ipv4}
```

To generate this file, we'll use a template with a variable in it, that Terraform will generate for us, using a `data` resource in `data.tf`—it simply contains the file interpolation of our template and passes it the variable we need from our AWS instance:

```
data "template_file" "ansible_hosts" {
```

```
template = "${file("hosts.tpl")}"

vars {
  host_public_ipv4 = "${aws_instance.centos.public_ip}"
}
}
```

The local-exec Terraform provisioner

This generates the template internally, meaning the data is available, but not dumped anywhere. That's where the `local-exec` provisioner comes in, by simply echoing the rendered template from the data source into the file we want (in `data.tf`):

```
resource "null_resource" "generate_ansible_hosts" {
  provisioner "local-exec" {
    command = "echo '${data.template_file.ansible_hosts.rendered}'
    > hosts"
  }
}
```

 We use `"null_resource"` for this purpose, so the generation of the template is independent of any other executing resource. In other situations, we can perfectly use the `"local-exec"` { } provisioner directly from inside a standard resource.

We can now `terraform apply` this setup. How does our `hosts` file look? Like this:

$ cat hosts

[centos7_hosts]

52.17.172.231

It's correctly populated!

Apply a configured Ansible

Our code repository is now ready for use by Ansible. Here's a sample Ansible role that simply installs Docker and starts it, so we can play with it, under `ansible/main.yml`:

```
---
- hosts: centos7_hosts
  become: yes
  tasks:
    - name: Install EPEL
      yum: name=epel-release state=present
    - name: Install Docker
```

```
        yum: name=docker state=present
    - name: Start docker
        service: name=docker state=started enabled=yes
```

Now you just have to execute Ansible when you want, it is all ready and configured!

```
$ ansible-playbook -i hosts -u centos ansible/main.yml

PLAY [centos7_hosts]
*********************************************************

[...]

PLAY RECAP
*************************************************************************

52.17.172.231                : ok=4    changed=0    unreachable=0
failed=0
```

Executing remote commands at bootstrap using Terraform

It's a very common practice to have a set of initial commands executed right after bootstrap, even before the proper configuration management system such as Chef or Ansible takes responsibility. It can include immediate full updating of the OS, initial registration on discovery systems such as Consul, or initial addition of local DNS servers. It really shouldn't go farther than delivering a system in a slightly more advanced and expected state for the next configuration system to take over. Under no circumstance should it replace a proper configuration management tool.

In this recipe, we'll launch a CentOS 7.2 system, then fully update it so it's as secure as possible, install EPEL so we have a greater library of available packages, add the Puppet Labs Yum repository and install a Puppet agent, and add a different name server so our system is ready for the next step (which we won't cover here, as it's probably executing Puppet code).

Getting ready

To step through this recipe, you will need the following:

▸ A working Terraform installation
▸ An AWS account with an SSH key configured in Terraform and a security group allowing SSH connections from outside (refer to the *chapter 2, Provisioning IaaS with Terraform* recipes)
▸ An Internet connection

How to do it...

Before diving into the provisioning part, let's start by describing a classic CentOS 7.2 AMI in `instances.tf`:

```
resource "aws_instance" "centos" {
  ami                       = "${lookup(var.aws_centos_ami,
  var.aws_region)}"
  instance_type             = "${var.aws_instance_type}"
  key_name                  =
  "${aws_key_pair.admin_key.key_name}"
  security_groups           =
  ["${aws_security_group.base_security_group.name}"]
  associate_public_ip_address = true

  tags {
    Name = "CentOS"
  }
}
```

The variables in the `variables.tf` file are as follows:

```
variable "aws_centos_ami" {
  type = "map"

  default = {
    eu-west-1 = "ami-7abd0209"
    us-east-1 = "ami-6d1c2007"
  }
}

variable "aws_instance_type" {
  default     = "t2.micro"
  description = "Instance Type"
}
```

Now, what are our immediate objectives for this system?:

▶ Fully update it: `sudo yum install -y`

▶ Enable the EPEL repository: `sudo yum install epel-release -y`

▶ Add a custom name server: `echo "nameserver 8.8.8.8" | sudo tee -a / etc/resolv.conf`

▶ Add the Puppet Labs repository: `sudo yum install https://yum. puppetlabs.com/puppetlabs-release-pc1-el-7.noarch.rpm -y`

▸ Install the Puppet agent: `sudo yum install puppet-agent -y`

▸ Display the Puppet version: `sudo /opt/puppetlabs/bin/puppet agent --version`

Let's add those commands inside a `remote-exec` provisioner inside our `aws_instance` resource, changing the default username to `centos`:

```
provisioner "remote-exec" {
    inline = [
      "echo \"nameserver 8.8.8.8\" | sudo tee -a
/etc/resolv.conf",
      "sudo yum update -y",
      "sudo yum install epel-release -y",
      "sudo yum install https://yum.puppetlabs.com/puppetlabs-
release-pc1-el-7.noarch.rpm -y",
      "sudo yum install puppet-agent -y",
      "sudo /opt/puppetlabs/bin/puppet agent --version"
    ]
    connection {
        user = "centos"
      }
  }
```

When you `terraform apply` this, you'll end up with a fully updated CentOS 7.2 system, with EPEL available, a custom DNS server added and Puppet agent installed.

Ready for the next stage of deployment with Puppet!

Using Docker with Terraform

Terraform can also be used to manipulate Docker. The classical usage is against an already running Docker server on the network, but it will work exactly the same locally with your own Docker installation. Using Terraform for controlling Docker, we'll be able to dynamically trigger Docker image updates, execute containers with every imaginable option, manipulate Docker networks, and use Docker volumes.

Here, we'll deploy an isolated blog container (Ghost) that will be publicly served by the `nginx-proxy` container over HTTP. This very useful `nginx-proxy` container is proposed by Jason Wilder from InfluxDB on his GitHub: `https://github.com/jwilder/nginx-proxy`.

Getting ready

To step through this recipe, you will need the following:

- A working Terraform installation.
- A working Docker installation (native Docker for Mac, Docker Engine on Linux, a remote server running Docker on TCP, and so on). Docker 1.12 is used for this recipe.
- An Internet connection.

How to do it...

Before starting to code anything using Terraform, ensure you can connect to any kind of Docker Engine, local or remote:

```
$ docker version
Client:
 Version:      1.12.0
 API version:  1.24
 Go version:   go1.6.3
 Git commit:   8eab29e
 Built:        Thu Jul 28 21:15:28 2016
 OS/Arch:      darwin/amd64

Server:
 Version:      1.12.0
 API version:  1.24
 Go version:   go1.6.3
 Git commit:   8eab29e
 Built:        Thu Jul 28 21:15:28 2016
 OS/Arch:      linux/amd64
```

If you have issues at this point, you need to fix them before going further.

Our goal is to serve, through an `nginx-proxy` container, a blog container (Ghost) that will not be directly available on the network.

If you're connecting to a remote Docker server, you need to configure the Docker provider (maybe in `provider.tf`). Alternatively, it can use the `DOCKER_HOST` environment variable, or just the local daemon if not specified. When using locally for this exercise, you can just forget about including the provider:

```
provider "docker" {
   host = "tcp://1.2.3.4:2375"
}
```

Let's start by declaring two data sources for each of our Docker images (in `docker.tf`). The `ghost` image will be in its `0.10` version tag, while `nginx-proxy` will use the `0.4.0` version tag. Using a data source will help us manipulate the image later:

```
data "docker_registry_image" "ghost" {
   name = "ghost:0.10"
}

data "docker_registry_image" "nginx-proxy" {
   name = "jwilder/nginx-proxy:0.4.0"
}
```

Now that we can access the image, let's exactly do that, using the `docker_image` resource. We're reusing all the information our data source is exposing to us, such as the image name or its SHA256, so we know if a new image is available to pull:

```
resource "docker_image" "ghost" {
   name         = "${data.docker_registry_image.ghost.name}"
   pull_trigger =
   "${data.docker_registry_image.ghost.sha256_digest}"
}

resource "docker_image" "nginx-proxy" {
   name         = "${data.docker_registry_image.nginx-proxy.name}"
   pull_trigger = "${data.docker_registry_image.nginx-
   proxy.sha256_digest}"
}
```

Let's now declare the private Ghost container (without any port mapping), using the `docker_container` resource. Let's use the image we just declared through the `docker_image` resource, and export an environment variable named `VIRTUAL_HOST`, to be used by the nginx-proxy container (refer to the nginx-proxy documentation for more information). Replace with the host you want if you're not running against a local Docker host:

```
resource "docker_container" "ghost" {
   name  = "ghost"
   image = "${docker_image.ghost.latest}"
   env   = ["VIRTUAL_HOST=localhost"]
}
```

Now let's start the `nginx-proxy` container. We know from its documentation that it needs to share the Docker socket in read-only mode (`/var/run/docker.sock`) to dynamically access the running containers, and we want it to run on the default HTTP port (`tcp/80`). Let's do that:

```
resource "docker_container" "nginx-proxy" {
  name  = "nginx-proxy"
  image = "${docker_image.nginx-proxy.latest}"

  ports {
    internal = 80
    external = 80
    protocol = "tcp"
  }

  volumes {
    host_path      = "/var/run/docker.sock"
    container_path = "/tmp/docker.sock"
    read_only      = true
  }
}
```

Now if you `terraform apply` this, you can navigate over to `http://localhost/admin` (replace `localhost` with the Docker server you used) and set up your Ghost blog!

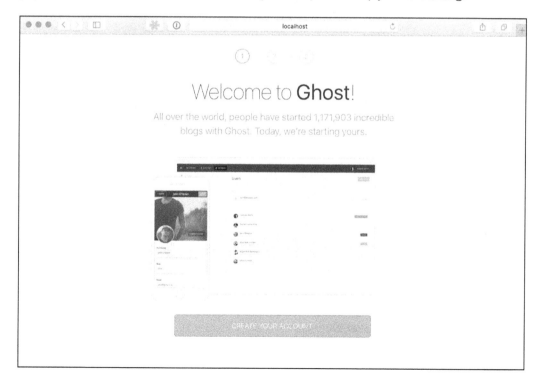

Simulating infrastructure changes using Terraform

In an earlier recipe, you learned how to manage different environments with Terraform, which is great. But how do we test for changes before applying them?

Terraform has a great internal mechanism that allows us to *plan* for changes by comparing what our infrastructure code wants and what the remote state includes. That way, we can safely check whether what we thought was a minor modification in our code has in fact a destructive impact (sometimes, some parameters in a resource trigger a full destruction of the resource!).

We'll cover different ways of anticipating, simulating, and targeting changes in our infrastructure, as an added safety check before applying the changes for good.

Getting ready

To step through this recipe, you will need the following:

▶ A working Terraform installation

▶ An AWS account with an SSH key configured in Terraform (refer to the *Chapter 2, Provisioning IaaS with Terraform* recipes)

▶ An Internet connection

How to do it...

Let's start with a simple CoreOS machine on AWS. We know the AMI ID, we want a single `t2.micro` host. Let's put that information in the `variables.tf` file:

```
variable "aws_coreos_ami" {
  default = "ami-85097ff6"
}

variable "cluster_size" {
  default     = "1"
  description = "Number of nodes in the cluster"
}

variable "aws_instance_type" {
  default     = "t2.micro"
  description = "Instance type"
}
```

The simplest `aws_instance` resource we can make is the following in `instances.tf`:

```
resource "aws_instance" "coreos" {
  count                       = "${var.cluster_size}"
  ami                         = "${var.aws_coreos_ami}"
  instance_type               = "${var.aws_instance_type}"
  key_name                    = "${aws_key_pair.admin_key.key_name}"
  associate_public_ip_address = true

  tags {
    Name = "coreos_${count.index+1}"
  }
}
```

Planning

Until now, we've used `terraform apply` for immediate action. There's another command: `terraform plan`. It does what it says. It plans for changes, but doesn't apply them:

```
$ terraform plan

Refreshing Terraform state in-memory prior to plan...

The refreshed state will be used to calculate this plan, but

will not be persisted to local or remote state storage.

The Terraform execution plan has been generated and is shown
below.

[...]


+ aws_instance.coreos

    ami:                            "ami-85097ff6"

    [...]


+ aws_key_pair.admin_key

    [...]


Plan: 2 to add, 0 to change, 0 to destroy.
```

So, by planning before applying, we can know what's about to happen to our infrastructure. We're happy about an instance with the right AMI being created, so let's `terraform apply`.

Now the infrastructure is created, if you run a plan again, it will say nothing should be modified:

```
$ terraform plan
```

```
Refreshing Terraform state in-memory prior to plan...
The refreshed state will be used to calculate this plan, but
will not be persisted to local or remote state storage.

aws_key_pair.admin_key: Refreshing state... (ID: admin_key)
aws_instance.coreos: Refreshing state... (ID: i-0f9106905e74a29f7)

No changes. Infrastructure is up-to-date. This means that Terraform
could not detect any differences between your configuration and
the real physical resources that exist. As a result, Terraform
doesn't need to do anything.
```

A normally operating infrastructure should always be in a state where a `terraform plan` doesn't want to change anything.

Now let's say we need our infrastructure to evolve, and create an S3 bucket. That would look like this in a file named `s3.tf`:

```
resource "aws_s3_bucket" "bucket" {
  bucket = "iacbook"

  tags {
    Name = "IAC Book Bucket"
  }
}
```

We're not sure about what's about to happen, so let's plan with Terraform, so it's telling us exactly what it's intending to do:

```
$ terraform plan
Refreshing Terraform state in-memory prior to plan...
[...]

aws_key_pair.admin_key: Refreshing state... (ID: admin_key)
aws_instance.coreos: Refreshing state... (ID: i-0f9106905e74a29f7)

[...]

+ aws_s3_bucket.bucket
    bucket:           "iacbook"
    tags.Name:        "IAC Book Bucket"
```

```
[...]
```

```
Plan: 1 to add, 0 to change, 0 to destroy.
```

The plan looks good—it seems to want to create an S3 bucket named the way we want! Let's `terraform apply` this and move on.

Quickly simulating changes

We now wonder what would happen if we were to change the number of instances. That's the `cluster_size` variable, currently set to `1`. Instead of messing with the code, we can test the impact of changing that value directly from the command line:

```
$ terraform plan -var 'cluster_size="2"'
[...]
+ aws_instance.coreos.1
    ami:                        "ami-85097ff6"

    instance_type:              "t2.micro"

    tags.Name:                  "coreos_2"

    [...]
Plan: 1 to add, 0 to change, 0 to destroy.
```

Good news! It looks like increasing the `cluster_size` value has the intended effect: creating a new instance.

Now, we wonder legitimately what would be the effect of changing the instance type, from `t2.micro` to `t2.medium`:

```
$ terraform plan -var aws_instance_type="t2.medium"
[...]
-/+ aws_instance.coreos
    [...]
    instance_type:              "t2.micro" => "t2.medium" (forces
    new resource)
```

```
Plan: 1 to add, 0 to change, 1 to destroy.
```

Ouch! Changing the instance type seems to be a destructive action. Let's work on that later, and add the change to a new file named `plan.tfvars`:

```
aws_instance_type="t2.medium"
```

We know we'd like to propose to change the number of instances to 2, so let's add that to the same file:

```
aws_instance_type="t2.medium"
cluster_size="2"
```

We can now test against this file containing all our changes, using the `-var-file` option:

```
$ terraform plan -var-file=plan.tfvars

-/+ aws_instance.coreos.0

    instance_type:                "t2.micro" => "t2.medium" (forces
    new resource)

    tags.Name:                    "coreos_1" => "coreos_1"

    [...]


+ aws_instance.coreos.1

    instance_type:                "t2.medium"

    tags.Name:                    "coreos_2"

    [...]

Plan: 2 to add, 0 to change, 1 to destroy.
```

Good! You learn that our first instance will be destroyed and recreated to move from `t2.micro` to `t2.medium`, and that a second instance will be created with the same values. Let's not apply this, as added fees will be incurred.

Targeting for a specific change

Our colleague asks us if we're sure our proposed changes have no impact specifically on the S3 bucket. Terraform allows us to get an answer to that question very specifically by targeting the resource directly in the planning phase:

```
$ terraform plan -var-file=plan.tfvars -
target="aws_s3_bucket.bucket"

[...]

aws_s3_bucket.bucket: Refreshing state... (ID: iacbook)

[...]

No changes. Infrastructure is up-to-date.

[...]
```

Our colleague is happy, and we're now sure that this change will do exactly what's intended. We can submit this change for review.

Teamwork – sharing Terraform infrastructure state

You probably work with a team, and now you're using Terraform to manage your infrastructure, you'll face an issue: how does your team work together on infrastructure-as-code? There're many answers to that, and one crucial question to address is: how is transmitted or synchronized the Terraform state?

We'll see here how we can share the state using Git (a version control system where developers can store code), AWS S3 (an Amazon Web Services storage system using HTTP) or Consul (a tool for service discovery and a key-value store), chosen among many other solutions.

Getting ready

To step through this recipe, you will need the following:

- ▸ A working Terraform installation
- ▸ An AWS account with an SSH key configured in Terraform (refer to the *Chapter 2, Provisioning IaaS with Terraform* recipes)
- ▸ A working Docker installation for the Consul simulation solution (optional)
- ▸ An Internet connection

How to do it...

Let's start by having an initial infrastructure running (a single virtual machine for this example). Here's an `aws_instance` resource in `instances.tf` for a CoreOS stable release taken from previous recipes:

```
resource "aws_instance" "coreos" {
  count                       = "${var.cluster_size}"
  ami                         = "${var.aws_coreos_ami}"
  instance_type               = "${var.aws_instance_type}"
  key_name                    = "${aws_key_pair.admin_key.key_name}"
  associate_public_ip_address = true

  tags {
    Name = "coreos_${count.index+1}"
  }
}
```

Here are example variables in `variables.tf`; feel free to adapt them:

```
variable "aws_coreos_ami" {
  default = "ami-85097ff6"
}

variable "cluster_size" {
  default     = "1"
  description = "Number of nodes in the cluster"
}

variable "aws_instance_type" {
  default     = "t2.micro"
  description = "Instance type"
}
```

Terraform stores its state by default in a file named `terraform.tfstate`, with a backup file named `terraform.tfstate.backup`:

```
$ ls terraform.tfstate*

terraform.tfstate          terraform.tfstate.backup
```

Sharing with Git

The simplest of all options is to share the state file using Git: you're already supposed to version your infrastructure code! Go and create an account somewhere. GitHub (https://github.com) doesn't have free private repositories, but GitLab (https://gitlab.com) or BitBucket (https://bitbucket.org) do. Follow the instructions to have your Git repository locally working.

Now, add the `tfstate` files:

```
$ git add *.tfstate*
```

Commit the files:

```
$ git commit -m "initial state creating the infrastructure"
[master (root-commit) 6f7e2ba] initial state creating the
infrastructure
 2 files changed, 193 insertions(+)
 create mode 100644 terraform.tfstate
 create mode 100644 terraform.tfstate.backup
```

Push the commit:

```
$ git push
```

Now your coworkers absolutely need to pull the changes before applying any action, or calamity might follow soon:

```
coworker@host $ git pull
```

Sharing remotely with S3

Sharing the state file through Git works, to some extent. You'll end up someday in a situation where someone forgets to push or pull. Merging conflicts in a state file is really not something nice to do.

One solution to stop thinking about it is using S3 to share the state file and use the remote state feature of Terraform.

Start by creating an S3 bucket just for that, in `s3.tf`, with versioning enabled (so you can roll back to a previous version of the infrastructure):

```
resource "aws_s3_bucket" "tfstate" {
  bucket = "iacbook-tfstate"

  versioning {
    enabled = true
  }

  tags {
    Name = "IAC Book TFState Bucket"
  }
}
```

Let's `terraform apply` this S3 bucket, and move on to the remote configuration with our information:

```
$ terraform remote config -backend=s3 -backend-
config="bucket=iacbook-tfstate" -backend-
config="key=terraform.tfstate"
Remote state management enabled
Remote state configured and pulled.
```

You can now see the terraform state file in the S3 browser:

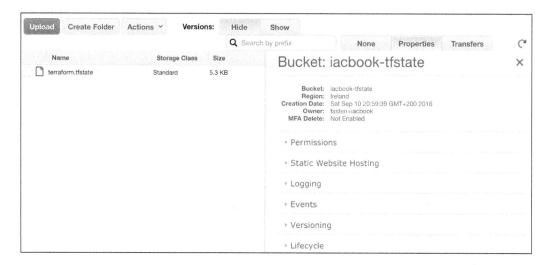

Now make any change to the infrastructure, such as adding a new S3 bucket, to see the file change in action:

```
resource "aws_s3_bucket" "bucket" {
  bucket = "iacbook-bucket"

  tags {
    Name = "IAC Book Bucket"
  }
}
```

After a `terraform apply`, simply push the changes:

```
$ terraform remote push
State successfully pushed!
```

See the history in the S3 browser:

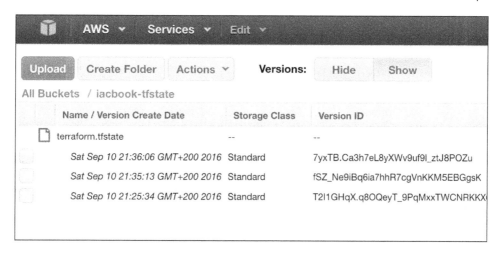

The coworker has to configure their environment and pull the information:

```
coworker@host $ terraform remote config -backend=s3 -backend-
config="bucket=iacbook-tfstate" -backend-
config="key=terraform.tfstate"
Initialized blank state with remote state enabled!
Remote state configured and pulled.
```

A local copy is now residing in the `.terraform` folder:

```
$ head .terraform/terraform.tfstate
```

Sharing remotely with Consul

A very nice way to share the state file is by using Consul, a powerful key/value storage from Hashicorp (`http://consul.io/`). Using Consul to store the Terraform states makes it easier to work with a team, as there's only a single replicated state. No risk of using an old state file if we forgot to synchronize our git repository.

Configuring a proper Consul in cluster for production is out of the scope of this book, but if you don't have a Consul cluster at hand to try this out, here's a way to quickly have one, using Docker and a Consul image:

```
$ docker run -it --rm -p 8400:8400 -p 8500:8500 -p 8600:53/udp -h
node1 progrium/consul -server -bootstrap
```

Now let's configure our Terraform remote for Consul, and name it `terraform/my_customer`, so we can manage multiple customers simultaneously:

```
$ terraform remote config -backend=consul -backend-
config="path=terraform/my_customer"
Remote state management enabled
Remote state configured and pulled.
```

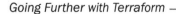
Job done! Your coworkers can now push and pull from the Consul source! In a production Consul cluster, it means replicated and synchronized states on each node, with added privacy.

Other state sharing options

There're many other ways to share the state, such as on Azure, using OpenStack Swift, any kind of HTTP server supporting REST, CoreOS's own etcd key-value store, Google Cloud storage, or Atlas, the commercial solution by Hashicorp.

Maintaining a clean and standardized Terraform code

Everyone has coding styles, but enforcing a standardized and commonly readable style is the key for a smooth collaborative team work. That's why Terraform has a command to ensure both format and style are all right.

I encourage readers to use it extensively, and even integrate it in **Continuous Integration (CI)** systems and in Makefiles.

Getting ready

To step through this recipe, you will need the following:

▸   A working Terraform installation
▸   An Internet connection

How to do it...

We'll intentionally write a simple Terraform code with non-standard style and with an error (a missing variable). This will help us manipulate the various tools Terraform offers to ensure the most consistent and homogenous code, so we can achieve more quickly a better quality and a higher level of standardization of our code.

Let's write a provider for AWS like this in `provider.tf` (deliberately on one line):

```
provider "aws" { region = "${var.aws_region}" }
```

Syntax validation

Try to validate that file, and it will notify us that we're missing a variable:

```
$ terraform validate
Error validating: 1 error(s) occurred:
```

```
* provider config 'aws': unknown variable referenced:
'aws_region'. define it with 'variable' blocks
```

The validation fails, and the return code is `1`:

```
$ echo $?
1
```

Let's add this variable to a `variables.tf` file:

```
variable "aws_region" { default = "eu-west-1" }
```

Hooray! A `terraform validate` is now happy:

```
$ terraform validate
$ echo $?
0
```

Style validation

This thing is, we solved the obvious problem (a missing variable), but what about style? The preceding style perfectly works, but style might not be canonical.

Let's use the `fmt` option to check for styling issues, displaying the `diff` onscreen, but not writing the files automatically:

```
$ terraform fmt -write=false -diff=true
provider.tf
diff a/provider.tf b/provider.tf
--- /var/folders/zn/bx_20cp90bq5_fqqmlvx3tq40000gn/T/598506546
2016-09-10 22:40:35.000000000 +0200
+++ /var/folders/zn/bx_20cp90bq5_fqqmlvx3tq40000gn/T/407676393
2016-09-10 22:40:35.000000000 +0200
@@ -1 +1,3 @@
-provider "aws" { region = "${var.aws_region}" }
+provider "aws" {
+   region = "${var.aws_region}"
+}
variables.tf
diff a/variables.tf b/variables.tf
--- /var/folders/zn/bx_20cp90bq5_fqqmlvx3tq40000gn/T/743564340
2016-09-10 22:40:35.000000000 +0200
+++ /var/folders/zn/bx_20cp90bq5_fqqmlvx3tq40000gn/T/095288323
2016-09-10 22:40:35.000000000 +0200
```

```
@@ -1 +1,3 @@
-variable "aws_region" { default = "eu-west-1" }
+variable "aws_region" {
+   default = "eu-west-1"
+}
```

We see our style was quite far away from the guidelines. Let's fix this and automatically format our files correctly:

```
$ terraform fmt
provider.tf
variables.tf
```

Our two files are now correctly formatted!

I highly recommend putting those two commands in your CI tests (you are running infrastructure code tests in CI, aren't you?), and even before reaching the CI, it's even better if it's in the project's Makefile.

Here's a simple Makefile example:

```
.DEFAULT_GOAL := all

all:
    terraform validate
    terraform fmt
```

Now you can just type make in the Terraform directory and you're sure your code both validates and is coherently styled.

One Makefile to rule them all

Some languages have environment or version managers such as RVM for Ruby, NVM for Node, or even Rackspace's DVM for Docker.

It's highly recommended to lock the Terraform version, so everyone in the team uses the same version, and updates can be painlessly handled. To do that, I suggest using a Terraform container, so we'll use here the one I use myself: `sjourdan/terraform:<version>` (from `https://github.com/sjourdan/terraform-docker`). But I understand replacing the simple `terraform` command by something such as `docker run -it --rm -v ˋpwdˋ:/data sjourdan/terraform:0.7.3` can feel not so appealing. That's why we can use a common Makefile for each project using Terraform.

Using a common entry point for manipulating the infrastructure code helps a lot of sharing practices, enforcing policies, and integrating third-party services such as CI systems.

Getting ready

To step through this recipe, you will need the following:

- A working Terraform installation
- An AWS account with an SSH key configured in Terraform (refer to the *Chapter 2, Provisioning IaaS with Terraform* recipes)
- An Internet connection

How to do it...

Let's begin by setting the Terraform version we want to use in a Makefile so it will be easy to manipulate for updates in the future:

```
TERRAFORM_VERSION = 0.7.3
```

Let's now create a `TERRAFORM_BIN` variable that will include the full Docker command, plus share our local folder:

```
TERRAFORM_BIN = docker run -it --rm -v "$(PWD)":/data
sjourdan/terraform:$(TERRAFORM_VERSION)
```

I like auto-documenting my Makefile, and I propose a popular technique: `make` by default calls `make help`, which in turn parses the `Makefile` for comments, and displays them. That way, I can choose what to output by simply adding a comment. Here's how it works:

```
.DEFAULT_GOAL := help

help:
	@grep -E '^[a-zA-Z_-]+:.*?## .*$$' $(MAKEFILE_LIST) | sort |
	awk 'BEGIN {FS = ":.*?## "}; {printf "\033[36m%-30s\033[0m
%s\n",
	$$1, $$2}'
```

Now simply use this feature to create an entry for the validation and formatting from the previous recipe:

```
validate: terraform-fmt terraform-validate  ## Validate syntax and
format

terraform-fmt:
  $(TERRAFORM_BIN) fmt -list

terraform-validate:
  $(TERRAFORM_BIN) validate
```

If you simply type `make`, you'll get an automatic help:

```
$ make
validate                        Validate syntax and format
```

Now, a simple `make validate` will both validate the syntax and format the code.

It would be great to have the `plan` and `apply` commands as well, and if you followed the recipe on environment management with Terraform, that would be awesome if it worked right from the `Makefile`, we'd save a lot of time.

Start by creating the `Makefile` main "help" entries:

```
plan: terraform-validate terraform-plan ## Plan changes
apply: terraform-validate terraform-apply ## Apply Changes
```

 We added the validation step at each step, so we're always absolutely sure it passes full validation (and you can add your own validation steps).

Let's check for an environment variable named `env`, passed at `make` execution (such as `make plan env=staging`), and returns an error if not set:

```
ifndef env
getenv=$(error var:"env=" is not set)
else
getenv=$(env)
endif
```

Now we can write what `terraform-plan` and `terraform-apply` are exactly running, with isolated Terraform states and environments:

```
terraform-plan:
    $(TERRAFORM_BIN) plan -state=$(call getenv).tfstate -var
    environment=$(call getenv)


terraform-apply:
    $(TERRAFORM_BIN) apply -state=$(call getenv).tfstate -var
    environment=$(call getenv)
```

By the way, you can add support for environments to our previous `terraform-validate` example:

```
terraform-validate:
    $(TERRAFORM_BIN) validate -var environment=$(call getenv)
```

Add as many features as you want to your project's `Makefile`; you'll soon realize this simple tool helps so much.

For example, I always add a `make destroy` command, so I can easily destroy a test infrastructure (be careful though!):

```
destroy: terraform-destroy  ## Destroy (careful!)
terraform-destroy:
  $(TERRAFORM_BIN) destroy -state=$(call getenv).tfstate -var
  environment=$(call getenv)
```

Our Makefile now looks like this:

```
$ make

apply                         Apply Changes

destroy                       Destroy (careful!)

plan                          Plan changes

validate                      Validate syntax and format
```

Also, it can be used like this:

```
$ make plan env=staging
$ make apply env=staging
```

 Add absolutely anything that might make your lives easier, such as releases, tests, and so on.

See also

- The auto documented Makefile: `http://marmelab.com/blog/2016/02/29/auto-documented-makefile.html`
- Rbenv: `https://github.com/rbenv/rbenv`
- RVM: `https://github.com/rvm/rvm`
- DVM: `https://github.com/getcarina/dvm`
- NVM: `https://github.com/creationix/nvm`

Team workflow example

Working with infrastructure code is very similar to working with software code. Countless books and methods exist on the subject and approaches are usually very opinionated.

A simple workflow I propose to use here for our infrastructure-as-code work is based on what's called the **GitHub Flow** (https://guides.github.com/introduction/flow/):

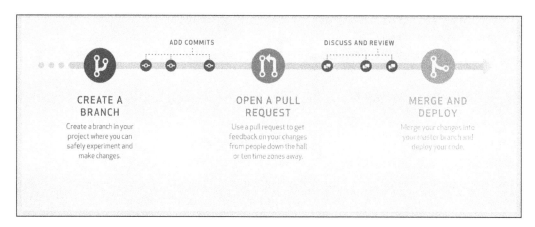

Getting ready

To step through this recipe, you will need the following:

- An account on some Git hosting (self-hosted or commercial)
- A working Terraform installation
- An AWS account with an SSH key configured in Terraform (refer to the *Chapter 2, Provisioning IaaS with Terraform* recipes)
- An Internet connection

How to do it...

Start by creating a new repository for use with your team. Use any service that works for you: GitLab, GitHub, BitBucket, and others. This example uses GitHub.

A simple Git repository

Create a new repository on GitHub:

We might be storing secrets in that repository, such as SSH private keys or passwords. It's probably a safer option to create a private Git repository for now.

Now import this new empty repository on your workstation, in a dedicated folder:

```
$ git clone <your_git_repostory_address>
Cloning into 'my_infrastructure_code'...
remote: Counting objects: 3, done.
remote: Compressing objects: 100% (2/2), done.
remote: Total 3 (delta 0), reused 0 (delta 0), pack-reused 0
Receiving objects: 100% (3/3), done.
Checking connectivity... done.
```

Initial infrastructure code

Create a new Git branch to work on an initial infrastructure:

```
$ git checkout -b new_infrastructure
Switched to a new branch 'new_infrastructure'
```

Add some Terraform code from the previous recipes, such as a single CoreOS instance. For the record, here's the `variables.tf` file:

```
variable "aws_region" {
  default = "eu-west-1"
}
```

```
variable "aws_ssh_admin_key_file" {
  default = "keys/aws_terraform"
}

variable "aws_coreos_ami" {
  default = "ami-85097ff6"
}

variable "cluster_size" {
  default     = "1"
  description = "Number of nodes in the cluster"
}

variable "aws_instance_type" {
  default     = "t2.micro"
  description = "Instance type"
}
```

Here's a deliberately badly formatted `provider.tf`:

```
provider "aws" { region = "${var.aws_region}" }
```

Also, here's a CoreOS instance in `instances.tf`:

```
resource "aws_instance" "coreos" {
  count                       = "${var.cluster_size}"
  ami                         = "${var.aws_coreos_ami}"
  instance_type               = "${var.aws_instance_type}"
  key_name                    = "${aws_key_pair.admin_key.key_name}"
  associate_public_ip_address = true

  tags {
    Name = "coreos_${count.index+1}"
  }
}
```

Terraform code validation

Let's be sure our code validates:

```
$ terraform validate
```

Thankfully, it does!

Does this code plan to do what we want it to do? Have a look:

```
$ terraform plan
[...]
+ aws_instance.coreos
[...]
+ aws_key_pair.admin_key
[...]
Plan: 2 to add, 0 to change, 0 to destroy.
```

This looks exactly like our objective. Let's continue.

Infrastructure code commit

What are the new files on this branch that aren't on master? Let's find out:

```
$ git status
[...]
        instances.tf
        keys.tf
        keys/
        provider.tf
        variables.tf
```

Good, those are the files we just created. Let's add them to a `commit`:

```
$ git add .
$ git commit -m "an initial infrastructure"
[new_infrastructure 2415ad4] an initial infrastructure
 6 files changed, 65 insertions(+)
 create mode 100644 instances.tf
 create mode 100644 keys.tf
 create mode 100644 keys/aws_terraform
 create mode 100644 keys/aws_terraform.pub
 create mode 100644 provider.tf
 create mode 100644 variables.tf
```

Now let's send the branch upstream so that our coworkers can see our work that's still not yet in production:

```
$ git push --set-upstream origin new_infrastructure
Counting objects: 9, done.
Delta compression using up to 4 threads.
Compressing objects: 100% (8/8), done.
Writing objects: 100% (9/9), 2.60 KiB | 0 bytes/s, done.
Total 9 (delta 0), reused 0 (delta 0)
To git@github.com:sjourdan /my_infrastructure_code.git
 * [new branch]       new_infrastructure -> new_infrastructure
Branch new_infrastructure set up to track remote branch
new_infrastructure from origin.
```

Make a pull request

Navigate to your repository, and you'll see something similar to the following screenshot, showing an information about the new branch being just pushed. GitHub proposes to easily create a pull request. A pull request is a request to merge the content of one branch to another branch. In our case, we want to ask our coworkers to merge our `new_infrastructure` branch into the master branch, to create some discussion:

When you open a pull request, GitHub automatically tries the requested merge (in our case, from our branch to master). Here, no conflicts are noted, so we can write a message explaining what our request is all about. A pull request is often composed of multiple commits, so a summary is more than welcome:

Now everyone from your team have access to your work and can discuss it right from GitHub if necessary:

A few minutes later, one of your coworkers reviews your code and sends you a remark:

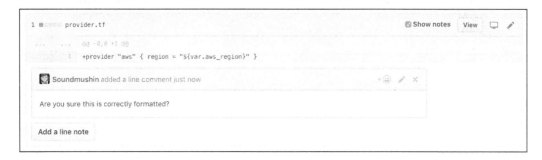

She might be right; let's find out with the Terraform formatter:

```
$ terraform fmt
provider.tf
```

Looks like there was a formatting issue! Use `git diff` to see what's the difference:

```
$ git diff
diff --git a/provider.tf b/provider.tf
index 59cdf2a..b54eb94 100644
--- a/provider.tf
+++ b/provider.tf
@@ -1 +1,3 @@
-provider "aws" { region = "${var.aws_region}" }
+provider "aws" {
+  region = "${var.aws_region}"
+}
```

We're happy with that; let's `add`, `commit`, and `push`. Pushing to our remote branch will automatically add our commit to the pull request as well:

```
$ git add provider.tf
$ git commit -m "fixed bad formatting"
[new_infrastructure b027825] fixed bad formatting
 1 file changed, 3 insertions(+), 1 deletion(-)
$ git push
```

Our coworker can now see in real time that we took her remark into account, as GitHub automatically marks it as outdated:

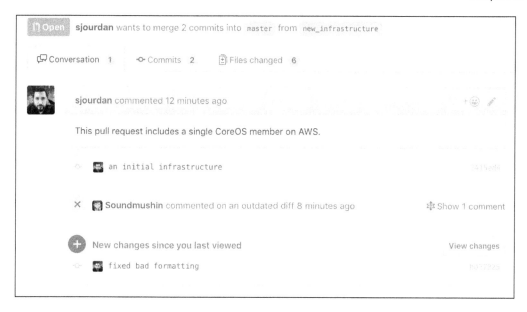

Now our coworker pulled the changes on her side, tried to plan the changes herself with Terraform, and announces she's happy with the results as well:

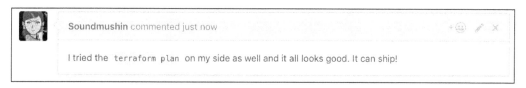

Apply the changes

So let's do that right now:

```
$ terraform apply
aws_key_pair.admin_key: Creating...
[...]
aws_instance.coreos: Creating...
[...]
Apply complete! Resources: 2 added, 0 changed, 0 destroyed.
```

Is there anything new in our repository? Have a look:

```
$ git status
terraform.tfstate
```

Sure, now we have to ship our infrastructure state to the pull request:

```
$ git add terraform.tfstate
$ git commit -m "initial terraform state"
$ git push
```

Our coworker sees that everything is all right, and she also checked the server is doing well. So, now she can merge our branch, close the pull request with a message, and then delete the now useless branch:

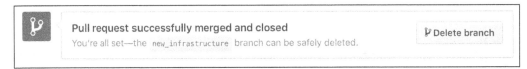

Our code and its fixes are now on master, along with the updated infrastructure state, all done in full collaboration with a coworker.

For any new feature, anything added to the infrastructure should follow the same pattern: create a branch, insert your changes, open a pull request, discuss the changes with the coworkers, apply the change, and merge to master. Master is now the reference again.

Managing GitHub with Terraform

There're many service providers to use with Terraform. GitHub is one of them, and we'll see how to manage members of an organization, various teams, and control repository access, right from our infrastructure code. That way, we have an automatic history log of who accesses what.

Getting ready

To step through this recipe, you will need the following:

- ▶ A working Terraform installation

- A GitHub account (with an API token)
- An Internet connection

How to do it...

We want to manage a GitHub organization named **ACME**. Here are the users and their groups:

GitHub username	GitHub team name	Membership level	Team privacy
John	Documentation	member	closed
Jane	Engineering	admin	secret

Here's the policy we decided concerning the Git repository named `infrastructure-repository`:

GitHub team name	Repository permissions
Documentation	pull
Engineering	admin

Configuring GitHub

Let's start by creating a `github` provider, as we used an `aws` provider for AWS in the previous recipes. The documentation lists the requirements: an API token and an organization name:

```
provider "github" {
  token        = "${var.github_token}"
  organization = "${var.github_organization}"
}
```

Set the generic variables in a `variables.tf` file:

```
variable "github_token" {
  default = "1a2b3c4d5"
  description = "GitHub API Token"
}

variable "github_organization" {
  default = "ACME Inc."
  description = "GitHub Organization Name"
}
```

Don't forget to override those variables to fit your own in the `terraform.tfvars` file.

Adding users to the GitHub organization

We want to add the username john as a member, and jane as an admin, in a file you can name github.tf (feel free to split managed GitHub features in many smaller files as your organization grows):

```
// john is a simple member of the organization
resource "github_membership" "membership_for_john" {
  username = "john"
  role     = "member"
}

// jane is an administrator of the organization
resource "github_membership" "membership_for_jane" {
  username = "jane"
  role     = "admin"
}
```

John and Jane are now part of the GitHub organization (they will receive invitations by e-mail).

Adding GitHub teams

Let's create our two teams, technical writers and engineering, with their respective privacy settings:

```
// An engineering team
resource "github_team" "engineering" {
  name        = "Engineering Team"
  description = "Our awesome engineers"
  privacy     = "secret"
}

// A documentation team
resource "github_team" "documentation" {
  name        = "Technical Writers Team"
  description = "Our awesome technical writers"
  privacy     = "closed"
}
```

Add our two members to their respective teams—Jane in engineering, John in documentation:

```
// Jane is a member of the engineering team
resource "github_team_membership" "eng_membership_jane" {
  team_id  = "${github_team.engineering.id}"
  username = "jane"
  role     = "member"
}

// John is a member of the documentation team
```

```
resource "github_team_membership" "doc_membership_john" {
  team_id  = "${github_team.documentation.id}"
  username = "john"
  role     = "member"
}
```

Setting Git repository access rights

The policy we've set is that members of the engineering group are admins of the repository, while technical writers can only pull the code:

```
// technical writers can pull the repo
resource "github_team_repository" "infrastructure_doc" {
  team_id    = "${github_team.documentation.id}"
  repository = "infrastructure-repository"
  permission = "pull"
}

// engineers are admin on the repo
resource "github_team_repository" "infrastructure_eng" {
  team_id    = "${github_team.engineering.id}"
  repository = "infrastructure-repository"
  permission = "admin"
}
```

You've just set the essentials to manage your GitHub organization right from Terraform!

External monitoring integration with StatusCake

External monitoring is helpful because it gives insights on how performant your infrastructure is, as seen from the outside, maybe from many places in the world. We can build our own availability monitoring systems, or we can use third-party services. StatusCake is a good example for us as they have a good API and a free service tier for us to try with Terraform. We'll monitor two things: host latency and HTTP availability.

Getting ready

To step through this recipe, you will need the following:

▸ A working Terraform installation
▸ A StatusCake account (`https://statuscake.com`)

▸ Optionally, an infrastructure managed by Terraform (refer to the previous recipes)

▸ An Internet connection

How to do it...

Start by setting the new `statuscake` provider, as we did with AWS or GitHub, using a username and API key:

```
provider "statuscake" {
  username = "${var.statuscake_username}"
  apikey   = "${var.statuscake_apikey}"
}
```

Declare the variables in `variables.tf`:

```
variable "statuscake_username" {
  default     = "changeme"
  description = "Sets the StatusCake Username"
}

variable "statuscake_apikey" {
  default     = "hackme"
  description = "Sets the StatusCake API Key"
}
```

Also, don't forget to set those variables to your own values in `terraform.tfvars`.

Creating an automated ping monitoring test

Let's create an initial test, a simple ICMP ping to a server whose IP is `1.2.3.4`, every 5 minutes:

```
resource "statuscake_test" "latency" {
  website_name = "My Server Latency"
  website_url  = "1.2.3.4"
  test_type    = "PING"
  check_rate   = 300
  paused       = false
}
```

The `website_name` or `website_url` can be a reference to an existing Terraform resource. If our AWS instance resource is named `centos`, you can access the value dynamically like this, instead of a static value:

```
website_url = "${aws_instance.centos.public_ip}"
```

If your resource has a `count` number, you can iterate through it so all the available instances are automatically monitored. It works like this:

```
resource "statuscake_test" "another_latency" {
  website_name = "${element(aws_instance.centos.*.public_ip,
  count.index)}"
  website_url  = "${element(aws_instance.centos.*.public_ip,
  count.index)}"
  test_type    = "PING"
  check_rate   = 300
  paused       = false
}
```

Another useful feature is to switch the value of `paused` to `true` for planned downtimes, so you're not hammered with alerts you're already aware of.

Creating an HTTPS test

A very common test we'll want to make is HTTP availability. It's really no different than an ICMP check;

```
resource "statuscake_test" "http" {
  website_name = "www.myweb.com Availability"
  website_url  = "https://www.myweb.com:443"
  test_type    = "HTTP"
  check_rate   = 300
}
```

4
Automating Complete Infrastructures with Terraform

In this chapter, we will cover the following recipes:

- ▶ Provisioning a complete CoreOS infrastructure on Digital Ocean with Terraform
- ▶ Provisioning a three-tier infrastructure on Google Compute Engine
- ▶ Provisioning a GitLab CE + CI runners on OpenStack
- ▶ Managing Heroku Apps and Add-ons using Terraform
- ▶ Creating a scalable Docker Swarm cluster on bare metal with Packet

Introduction

In this chapter, we'll describe complete infrastructures using Terraform, how it looks when everything is tied together, with a real project in mind. Most examples from previous chapters on Terraform were on Amazon Web Services, so to try to be more diverse and complete, this chapter is dedicated to other infrastructure services, namely Digital Ocean, Google Cloud, Heroku, and Packet. On Digital Ocean, we'll build a fully working and monitored CoreOS cluster with DNS dynamically updated. On Google Cloud, we'll build a three-tier infrastructure with two HTTP nodes behind a load balancer and an isolated MySQL managed database. Using OpenStack, we'll deploy a GitLab CE and two GitLab CI runners, using different storage solutions. We'll see how we can integrate and automate a Heroku environment. We'll end this chapter with a powerful and scalable Docker Swarm cluster on bare metal using Packet, capable of scaling hundreds of containers.

The Terraform version in use for this book is 0.7.4.

Provisioning a complete CoreOS infrastructure on Digital Ocean with Terraform

In this recipe, we'll build from scratch a fully working CoreOS cluster on Digital Ocean in their New York region, using Terraform and cloud-init. We'll add some latency monitoring as well with StatusCake, so we have a good foundation of using Terraform on Digital Ocean.

Getting ready

To step through this recipe, you will need the following:

- ▶ A working Terraform installation
- ▶ A Digital Ocean account
- ▶ A StatusCake account
- ▶ An Internet connection

How to do it...

Let's start by creating the `digitalocean` provider (it only requires an API token) in a file named `providers.tf`:

```
provider "digitalocean" {
  token = "${var.do_token}"
}
```

Declare the `do_token` variable in a file named `variables.tf`:

```
variable "do_token" {
  description = "Digital Ocean Token"
}
```

Also, don't forget to set it in a private `terraform.tfvars` file:

```
do_token = "a1b2c3d4e5f6"
```

Handling the SSH key

We know that we'll need an SSH key to log into the cluster members. With Digital Ocean, the resource is named `digitalocean_ssh_key`. I propose that we name the SSH key file `iac_admin_sshkey` in the `keys` directory, but as you might prefer something else, let's use a variable for that as well. Let's write this in a `keys.tf` file:

```
resource "digitalocean_ssh_key" "default" {
  name       = "Digital Ocean SSH Key"
  public_key = "${file("${var.ssh_key_file}.pub")}"
}
```

Create the related variable in `variables.tf`, with our suggested default:

```
variable "ssh_key_file" {
  default     = "keys/iac_admin_sshkey"
  description = "Default SSH Key file"
}
```

It's now time to effectively override the value in the `terraform.tfvars` file if you feel like it:

```
ssh_key_file = "./keys/my_own_key"
```

Creating the CoreOS cluster members

Here's the core of our infrastructure: three nodes running in the New York City data center NYC1, with private networking enabled, no backups activated (set it to `true` if you feel like it!), the SSH key we previously created, and a cloud-init file to initiate configuration. A virtual machine at Digital Ocean is named a *droplet*, so the resource to launch a droplet is `digitalocean_droplet`. All variables' names relate to what we just enumerated:

```
resource "digitalocean_droplet" "coreos" {
  image               = "${var.coreos_channel}"
  count               = "${var.cluster_nodes}"
  name                = "coreos-${count.index+1}"
  region              = "${var.do_region}"
  size                = "${var.do_droplet_size}"
  ssh_keys            = ["${digitalocean_ssh_key.default.id}"]
  private_networking  = true
  backups             = false
  user_data           = "${file("cloud-config.yml")}"
}
```

Declare all the variables in the `variables.tf` file, with some good defaults (the smallest 512 MB droplet, a three-node cluster), and some defaults we'll want to override (AMS3 data center or the stable CoreOS channel):

```
variable "do_region" {
```

```
    default     = "ams3"
    description = "Digital Ocean Region"
}

variable "do_droplet_size" {
    default     = "512mb"
    description = "Droplet Size"
}

variable "coreos_channel" {
    default     = "coreos-stable"
    description = "CoreOS Channel"
}

variable "cluster_nodes" {
    default     = "3"
    description = "Number of nodes in the cluster"
}
```

Here are our overridden values in `terraform.tfvars` (but feel free to put your own values, such as using another data center or CoreOS release):

```
do_region = "nyc1"
coreos_channel = "coreos-beta"
```

Adding useful output

It would be awesome to automatically have a few auto-documented lines on how to connect to our CoreOS cluster. As we can do that with the Terraform outputs, let's use this example for a start, in `outputs.tf`. This is constructing an SSH command line with dynamic information from Terraform that we'll be able to use easily (it's simply iterating over every `digitalocean_droplet.coreos.*` available):

```
output "CoreOS Cluster Members" {
  value = "${formatlist("ssh core@%v -i ${var.ssh_key_file}",
digitalocean_droplet.coreos.*.ipv4_address)}"
}
```

The output will look like this:

```
CoreOS Cluster Members = [
    ssh core@192.241.128.44 -i ./keys/iac_admin_sshkey,
    ssh core@192.241.130.33 -i ./keys/iac_admin_sshkey,
    ssh core@198.199.120.212 -i ./keys/iac_admin_sshkey
]
```

Dynamic DNS Integration

One of the attractive features of Digital Ocean is the easy DNS integration. For example, if our domain is `infrastructure-as-code.org` and we launch a *blog* droplet, we'll end up registering it automatically under the public DNS name `blog.infrastructure-as-code.org`. Pretty easy and dynamic! To give Digital Ocean power on our domain, we need to go to our registrar (where we bought our domain), and configure our domain to be managed by Digital Ocean, using their own nameservers, which are as follows:

- `ns1.digitalocean.com`
- `ns2.digitalocean.com`
- `ns3.digitalocean.com`

This prerequisite being done, let's declare our domain in the `dns.tf` file using the `digitalocean_domain` resource, automatically using a `cluster_domainname` variable for the domain name, and an initial IP address matching, that we can either set to a value you already know or to an arbitrary droplet:

```
resource "digitalocean_domain" "cluster_domainname" {
  name       = "${var.cluster_domainname}"
  ip_address = "${digitalocean_droplet.coreos.0.ipv4_address}"
}
```

Add the new variable in `variables.tf`:

```
variable "cluster_domainname" {
  default     = "infrastructure-as-code.org"
  description = "Domain to use"
}
```

Don't forget to override it as necessary in `terraform.tfvars`.

The next step is to register automatically every droplet in the DNS. By iterating over each droplet, and extracting their `name` and `ipv4_address` attributes, we'll add this `digitalocean_record` resource into the mix:

```
resource "digitalocean_record" "ipv4" {
  count  = "${var.cluster_nodes}"
  domain = "${digitalocean_domain.cluster_domainname.name}"
  type   = "A"
  name   = "${element(digitalocean_droplet.coreos.*.name,
  count.index)}"
  value  = "${element(digitalocean_droplet.coreos.*.ipv4_address,
  count.index)}"
}
```

This will automatically register every droplet under the name core-[1,2,3].mydomain.com, for easier access and reference.

If you like, you can access the `fqdn` attribute of this resource right from the outputs (`outputs.tf`):

```
output "CoreOS Cluster Members DNS" {
  value = "${formatlist("ssh core@%v -i ${var.ssh_key_file}",
digitalocean_record.ipv4.*.fqdn)}"
}
```

Integrating cloud-init

We need to build a fully working `cloud-config.yml` file for our CoreOS cluster. Refer to the cloud-init part of this book in *Chapter 5, Provisioning the Last Mile with Cloud-Init* for more information on the `cloud-config.yml` file, and especially on configuring CoreOS with it.

What we need for a fully usable CoreOS cluster are the following:

▶ A working etcd cluster on the local network interface (`$private_ipv4`)

▶ A working fleet cluster on the local network interface (`$private_ipv4`)

    Fleet is a distributed init system. You can think of it as systemd for a whole cluster

To configure etcd, we first need to obtain a new token. This token is unique and can be distributed through different channels. It can be easily obtained through the `https://coreos.com/os/docs/latest/cluster-discovery.html` etcd service. Then we'll start 2 units—etcd and fleet.

```
$ curl -w "\n" 'https://discovery.etcd.io/new?size=3'
https://discovery.etcd.io/b04ddb7ff454503a66ead486b448afb7
```

Note this URL carefully and copy paste it in the following `cloud-config.yml` file:

```
#cloud-config
# https://coreos.com/validate/
coreos:
  etcd2:
    discovery:
    "https://discovery.etcd.io/b04ddb7ff454503a66ead486b448afb7"
    advertise-client-urls: "http://$private_ipv4:2379"
    initial-advertise-peer-urls: "http://$private_ipv4:2380"
    listen-client-urls: http://0.0.0.0:2379
    listen-peer-urls: http://$private_ipv4:2380
  units:
    - name: etcd2.service
      command: start
    - name: fleet.service
      command: start
  fleet:
    public-ip: "$public_ipv4"
    metadata: "region=ams,provider=digitalocean"
```

This will be enough to start an etcd + fleet cluster on CoreOS. *Chapter 5, Provisioning the Last Mile with Cloud-Init*, for in-depth details on cloud-init.

Integrating dynamic StatusCake monitoring

We can reuse our knowledge from previous chapters to easily integrate full latency monitoring to the hosts of our CoreOS cluster, using a free StatusCake account (`https://statuscake.com`).

Start by configuring the provider in `providers.tf`:

```
provider "statuscake" {
  username = "${var.statuscake_username}"
  apikey   = "${var.statuscake_apikey}"
}
```

Declare the required variables in `variables.tf`:

```
variable "statuscake_username" {
  default     = "changeme"
  description = "StatusCake Account Username"
}

variable "statuscake_apikey" {
  default     = "hackme"
  description = "StatusCake Account API Key"
}
```

Also, override with your own values in `terraform.tfvars`.

Now we can use the `statuscake_test` resource to activate immediate latency (ping) monitoring on every droplet by iterating over each `digitalocean_droplet.coreos.*` resource value:

```
resource "statuscake_test" "coreos_cluster" {
  count        = "${var.cluster_nodes}"
  website_name = "${element(digitalocean_droplet.coreos.*.name,
  count.index)}.${var.cluster_domainname}"
  website_url  =
"${element(digitalocean_droplet.coreos.*.ipv4_address,
count.index)}"
  test_type    = "PING"
  check_rate   = 300
  paused       = false
}
```

It's time to `terraform apply` this:

```
$ terraform apply
[...]


CoreOS Cluster Members = [
    ssh core@159.203.189.142 -i ./keys/iac_admin_sshkey,
    ssh core@159.203.189.146 -i ./keys/iac_admin_sshkey,
    ssh core@159.203.189.131 -i ./keys/iac_admin_sshkey
]
CoreOS Cluster Members DNS = [
    ssh core@coreos-1.mydomain.com -i ./keys/iac_admin_sshkey,
    ssh core@coreos-2.mydomain.com -i ./keys/iac_admin_sshkey,
    ssh core@coreos-3.mydomain.com -i ./keys/iac_admin_sshkey
]
```

Confirm that we can connect to a member using the command line from the output:

```
$ ssh core@159.203.189.142 -i ./keys/iac_admin_sshkey
```

Verify the etcd cluster health:

```
$ core@coreos-1 ~ $ etcdctl cluster-health
member 668f889d5f96b578 is healthy: got healthy result from
http://10.136.24.178:2379
member c8e8906e0f3f63be is healthy: got healthy result from
http://10.136.24.176:2379
member f3b53735aca3062e is healthy: got healthy result from
http://10.136.24.177:2379
cluster is healthy
```

Check that all fleet members are all right:

```
core@coreos-1 ~ $ fleetctl list-machines
MACHINE          IP               METADATA
24762c02...      159.203.189.146  provider=digitalocean,region=ams
3b4b0792...      159.203.189.142  provider=digitalocean,region=ams
59e15b88...      159.203.189.131  provider=digitalocean,region=ams
```

Enjoy, in less than a minute, you're ready to use a CoreOS cluster with basic monitoring, using only fully automated Terraform code!

Provisioning a three-tier infrastructure on Google Compute Engine

We'll provision a ready to use, three-tier, load-balanced web infrastructure on Google Compute Engine, using two CentOS 7.2 servers for the web and one master Google MySQL instance. The MySQL instance will allow connections only from the two web servers (with valid credentials), and all three instances (SQL and HTTP) will be accessible from a single *corporate* network (our company's network). The topology looks like this:

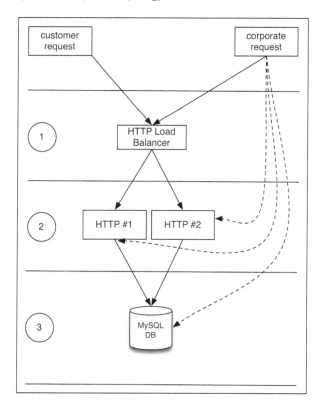

Getting ready

To step through this recipe, you will need the following:

- A working Terraform installation
- A Google Compute Engine account with a project
- An Internet connection

How to do it...

The first thing we need to do is to get our credentials from the console.

Generating API credentials for a Google project

Navigate to your Google Cloud project, and in the *API Manager*, select **Credentials | Create credentials | Service Account Key**. Now choose **Compute Engine default service account** from the dropdown list, in the JSON format. Save this file as `account.json` at the root of the infrastructure repository.

Create the variables to define our credentials file in `variables.tf`, store the region we're running in, and the Google Compute project name:

```
variable "credentials_file" {
  default     = "account.json"
  description = "API credentials JSON file"
}
variable "region" {
  default     = "europe-west"
  description = "Region name"
}
variable "project_name" {
  default     = "default-project"
  description = "Project ID to use"
}
```

Don't forget to override those values in `terraform.tfvars` if you want to:

```
project_name = "iac-book-infra"
region = "us-east1"
```

Now, in a `providers.tf` file, add the `google` provider:

```
provider "google" {
  credentials = "${file("${var.credentials_file}")}"
  project     = "${var.project_name}"
  region      = "${var.region}"
}
```

Our `google` provider is now configured!

Creating Google Compute HTTP instances

Here's the checklist of our requirements for these HTTP hosts:

- We want two of them

- Their type is `n1-standard-1` (3.75 GB of RAM, one vCPU)
- Their region and zone is: us-east1-d
- They are running CentOS 7.2 (official image is: centos-cloud/centos 7)
- The default SSH username is `centos`
- The SSH key known to us is (`keys/admin_key`)
- We want a fully updated system with Docker installed and running

Let's define generic variables for all these requirements in a `variables.tf` file:

```
variable "machine_type" {
  default     = "f1-micro"
  description = "Machine type"
}

variable "zone" {
  default     = "c"
  description = "Region Zone"
}

variable "disk_image" {
  default     = "centos-cloud/centos-7"
  description = "Disk image"
}

variable "ssh_key" {
  default     = "keys/admin_key"
  description = "SSH key"
}

variable "ssh_username" {
  default     = "root"
  description = "The SSH username to use"
}

variable "www_servers" {
  default = "2"
  description = "Amount of www servers"
}
```

Now let's override in `terraform.tfvars` the generic values we just set:

```
machine_type = "n1-standard-1"
zone = "d"
ssh_username = "centos"
```

Google Cloud instances are called from Terraform using the resource `google_compute_instance`:

Let's add what we already know in this resource:

```
resource "google_compute_instance" "www" {
    count         = "${var.www_servers}"
    name          = "www-${count.index+1}"
    machine_type  = "${var.machine_type}"
    zone          = "${var.region}-${var.zone}"

    disk {
        image = "${var.disk_image}"
    }

    metadata {
        ssh-keys = "${var.ssh_username}:${file("${var.ssh_key}.pub")}"
    }
}
```

This could be enough, but we want to go much farther.

For example, we'll later add a firewall, whose rule will apply to a target defined by its tags. Let's add a tag right now, so we can use it later:

```
    tags          = ["www"]
```

We have to configure networking. It's necessary in our case to have a public IPv4, because we need to access the servers by SSH from outside. We might have chosen to not have publicly exposed servers and use a bastion host instead. To create a network interface in our default network, mapped behind a public IPv4, add the following to the `google_compute_instance` resource:

```
    network_interface {
        network = "default"

        access_config {
            nat_ip = ""
        }
    }
```

Let's finish by connecting automatically to each instance and fully update it, then install, enable, and start Docker. We do this using the `remote-exec` provisioner, correctly configured with the right SSH username and private key:

```
    provisioner "remote-exec" {
        connection {
```

```
    user        = "${var.ssh_username}"
    private_key = "${file("${var.ssh_key}")}"
  }

  inline = [
    "sudo yum update -y",
    "sudo yum install -y docker",
    "sudo systemctl enable docker",
    "sudo systemctl start docker",
  ]
}
```

We're finally done, with our two instances automatically provisioned!

Creating a Google Compute Firewall rule

Our goal is simple: we want to allow anyone (0.0.0.0/0) to access using HTTP (TCP port 80) any instance with the tag www in the default network. To do this, let's use the `google_compute_firewall` resource:

```
resource "google_compute_firewall" "fw" {
  name    = "www-firewall"
  network = "default"

  allow {
    protocol = "tcp"
    ports    = ["80"]
  }

  source_ranges = ["0.0.0.0/0"]
  target_tags   = ["www"]
}
```

Load balancing Google Compute instances

To load balance requests across our two instances, we'll need to create a *pool* of hosts, where membership will be handled by a simple health check: an HTTP GET on / every second, with an immediate timeout (1 second), and removal after 3 errors. We can do this in a file named pool.tf with the `google_compute_http_health_check` resource:

```
resource "google_compute_http_health_check" "www" {
  name                = "http"
  request_path        = "/"
  check_interval_sec  = 1
  healthy_threshold   = 1
  unhealthy_threshold = 3
  timeout_sec         = 1
}
```

Feel free to transform those values into variables for better tuning on your end!

Now, let's define the pool, which is defined by the results of the health checks and instances inclusion. This is done using the `google_compute_target_pool` resource:

```
resource "google_compute_target_pool" "www" {
  name          = "www-pool"
  instances     = ["${google_compute_instance.www.*.self_link}"]
  health_checks = ["${google_compute_http_health_check.www.name}"]
}
```

 The `self_link` attribute returns the URI of the resource.

Now we have our pool of hosts with health checks, let's create the load balancer itself. It's done using the `google_compute_forwarding_rule` resource, simply pointing to the pool of hosts we created earlier. Add the following in a `loadbalancer.tf` file:

```
resource "google_compute_forwarding_rule" "http" {
  name       = "http-lb"
  target     = "${google_compute_target_pool.www.self_link}"
  port_range = "80"
}
```

Creating a Google MySQL database instance

Our typical target application needs a database to store and access data. We won't get into database replication here, but it can also be done quite simply with Terraform on Google Cloud.

 Double-check you have the SQL API activated in the Google Cloud Console: `https://console.cloud.google.com/apis/library`. By default, it isn't.

Here's a checklist of what we know about our MySQL database:

- It's running on us-east1 region
- It's running MySQL 5.6
- It's type is *D2* (1 GB of RAM)
- Our own network and both HTTP servers can access it
- We want a database named `app_db`
- We want a user with a password to be allowed to connect from the HTTP servers

Let's put all these variables in the `variables.tf` file:

```
variable "db_type" {
  default     = "D0"
  description = "Google SQL DB type"
}

variable "db_authorized_network" {
  default     = "0.0.0.0/0"
  description = "A corporate network authorized to access the DB"
}

variable "db_username" {
  default     = "dbadmin"
  description = "A MySQL username"
}

variable "db_password" {
  default     = "changeme"
  description = "A MySQL password"
}

variable "db_name" {
  default     = "db_name"
  description = "MySQL database name"
}
```

Don't forget to override each generic value in the `terraform.tfvars`:

```
db_authorized_network = "163.172.161.158/32"
db_username = "sqladmin"
db_password = "pwd1970"
db_name = "app_db"
db_type = "D2"
```

Now we can build our database using the `google_sql_database_instance` resource in a `db.tf` file:

```
resource "google_sql_database_instance" "master" {
  name             = "mysql-mastr-1"
  region           = "${var.region}"
  database_version = "MYSQL_5_6"

  settings = {
    tier              = "${var.db_type}"
    activation_policy = "ALWAYS"          // vs "ON_DEMAND"
```

```
    pricing_plan       = "PER_USE"           // vs "PACKAGE"

    ip_configuration {
      ipv4_enabled = true

      authorized_networks {
        name  = "authorized_network"
        value = "${var.db_authorized_network}"
      }

      authorized_networks {
        name  = "${google_compute_instance.www.0.name}"
        value = "${google_compute_instance.www.0.network_
interface.0.access_config.0.assigned_nat_ip}"
      }

      authorized_networks {
        name  = "${google_compute_instance.www.1.name}"
        value = "${google_compute_instance.www.1.network_
interface.0.access_config.0.assigned_nat_ip}"
      }
    }
  }
}
```

 The `pricing_plan` `"PACKAGE"` is more interesting for a long-lasting database. Also, the `authorized_network` block doesn't currently support a `count` value, so we can't iterate dynamically over every HTTP host. For now, we have to duplicate the block, but that may very well change in a newer Terraform version.

Let's now create a database, using a `google_sql_database` resource:

```
resource "google_sql_database" "db" {
  name     = "${var.db_name}"
  instance = "${google_sql_database_instance.master.name}"
}
```

Finish by creating the SQL user with host restriction. Like the `authorized_network` block, the `google_sql_user` resource doesn't support a `count` value yet, so we have to duplicate the code for each HTTP server for now:

```
resource "google_sql_user" "user_www_1" {
  name     = "${var.db_username}"
  password = "${var.db_password}"
```

```
  instance = "${google_sql_database_instance.master.name}"
  host     = "${google_compute_instance.www.0.network_
interface.0.access_config.0.assigned_nat_ip}"
}

resource "google_sql_user" "user_www_2" {
  name     = "${var.db_username}"
  password = "${var.db_password}"
  instance = "${google_sql_database_instance.master.name}"
  host     = "${google_compute_instance.www.1.network_
interface.0.access_config.0.assigned_nat_ip}"
}
```

Adding some useful outputs

It would be awesome to have some useful information such as IPs for all our instances and services and usernames and passwords. Let's add some outputs in outputs.tf:

```
output "HTTP Servers" {
  value = "${join(" ", google_compute_instance.www.*.network_
interface.0.access_config.0.
assigned_nat_ip)}"
}

output "MySQL DB IP" {
  value = "${google_sql_database_instance.master.ip_address.0.ip_
address}"
}

output "Load Balancer Public IPv4" {
  value = "${google_compute_forwarding_rule.http.ip_address}"
}

output "DB Credentials" {
  value = "Username=${var.db_username} Password=${var.db_password}"
}
```

Here we are!

```
$ terraform apply
[...]
Outputs:

DB Credentials = Username=sqladmin Password=pwd1970
HTTP Servers = 104.196.180.192 104.196.157.246
```

```
Load Balancer Public IPv4 = 104.196.45.46

MySQL DB IP = 173.194.111.120
```

Simply deploy our application on the HTTP servers and we're done! To test drive the load balancer and the HTTP instances, you can simply deploy the NGINX container on each server and see the traffic flow:

```
$ sudo docker run -it --rm -p 80:80 --name web nginx
```

Provisioning a GitLab CE + CI runners on OpenStack

OpenStack is a very popular open source cloud computing solution. Many providers are based on it, and you can roll your own in your data center. In this example, we'll use the public OpenStack by OVH, located in Montreal, QC (Canada), but we can use any other OpenStack. There're differences in implementation for every custom deployment, but we'll stick with very stable features.

We'll launch one compute instance running Ubuntu LTS 16.04 for GitLab, with a dedicated block device for Docker, and two other compute instances for GitLab CI runners. Security will allow HTTP for everyone, but SSH only for a known IP from our corporate network. To store our builds or releases, we'll create a *container*, which is in OpenStack terminology—an object storage. The equivalent with AWS S3 is a *bucket*.

Getting ready

To step through this recipe, you will need the following:

▸ A working Terraform installation.
▸ An OpenStack account on any OpenStack provider (public or private). This recipe uses an account on OVH's public OpenStack (https://www.ovh.com/us/).
▸ An Internet connection.

How to do it...

We'll create:

▸ Three compute instances (virtual machines)
▸ One keypair
▸ One block storage device
▸ One security group
▸ One object storage bucket

Configuring the OpenStack provider

Let's start by configuring the OpenStack provider. We need four pieces of information: a username, a password, an OpenStack tenant name, and an OpenStack authentication endpoint URL. To make the code very dynamic, let's create variables for those in `variables.tf`:

```
variable "user_name" {
  default     = "changeme"
  description = "OpenStack username"
}

variable "password" {
  default     = "hackme"
  description = "OpenStack password"
}

variable "tenant_name" {
  default     = "123456"
  description = "OpenStack Tenant name"
}

variable "auth_url" {
  default     = "https://openstack.url/v2.0"
  description = "OpenStack Authentication Endpoint"
}
```

Don't forget to override the default values with your own in the `terraform.tfvars` file!

```
user_name   = "***"
tenant_name = "***"
password    = "***"
auth_url    = "https://auth.cloud.ovh.net/v2.0/"
```

Now we're good to go.

Creating a key pair on OpenStack

To authenticate ourselves on the instances, we need to provide the public part of the key pair to OpenStack. This is done using the `openstack_compute_keypair_v2` resource, specifying in which region we want the key, and where the key is. Let's add both variables in `variables.tf`:

```
variable "region" {
  default     = "GRA1"
  description = "OpenStack Region"
}
```

```
variable "ssh_key_file" {
  default     = "keys/admin_key"
  description = "Default SSH key"
}
```

Next, override them in the `terraform.tfvars` file:

```
region       = "BHS1"
```

Now we can build our resource in the `keys.tf` file:

```
resource "openstack_compute_keypair_v2" "ssh" {
  name       = "Admin SSH Public Key"
  region     = "${var.region}"
  public_key = "${file("${var.ssh_key_file}.pub")}"
}
```

Creating a security group on OpenStack

We know our requirements are to allow HTTP (TCP/80) from anywhere, but SSH (TCP/22) only from one corporate network. Add it right now in `variables.tf` so we can use it:

```
variable "allowed_network" {
  default = "1.2.3.4/32"
  description = "The Whitelisted Corporate Network"
}
```

Don't forget to override with your own network in `terraform.tfvars`.

Let's create a first security group allowing HTTP for everyone in our region, using the `openstack_compute_secgroup_v2` resource in a `security.tf` file:

```
resource "openstack_compute_secgroup_v2" "http-sg" {
  name        = "http-sg"
  description = "HTTP Security Group"
  region      = "${var.region}"

  rule {
    from_port   = 80
    to_port     = 80
    ip_protocol = "tcp"
    cidr        = "0.0.0.0/0"
  }
}
```

Following the same pattern, create another security group to allow SSH only from our corporate network:

```
resource "openstack_compute_secgroup_v2" "base-sg" {
  name        = "base-sg"
  description = "Base Security Group"
  region      = "${var.region}"

  rule {
    from_port  = 22
    to_port    = 22
    ip_protocol = "tcp"
    cidr       = "${var.allowed_network}"
  }
}
```

Creating block storage volumes on OpenStack

In our requirements, we want a dedicated volume to be available to our GitLab instance, for Docker. We decide this one will be `10` GB in size. This volume will be mounted by the compute instance under a dedicated device (likely `/dev/vdb`). The whole thing is done using the `openstack_blockstorage_volume_v2` resource:

```
resource "openstack_blockstorage_volume_v2" "docker" {
  region      = "${var.region}"
  name        = "docker-vol"
  description = "Docker volume"
  size        = 10
}
```

Add a simple output in `outputs.tf` so we know the volume description, name, and size:

```
output "Block Storage" {
  value = "${openstack_blockstorage_volume_v2.docker.description}:
${openstack_blockstorage_volume_v2.docker.name},
${openstack_blockstorage_volume_v2.docker.size}GB"
}
```

We now have every requirement to launch our compute instances.

Creating compute instances on OpenStack

It's now time to create the instances. We know they have to be Ubuntu 16.04, and we decide on a flavor name: a flavor is the type of the machine. It varies from every other OpenStack installation. In our case, it's named `vps-ssd-1`. Let's define some defaults in the `variables.tf` file:

```
variable "image_name" {
```

```
    default     = "CentOS"
    description = "Default OpenStack image to boot"
}


variable "flavor_name" {
  default     = "some_flavor"
  description = "OpenStack instance flavor"
}
```

Also, override them with good values in `terraform.tfvars`:

```
image_name  = "Ubuntu 16.04"
flavor_name = "vps-ssd-1"
```

To create a compute instance, we use a resource named `openstack_compute_instance_v2`. This resource takes all the parameters we previously declared (name, image, flavor, SSH key, and security groups). Let's try this in `instances.tf`:

```
resource "openstack_compute_instance_v2" "gitlab" {
  name             = "gitlab"
  region           = "${var.region}"
  image_name       = "${var.image_name}"
  flavor_name      = "${var.flavor_name}"
  key_pair         = "${openstack_compute_keypair_v2.ssh.name}"
  security_groups  = ["${openstack_compute_secgroup_v2.base-
  sg.name}", "${openstack_compute_secgroup_v2.http-sg.name}"]
}
```

To attach the block storage volume we created, we need to add a `volume {}` block inside the resource:

```
volume {
  volume_id = "${openstack_blockstorage_volume_v2.docker.id}"
  device    = "/dev/vdb"
}
```

Now, an optional but fun part is that the commands needed to format the volume, mount it at the right place, fully update the system, install Docker, and run the GitLab CE container. This is done using the `remote-exec` provisioner and requires a SSH username. Let's set it as `variables.tf`:

```
variable "ssh_username" {
  default     = "ubuntu"
  description = "SSH username"
}
```

Now we can just type in all the commands to be executed when the instance is ready:

```
provisioner "remote-exec" {
  connection {
    user        = "${var.ssh_username}"
    private_key = "${file("${var.ssh_key_file}")}"
  }

  inline = [
    "sudo mkfs.ext4 /dev/vdb",
    "sudo mkdir /var/lib/docker",
    "sudo su -c \"echo '/dev/vdb /var/lib/docker ext4 defaults 0
    0' >> /etc/fstab\"",
    "sudo mount -a",
    "sudo apt update -y",
    "sudo apt upgrade -y",
    "sudo apt install -y docker.io",
    "sudo systemctl enable docker",
    "sudo systemctl start docker",
    "sudo docker run -d -p 80:80 --name gitlab gitlab/gitlab-
    ce:latest",
  ]
}
```

Add a simple output in the `outputs.tf` file, so we easily know the GitLab instance public IP:

```
output "GitLab Instance" {
  value = "gitlab:
  http://${openstack_compute_instance_v2.gitlab.access_ip_v4}"
}
```

The runner instances are the same, but a little simpler, as they don't need a local volume. However, we need to set the amount of runners we want in `variables.tf`:

```
variable "num_runners" {
  default     = "1"
  description = "Number of GitLab CI runners"
}
```

Override the value to have more runners in `terraform.tfvars`:

```
num_runners = "2"
```

Now we can create our runner instances using the `openstack_compute_instance_v2` resource:

```
resource "openstack_compute_instance_v2" "runner" {
  count            = "${var.num_runners}"
```

```
    name              = "gitlab-runner-${count.index+1}"
    region            = "${var.region}"
    image_name        = "${var.image_name}"
    flavor_name       = "${var.flavor_name}"
    key_pair          = "${openstack_compute_keypair_v2.ssh.name}"
    security_groups = ["${openstack_compute_secgroup_v2.base-
    sg.name}", "${openstack_compute_secgroup_v2.http-sg.name}"]

    provisioner "remote-exec" {
      connection {
        user        = "${var.ssh_username}"
        private_key = "${file("${var.ssh_key_file}")}"
      }

      inline = [
        "sudo apt update -y",
        "sudo apt upgrade -y",
        "sudo apt install -y docker.io",
        "sudo systemctl enable docker",
        "sudo systemctl start docker",
        "sudo docker run -d --name gitlab-runner -v
      /var/run/docker.sock:/var/run/docker.sock gitlab/gitlab-
      runner:latest",
      ]
    }
  }
}
```

This will launch a GitLab CI runner, so builds can be triggered by GitLab! (there's one last step of configuration, though. It's out of the scope of this book, but we need to register each runner to the main GitLab instance by executing `docker exec -it gitlab-runner gitlab-runner register` and answering the questions).

Add the following output to `outputs.tf` so we know all the IP addresses of our runners:

```
output "GitLab Runner Instances" {
  value = "${join(" ",
  openstack_compute_instance_v2.runner.*.access_ip_v4)}"
}
```

Creating an object storage container on OpenStack

This one is very simple: it only requires a name and a region. As it's to store releases, let's call it `releases`, using the `openstack_objectstorage_container_v1` resource, in an `objectstorage.tf` file:

```
resource "openstack_objectstorage_container_v1" "releases" {
  region = "${var.region}"
```

```
    name   = "releases"
  }
```

Add a simple output in `outputs.tf` so we remember the `Object Storage` container name:

```
output "Object Storage" {
  value = "Container name:
  ${openstack_objectstorage_container_v1.releases.name}"
}
```

Applying

In the end, do a `terraform apply`:

```
$ terraform apply
[...]

Outputs:

Block Storage = Docker volume: docker-vol, 10GB

GitLab Instance = gitlab: http://158.69.95.202

GitLab Runner Instances = 158.69.95.200 158.69.95.201

Object Storage = Container name: releases
```

Connect to the GitLab instance and enjoy the runners (after GitLab token registration)!

Managing Heroku apps and add-ons using Terraform

Heroku is a popular **Platform-as-a-Service** (**PaaS**), where you have absolutely no control over the infrastructure. But even for such platforms, Terraform can automate and manage things for you, so Heroku can do the rest. We'll create an app (a simple GitHub Hubot: `http://hubot.github.com/`), but feel free to use your own. On top of this app, we'll automatically plug a Heroku add-on (redis) and deploy everything.

Getting ready

To step through this recipe, you will need the following:

- A working Terraform installation
- A Heroku account (`https://www.heroku.com/`)

- ▸ An optional Slack Token
- ▸ An Internet connection

How to do it...

First things first: we need to define the Heroku provider. It consists of an e-mail address and an API key. Let's create generic variables for that in `variables.tf`:

```
variable "heroku_email" {
  default     = "user@mail.com"
  description = "Heroku account email"
}

variable "heroku_api_key" {
  default     = "12345"
  description = "Heroku account API key"
}
```

Don't forget to override them in `terraform.tfvars`:

```
heroku_email = "me@gmail.com"
heroku_api_key = "52eef461-5e34-47d8-8191-ede7ef6cf9bg"
```

Now we can create the Heroku provider with the information we have:

```
provider "heroku" {
  email   = "${var.heroku_email}"
  api_key = "${var.heroku_api_key}"
}
```

Creating a Heroku application with Terraform

Instead of clicking through Heroku to create an application, let's do it right from Terraform. We want to run our app in Europe and we want Hubot to connect to Slack, so we need to provide a Slack token as well. Let's start by creating default values in `variables.tf`:

```
variable "heroku_region" {
  default = "us"
  description = "Heroku region"
}

variable "slack_token" {
  default = "xoxb-1234-5678-1234-5678"
  description = "Slack Token"
}
```

Now we can create our first Heroku app with its variables using the `heroku_app` resource, in `heroku.tf`:

```
resource "heroku_app" "hubot" {
  name    = "iac-book-hubot"
  region = "${var.heroku_region}"

  config_vars {
    HUBOT_SLACK_TOKEN = "${var.slack_token}"
  }
}
```

That's it! As simple as it seems.

Add some output in `outputs.tf` so we have better information about our app, like the Heroku app URL and environment variables:

```
output "heroku URL" {
  value = "${heroku_app.hubot.web_url}"
}

output "heroku_vars" {
  value = "${heroku_app.hubot.all_config_vars}"
}

output "heroku Git URL" {
  value = "${heroku_app.hubot.git_url}"
}
```

Adding Heroku add-ons using Terraform

Some add-ons need Redis to store data. Instead of going through the web application and enabling add-ons, let's instead use the `heroku_addon` resource. It takes a reference to the app to link the add-on to, and a plan (`hobby-dev` is free, so let's use that):

```
resource "heroku_addon" "redis" {
  app  = "${heroku_app.hubot.name}"
  plan = "heroku-redis:hobby-dev"
}
```

Using Heroku with Terraform

It's out of the scope of this book to show Heroku usage, but let's apply this terraform code:

```
$ terraform apply
[...]
Outputs:
```

```
heroku Git URL = https://git.heroku.com/iac-book-hubot.git
heroku URL = https://iac-book-hubot.herokuapp.com/
heroku_vars = {
  HUBOT_SLACK_TOKEN = xoxb-1234-5678-91011-00e4dd
}
```

If you don't have an application ready to ship on Heroku, let's try to deploy GitHub's chat robot *Hubot*. It's an easy application ready to use on Heroku. Quickly reading through the Hubot documentation, let's install the Hubot generator:

```
$ npm install -g yo generator-hubot
```

Create a new `hubot`:

```
$ mkdir src; cd src
```

```
$ yo hubot
```

Answer the questions and when you're done, using the usual `heroku` command, add the Heroku git remote for our Heroku app:

```
$ heroku git:remote --app iac-book-hubot
```

Now you can `git push heroku` and see your application being deployed, all using Terraform.

Creating a scalable Docker Swarm cluster on bare metal with Packet

IaaS clouds have been popularized through heavy usage of virtual machines. Recent initiatives are targeting bare metal servers with an API, so we get the best of both worlds—on-demand servers through an API and incredible performance through direct access to the hardware. `https://www.packet.net/` is a bare metal IaaS provider (`https://www.scaleway.com/` is another) very well supported by Terraform with an awesome global network. Within minutes we have new hardware ready and connected to the network.

We'll build a fully automated and scalable Docker Swarm cluster, so we can operate highly scalable and performant workloads on bare metal: this setup can scale thousands of containers in just a few minutes. This cluster is composed of *Type 0* machines (4 cores and 8 GB RAM), for one manager and 2 nodes, totaling 12 cores and 24 GB of RAM, but we can use more performant machines if we want: the same cluster with *Type 2* machines will have 72 cores and 768 GB of RAM (though the price will adapt accordingly).

Getting ready

To step through this recipe, you will need the following:

- A working Terraform installation
- A Packet.net account with an API key
- An Internet connection

How to do it...

Let's start by creating the `packet` provider, using the API key (an authentication token). Create the variable in `variables.tf`:

```
variable "auth_token" {
  default     = "1234"
  description = "API Key Auth Token"
}
```

Also, be sure to override the value in `terraform.tfvars` with the real token:

```
auth_token = "JnN7e6tPMpWNtGcyPGT93AkLuguKw2eN"
```

Creating a Packet project using Terraform

Packet, like some other IaaS providers, uses the notion of *project* to group machines. Let's create a project named `Docker Swarm Bare Metal Infrastructure`, since that's what we want to do, in a `projects.tf` file:

```
resource "packet_project" "swarm" {
  name = "Docker Swarm Bare Metal Infrastructure"
}
```

This way, if you happen to manage multiple projects or customers, you can split them all into their own projects.

Handling Packet SSH keys using Terraform

To connect to the machines using SSH, we need at least one public key uploaded to our Packet account. Let's create a variable to store it in `variables.tf`:

```
variable "ssh_key" {
  default     = "keys/admin_key"
  description = "Path to SSH key"
}
```

Don't forget to override the value in `terraform.tfvars` if you use another name for the key.

Let's use the `packet_ssh_key` resource to create the SSH key on our Packet account:

```
resource "packet_ssh_key" "admin" {
  name       = "admin_key"
  public_key = "${file("${var.ssh_key}.pub")}"
}
```

Bootstraping a Docker Swarm manager on Packet using Terraform

We'll create two types of servers for this Docker Swarm cluster: managers and nodes. Managers are controlling what's executed on the nodes. We'll start by bootstrapping the Docker Swarm manager server, using the Packet service (more alternatives are available from Packet API):

 ▸ We want the cheapest server (`baremetal_0`)
 ▸ We want the servers in Amsterdam (`ams1`)
 ▸ We want the servers to run Ubuntu 16.04 (`ubuntu_16_04_image`)
 ▸ Default SSH user is `root`
 ▸ Billing will be `hourly`, but that can be `monthly` as well

Let's put generic information in `variables.tf` so we can manipulate them:

```
variable "facility" {
  default     = "ewr1"
  description = "Packet facility (us-east=ewr1, us-west=sjc1, eu-
west=ams1)"
}

variable "plan" {
  default     = "baremetal_0"
  description = "Packet machine type"
}

variable "operating_system" {
  default     = "coreos_stable"
  description = "Packet operating_system"
}

variable "ssh_username" {
  default     = "root"
  description = "Default host username"
}
```

Also, override them in `terraform.tfvars` to match our values:

```
facility = "ams1"
operating_system = "ubuntu_16_04_image"
```

To create a server with Packet, let's use the `packet_device` resource, specifying the chosen plan, facility, operating system, billing, and the project in which it will run:

```
resource "packet_device" "swarm_master" {
  hostname          = "swarm-master"
  plan              = "${var.plan}"
  facility          = "${var.facility}"
  operating_system  = "${var.operating_system}"
  billing_cycle     = "hourly"
  project_id        = "${packet_project.swarm.id}"
}
```

Now, let's create two scripts that will execute when the server is ready. The first one will update Ubuntu (`update_os.sh`) while the second will install Docker (`install_docker.sh`).

```
#!/usr/bin/env bash
# file: ./scripts/update_os.sh
sudo apt update -yqq
sudo apt upgrade -yqq
```

This script will install and start Docker:

```
#!/usr/bin/env bash
# file: ./scripts/install_docker.sh
curl -sSL https://get.docker.com/ | sh
sudo systemctl enable docker
sudo systemctl start docker
```

We can now call those scripts as a `remote-exec` provisioner inside the `packet_device` resource:

```
provisioner "remote-exec" {
  connection {
    user        = "${var.ssh_username}"
    private_key = "${file("${var.ssh_key}")}"
  }

  scripts = [
    "scripts/update_os.sh",
```

```
        "scripts/install_docker.sh",
    ]
}
```

At this point, the system is fully provisioned and functional, with Docker running.

To initialize a Docker Swarm cluster, starting with Docker 1.12, we can just issue the following command:

$ docker swarm init --advertise-addr docker.manager.local.ip

A server at Packet has one interface sharing both public and private IP addresses. The private IP is the second one, and is available through the following exported attribute: `${packet_device.swarm_master.network.2.address}`. Let's create another `remote-exec` provisioner, so the Swarm manager is initialized automatically, right after bootstrap:

```
    provisioner "remote-exec" {
      connection {
        user        = "${var.ssh_username}"
        private_key = "${file("${var.ssh_key}")}"
      }

      inline = [
          "docker swarm init --advertise-addr ${packet_device.swarm_master.network.2.address}",
        ]
    }
```

At this point, we have a Docker cluster running, with only one node—the manager itself.

The last step is to store the Swarm token, so the nodes can join. The token can be obtained with the following command:

$ docker swarm join-token worker -q

We'll store this token in a simple file in our infrastructure repository (`worker.token`), so we can access it and version it. Let's create a variable to store our token in a file in `variables.tf`:

```
    variable "worker_token_file" {
      default     = "worker.token"
      description = "Worker token file"
    }
```

We will execute the previous `docker swarm` command through SSH when everything else is done, using a `local-exec` provisioner. As we can't interact with the process, let's skip the host key checking and other initial SSH checks:

```
    provisioner "local-exec" {
```

```
   command = "ssh -t -o UserKnownHostsFile=/dev/null -o
   StrictHostKeyChecking=no -i ${var.ssh_key}
   ${var.ssh_username}@${packet_device.swarm_master.
network.0.address} \"docker swarm join-token worker -q\" >
${var.worker_token_file}"
  }
```

We're now done with the Docker Swarm manager!

Bootstraping Docker Swarm nodes on Packet using Terraform

We need nodes to join the swarm, so the workload can be spread. For convenience, the machine specs for the nodes will be the same as that of the master. Here's what will happen:

- ▸ Two nodes are created
- ▸ The token file is sent to each node
- ▸ The operating system is updated, and Docker is installed
- ▸ The node joins the swarm

Let's start by creating a variable for the number of nodes we want, in `variables.tf`:

```
variable "num_nodes" {
  default     = "1"
  description = "Number of Docker Swarm nodes"
}
```

Override that value as the cluster grows in `terraform.tfvars`:

```
num_nodes = "2"
```

Create the nodes using the same `packet_device` resource we used for the master:

```
resource "packet_device" "swarm_node" {
  count             = "${var.num_nodes}"
  hostname          = "swarm-node-${count.index+1}"
  plan              = "${var.plan}"
  facility          = "${var.facility}"
  operating_system  = "${var.operating_system}"
  billing_cycle     = "hourly"
  project_id        = "${packet_project.swarm.id}"
}
```

Add a `file` provisioner to copy the token file:

```
provisioner "file" {
  source      = "${var.worker_token_file}"
  destination = "${var.worker_token_file}"
}
```

Using the same update and Docker installation scripts as the master, create the same `remote-exec` provisioner:

```
provisioner "remote-exec" {
  connection {
    user        = "${var.ssh_username}"
    private_key = "${file("${var.ssh_key}")}"
  }

  scripts = [
    "scripts/update_os.sh",
    "scripts/install_docker.sh",
  ]
}
```

The operating system is now fully updated and Docker is running.

Now we want to join the Docker Swarm cluster. To do this, we need two pieces of information: the token and the local IP of the master. We already have the token in a file locally, and Terraform knows the local IP of the swarm manager. So a trick is to create a simple script (I suggest you write a more robust one!), that reads the local token, and takes the local manager IP address as an argument. In a file named `scripts/join_swarm.sh`, enter the following lines:

```
#!/usr/bin/env bash
# file: scripts/join_swarm.sh
MASTER=$1
SWARM_TOKEN=$(cat worker.token)
docker swarm join --token ${SWARM_TOKEN} ${MASTER}:2377
```

Now we just have to send this file to the nodes using the `file` provisioner:

```
provisioner "file" {
  source      = "scripts/join_swarm.sh"
  destination = "join_swarm.sh"
}
```

Use it as a last step through a `remote-exec` provisioner, sending the local Docker master IP (`${packet_device.swarm_master.network.2.address}"`) as an argument to the script:

```
provisioner "remote-exec" {
  connection {
    user        = "${var.ssh_username}"
    private_key = "${file("${var.ssh_key}")}"
  }
```

```
    inline = [
      "chmod +x join_swarm.sh",
      "./join_swarm.sh ${packet_device.swarm_master.
  network.2.address}",
    ]
  }//.
```

Launch the whole infrastructure:

$ terraform apply

Outputs:

Swarm Master Private IP = 10.80.86.129

Swarm Master Public IP = 147.75.100.19

Swarm Nodes = Public: 147.75.100.23,147.75.100.3, Private:
10.80.86.135,10.80.86.133

Our cluster is running.

Using the Docker Swarm cluster

Using our Docker Swarm cluster is out of the scope of this book, but now we have it, let's take a quick look to scale a container to the thousands!

Verify we have our 3 nodes:

```
# docker node ls
ID                             HOSTNAME               STATUS
AVAILABILITY  MANAGER STATUS
9sxqi2f1pywmofgf63184n7ps *    swarm-master.local.lan  Ready
Active          Leader
ag07nh1wzsbsvnef98sqf5agy      swarm-node-1.local.lan  Ready
Active
cppk5ja4spysu6opdov9f3x8h      swarm-node-2.local.lan  Ready
Active
```

We want a common network for our containers, and we want to scale to the thousands. So a typical /24 network won't be enough (that's the docker network default). Let's create a /16 overlay network, so we have room for scale!

 # docker network create -d overlay --subnet 172.16.0.0/16 nginx-network

Create a Docker service that will simply launch an nginx container on this new overlay network, with 3 replicas (3 instances of the container running at the same time):

 # docker service create --name nginx --network nginx-network --replicas 3 -p 80:80/tcp nginx

Verify if it's working:

```
# docker service ls
ID              NAME    REPLICAS    IMAGE    COMMAND
aeq91spl0mpg  nginx   3/3         nginx
```

Now, accessing by HTTP any of the public IPs of the cluster, any container of any node can answer: we can make an HTTP request to node-1, and it can be a container on node-2 responding. Nice!

Let's scale our service now, from 3 replicas to 100:

```
# docker service scale nginx=100
nginx scaled to 100
# docker service ls
ID              NAME    REPLICAS    IMAGE    COMMAND
aeq91spl0mpg  nginx   100/100     nginx
```

We just scaled to a hundred containers in a few seconds and split them on all 3 bare metal machines.

Now, you know you can scale, and with such a configuration you can push the nginx service to 500, 1000, or maybe more!

5
Provisioning the Last Mile with Cloud-Init

In this chapter, we will cover the following recipes:

- ▶ Using cloud-init on AWS, Digital Ocean, or OpenStack
- ▶ Handling files using cloud-init
- ▶ Configuring the server's time zone using cloud-init
- ▶ Managing users, keys, and credentials using cloud-init
- ▶ Managing repositories and packages using cloud-init
- ▶ Running commands during boot using cloud-init
- ▶ Configuring CoreOS using cloud-init
- ▶ Deploying Chef client from start to finish using cloud-init
- ▶ Deploying a remote Docker server using cloud-init

Introduction

Cloud-init is a cloud instance initialization system, standard across most Linux distributions. It's supported by all recent distributions (Ubuntu, Arch, CentOS/Red Hat, Fedora, and more), as well as a variant found on CoreOS systems.

With cloud-init, a number of actions are taken during the initialization phases of booting a cloud instance (new or not): installing packages, copying files or SSH keys, deploying Chef, defining repositories, or rebooting (when done).

The scope of action of cloud-init is really intended for the initialization phase; it's not a configuration management tool and is globally not meant to be run again afterwards to update configuration, like one would with Ansible or Chef. It's only used to obtain an instance properly configured for the next step to happen, and to ensure a set of commands are executed in order during boot. In other words, Terraform (the tool covered in *Chapter 2, Provisioning IaaS with Terraform, Chapter 3, Going Further with Terraform*, and *Chapter 4, Automating Complete Infrastructures with Terraform*) is perfect to define all the aspects of the underlying infrastructure, but cloud-init can be an easy and awesome solution for handling the first and subsequent boots before letting a full-fledged configuration management tool such as Chef or Ansible play its part for the rest of the instance life.

Cloud-init is defined as a simple YAML file (cloud-config), sent in the **user-data** field of a cloud instance. We'll see how this works in the coming sections.

In this chapter, we will present the most useful use cases with cloud-init, such as copying files, creating users, managing SSH keys, adding repositories and installing packages, running arbitrary commands, bootstrapping a Chef client, or managing CoreOS and Docker with it.

Using cloud-init on AWS, Digital Ocean, or OpenStack

As cloud-init is an initialization system for cloud instances, we need to find a way to send the cloud-config YAML file to the bootstrapping process. On all IaaS providers supporting cloud-init, there's a field where we can paste our file. We'll review how cloud-init works on three important IaaS providers—AWS, Digital Ocean, and OpenStack.

Getting ready

To step through this recipe, you will need an account on Amazon Web Services, Digital Ocean, or some OpenStack deployment, or on all of them if you want to try them all!

How to do it...

To illustrate cloud-init usage, we'll create the simplest cloud-config file on Ubuntu 16.04 and CentOS 7.2, installing packages such as `htop`, `tcpdump`, `docker`, or `nmap` that aren't usually installed by default on most Linux distributions. This is how a very simple cloud-config file looks:

```
#cloud-config
# Install packages on first boot
packages:
    - tcpdump
    - docker
    - nmap
```

Using cloud-init on Amazon Web Services

Using the AWS Console, when launching your instance, click on **Advanced Details** and we'll be able to paste our sample (and simple) cloud-config YAML file, or even simply upload it:

In this case, the Ubuntu 16.04 instance we just launched will already have the `htop` and `tcpdump` system tools installed, along with the Linux distribution's supported version of Docker:

```
ubuntu@ip-172-31-40-77:~$ which htop
/usr/bin/htop
ubuntu@ip-172-31-40-77:~$ which tcpdump
/usr/sbin/tcpdump
ubuntu@ip-172-31-40-77:~$ docker --version
Docker version 1.11.2, build b9f10c9
```

 We can manually update `cloud-config.yml` of a particular instance by powering off the instance, then under the **Actions** menu, navigate to **Instance Settings | View/Change User Data**. Start the EC2 instance again and the updated configuration is applied.

Using cloud-init on Digital Ocean

The situation is similar on Digital Ocean. When creating a new **droplet**, be sure to tick the **User data** checkbox under the **Select additional options** section and paste the cloud-config file content:

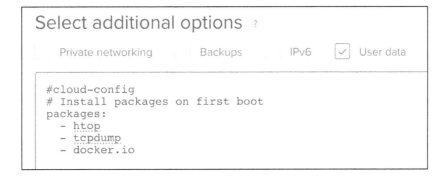

After a few seconds of boot time and package installation, our customized Ubuntu distribution is available:

```
root@ubuntu-512mb-nyc3-01:~# which htop
/usr/bin/htop
root@ubuntu-512mb-nyc3-01:~# which tcpdump
/usr/sbin/tcpdump
root@ubuntu-512mb-nyc3-01:~# docker --version
Docker version 1.11.2, build b9f10c9
```

Using cloud-init on OpenStack

When creating an instance on OpenStack, using the Horizon dashboard, click on the **Post-Creation** tab, and paste the cloud-config YAML content in the text box. Alternatively, it is possible to upload the file:

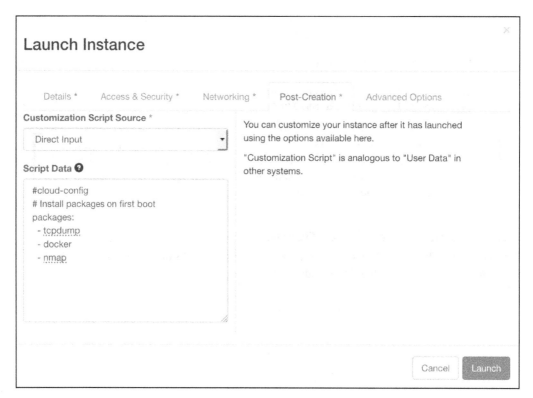

Verify the requested packages were installed, this time on a CentOS 7.2 box:

```
[centos@cloud-init-demo ~]$ which nmap
/usr/bin/nmap
[centos@cloud-init-demo ~]$ docker --version
Docker version 1.10.3, build cb079f6-unsupported
[centos@cloud-init-demo ~]$ which tcpdump
/usr/sbin/tcpdump
```

Combining cloud-init and Terraform for any IaaS

In the previous chapters about Terraform, we've in fact already used a `cloud-init` file a few times.

On Amazon Web Services, using the `aws_instance` resource to launch an EC2 VM, we use the `user_data` argument to pass the cloud-config file content, and in this case, using the `file()` interpolation:

```
resource "aws_instance" "vm" {
  ami           = "ami-643d4217"
  instance_type = "t2.micro"
  key_name      = "manual cloud init"
  user_data     = "${file("cloud-config.yml")}"
}
```

The equivalent for a Digital Ocean VM is the `user_data` argument as well:

```
resource "digitalocean_droplet" "vm" {
  image         = "ubuntu-14-04-x64"
  name          = "ubuntu"
  region        = "ams3"
  size          = "512mb"
  ssh_keys      = ["keys/admin_key"]
  user_data     = "${file("cloud-config.yml")}"
}
```

Handling files using cloud-init

An early need we all face is to have a file, a license, or a script in place right from the beginning of the instance life. Cloud-init proposes different ways of sending those files over the new instance. We'll see how to send files using plain text and base64 data encodings.

Getting ready

To step through this recipe, you will need:

▸ Access to a cloud-config enabled infrastructure

How to do it...

The first file we'll write is a **MOTD** (short for **Message Of The Day**) with root read-write permissions, read-only for everyone else. This file will have its content declared right from the cloud-config file:

```
#cloud-config
write_files:
  - path: /etc/motd
    content: |
        This server is configured using cloud-init.
        Welcome.
    owner: root:root
    permissions: '0644'
```

This machine, when booted, will have `/etc/motd` in place and display the string at login:

```
$ ssh ubuntu@server_ip
Welcome to Ubuntu 16.04.1 LTS (GNU/Linux 4.4.0-36-generic x86_64)
[...]
This server is configured using cloud-init.
Welcome.
[...]
ubuntu@ip-172-31-44-177:~$
```

Another way of including file content is to encode it in base64. Let's say we want to create a file named `/etc/server-id` with the content `abc-123`, with permissions `0600`. Begin by obtaining the base64 version of the file:

```
$ base64 server-id
YWJjLTEyMwo=
```

This is the output we'll integrate into the `content` field of the cloud-config file:

```
- path: /etc/server-id
  content: YWJjLTEyMwo=
  encoding: b64
  permissions: '0600'
```

Let's verify the remote content is what we expected:

```
$ ls -al /etc/server-id
-rw------- 1 root root 8 Sep 20 10:15 /etc/server-id
$ sudo cat /etc/server-id
abc-123
```

It works! Our file is read/write for the owner only, and the content is `abc-123`.

Another possibility is to compress the file using `gzip`, or even to base64 encode the resulting compressed gzip file.

Configuring the server's time zone using cloud-init

One very common configuration step on a new instance is setting the time zone. This time we'll explicitly set the EDT (New York) time zone for our server (even if the server is running in Europe or somewhere else). It is sometimes important to have as early as possible a correct date and time set up (for things like registration times, delays, and other issues depending on dates and times).

 In most setups, I personally prefer to ensure all the systems are set to GMT, wherever they are on the planet, GMT or not. This way, it's much easier to debug, compare logs or behavior when failures arise, without losing time doing the math of the time zones.

Getting ready

To step through this recipe, you will need:

► Access to a cloud-config enabled infrastructure

How to do it...

To set the server's time zone automatically to `America/New_York`, use the `timezone` directive:

```
#cloud-config
timezone: "America/New_York"
```

That is it! Our server is now configured from the beginning to use the correct time zone:

```
$ date
Sun Sep 25 10:48:32 EDT 2016
```

This, in fact, has simply set the `/etc/timezone` file to the correct value:

```
$ cat /etc/timezone
America/New_York
```

Managing users, keys, and credentials using cloud-init

There's a high probability we won't plan to use the default root account, or even the default user account from our distribution (those ubuntu or centos users). There's an even higher probability we'll need a Unix account very early in the process, even before the proper configuration management tool enters the game.

Let's say our IT security policy wants us to have an `emergency` user account in a group named `infosec` for the IT security team with passwordless `sudo` rights and the simple `/bin/sh` shell. This account has one authorized public key automatically populated. The policy is also to remove the default `ubuntu` account.

Getting ready

To step through this recipe, you will need:

▶ Access to a cloud-config enabled infrastructure

How to do it...

To create a group, we use a directive simply named `groups`, taking a list of groups. Any group can have a sublist of users to put in that group:

```
#cloud-config
groups:
  - infosec: [emergency]
```

To create a user, let's use a directive named `users`, taking a list of users. This list of users has a set of keys, such as `groups` the user is a member of, `sudo` rights, which `shell` to default to, or an SSH public key to authorize. Here's how it looks for our user `emergency`:

```
users:
  - name: emergency
    groups: sudo
    shell: /bin/sh
    sudo: ['ALL=(ALL) NOPASSWD:ALL']
    ssh-authorized-keys:
      - ssh-rsa
AAAAB3NzaC1yc2EAAAADAQABAAABAQC+fAfzjw5+mUZ7nGokB0tzO9fOLKrjHGVlabpRUxvs
IN/dRRmiBA9NDh5YRZ/ThAhn+RvPKGTBrXmuv3qWd/iWc3nie0fc2zDX1/Dc8EAIF9ybXfSxT
2DXOWWLOvNdUVOZNifmsmCQ1z0p9hg3bo65c0ZEBpXHIk+l75uFWAIYZ/
4jnXyFWz1ptmQR7gnAk2KBK19sj1Ii0pNjGyVbl5bNitWb3ulaviIT3FCswZoOsYvc
LpOwQrMA3k12kEAb30CYpesGcq6WDHAZSpWkFvc3Cd/AET4/
SjtyYpQVEhUn84v106WbNeDyJpUX6cz2WG2UaEqZc0VqZVhI63jG7wUR emergency@host
```

Once logged in as `emergency` using the private key, let's verify cloud-init did the job:

```
$ whoami
emergency
$ groups emergency
emergency : emergency sudo
$ echo $SHELL
/bin/sh
$ sudo whoami
root
```

We never explicitly asked to remove the default `ubuntu` user account: it's automatic as soon as we create an initial user.

However, if we wanted to keep the default user from our Linux distribution, we'd just have to add the following `default` user to the `users` directive:

```
users:
  - default
```

Managing repositories and packages using cloud-init

Unless we need a very specific release of a Linux distribution, it's highly probable we'll expect a fully updated system as soon as possible (think security patches and other bug fixes). Similarly, we usually expect a set of tools to be available in the new system. However, things might change, default tools might be removed – better to be safe than sorry. If one of our bootstrap scripts needs `wget` or `curl` and `nmap`, let's ensure those are present long before the proper configuration management tool starts its job (such as Chef or Puppet). We may also want to reboot the server after applying critical initial packages such as the kernel, or add a custom package repository.

Getting ready

To step through this recipe, you will need:

- Access to a cloud-config enabled infrastructure

How to do it...

To upgrade all the packages right after bootstrap, simply set the `package_upgrade` directive to `true`:

```
#cloud-config
package_upgrade: true
```

Another useful directive is to reboot the system if required by the package manager (common case with kernel updates). It's often better to reboot as soon as possible with the most secure kernel, but proceed with caution according to your own environment (you might not want to reboot while another action is taking place, maybe a Chef run or similar management software):

```
apt_reboot_if_required: true
```

To ensure the required packages are installed, use the `packages` directive:

```
packages:
    - htop
    - nmap
    - curl
    - wget
```

We can also add a custom APT repository using `apt_sources`:

```
apt_sources:
    - source: "ppa:nginx/stable"
```

Let's launch a new instance and verify it's fully updated, so no updates can be applied:

```
$ sudo apt-get dist-upgrade
Reading package lists... Done
Building dependency tree
Reading state information... Done
Calculating upgrade... Done
0 upgraded, 0 newly installed, 0 to remove and 0 not upgraded.
```

Verify our required tools are available:

```
$ which nmap
/usr/bin/nmap
$ which htop
/usr/bin/htop
$ which curl
/usr/bin/curl
$ which wget
/usr/bin/wget
```

Good thing! Now we're sure to always have a fully updated system with the required set of tools installed, even our own, right from the beginning.

Running commands during boot using cloud-init

When bootstrapping a new server or instance, the first boot is often very different from all the other boots the instance will experience in its life, and most often we want some commands to be executed very early or very late in the boot process. For example, let's say our cloud instance is launched with an attached block storage. We might want to format this storage space and be sure it's mounted on the host, but while we always want the disk to mount, we probably don't want it to be formatted at each boot! The bootcmd directive is there to handle everything related to commands to be executed very early in the boot process, while the runcmd directive is executed much later in the boot process (and only once).

 bootcmd will be executed at every boot of the instance.

Getting ready

To step through this recipe, you will need:

▸ Access to a cloud-config enabled infrastructure

How to do it...

We'll launch three commands during boot. The first one is a simple file with a dynamic content (the $INSTANCE_ID variable made available to us by cloud-init), which will always be rewritten, no matter what, at each boot. The second command is printing the date in the logs (so we know when the boot process started). The final command is the ext4 formatting of a block device attached on /dev/xvdb. For the sake of the exercise, we'll also mount the new device under /srv/www on the host.

To launch any command at boot time that will be run as early as possible, every time the machine boots, simply add it to the list of the bootcmd directive:

```
#cloud-config
bootcmd:
  - echo bootcmd started at $(date)
  - echo $INSTANCE_ID > /etc/instance_id
```

If we delete or modify this file, at the next reboot it will be overwritten.

On the other hand, if we want to run a command only once inside the bootcmd directive, we can use the helper script cloud-init-per. You can choose to launch the command once per boot or once per instance. In our case, we want to format the /dev/xvdb device (so, unless we want to format our drive each time we reboot, we probably want this to happen only once on this instance. So let's add the instance argument to the cloud-init-per helper script):

```
#cloud-config
bootcmd:
  - cloud-init-per instance mkfs-xvdb mkfs -t ext4 /dev/xvdb
```

Finally, let's use the mounts directive to mount the now formatted /dev/xvdb on the /srv/www folder:

```
mounts:
  - [ /dev/xvdb, /srv/www ]
```

After boot, let's verify the block device is mounted:

```
# df -h /srv/www/
Filesystem      Size  Used Avail Use% Mounted on
/dev/xvdb       4.8G   10M  4.6G   1% /srv/www
```

We can also test the existence of the file we created:

```
# cat /etc/instance_id
i-03005dd324599df11
```

Try to delete this file and reboot the server: the file will be there again.

Now, let's take a look at how different the runcmd directive is. Let's add a very similar command to the date output in the bootcmd directive:

```
runcmd:
  - 'echo runcmd started at $(date)'
```

Start a new instance, and observe the difference in timestamps:

```
$ grep "started at" /var/log/cloud-init-output.log
bootcmd started at Fri Sep 23 07:02:35 UTC 2016
+ echo runcmd started at Fri Sep 23 07:02:47 UTC 2016
runcmd started at Fri Sep 23 07:02:47 UTC 2016
```

The runcmd directive started 12 seconds later than the bootcmd directive.

Now reboot the instance, and observe that `runcmd` didn't run again:

```
$ grep "started at" /var/log/cloud-init-output.log
bootcmd started at Fri Sep 23 07:04:31 UTC 2016
```

Now we know what directive to use in each case.

Configuring CoreOS using cloud-init

CoreOS supports its own version of cloud-init, with added support for the CoreOS environment, and without everything else incompatible with its environment, so we can boot a fully configured system and cluster.

We'll take a look at the CoreOS specificities, as we can refer to earlier tips on how to manage users, files, authorized SSH keys, and other standard cloud-init directives. At the end of this part, you'll know how to configure the etcd key value store, the fleet cluster manager, the flannel overlay network, control the update mechanism, and ensure systemd units are started as early as possible.

 CoreOS proposes a very useful cloud-config file validator at `https://coreos.com/validate/`. It's super useful when we're not sure if a directive is supported or not in the distribution.

Getting ready

To step through this recipe, you will need:

- Access to a cloud-config enabled infrastructure

How to do it...

We'll get through the most important configuration options that can be manipulated for CoreOS. This includes the etcd distributed key value store, the fleet scheduler, the fleet network, the update strategy, and some systemd unit configuration.

Configuring etcd using cloud-init

The etcd key value store is used in CoreOS to share multiple configuration data between members of a same cluster. To begin with, we need a discovery token, that can be obtained from `https://discovery.etcd.io/new`.

```
$ curl -w "\n" 'https://discovery.etcd.io/new'
https://discovery.etcd.io/638d980c4edf94d6ddff8d6e862bc7d9
```

 We can specify the minimum required size of the CoreOS cluster by adding the `size=` argument to the URL `https://discovery.etcd.io/new?size=3`.

Now we have a valid discovery token, let's add it to our `cloud-config.yml` file under the `etcd2` directive:

```
#cloud-config
coreos:
  etcd2:
    discovery:
"https://discovery.etcd.io/638d980c4edf94d6ddff8d6e862bc7d9"
```

The next step is to configure etcd:

- How should etcd listen for peer traffic? (`listen-peer-urls`). We want the local interface on the default port (TCP/`2380`).

- How should etcd listen for client traffic? (`listen-client-urls`). We want all available interfaces on the default port (TCP/`2379`).

- How should etcd initially advertise to the rest of the cluster? (`initial-advertise-peer-urls`). We want the local interface, using the same peer traffic port (TCP/`2380`).

- How should etcd advertise the client URLs to the rest of the cluster? (`advertise-client-urls`). We want the local interface, using the same client traffic port (TCP/`2379`).

To make it more dynamic, we can use variables compatible with most IaaS providers—`$private_ipv4` and `$public_ipv4`.

This is how our `cloud-config.yml` file looks with all the etcd configuration:

```
#cloud-config
coreos:
  etcd2:
```

```
        discovery:
   "https://discovery.etcd.io/b8724b9a1456573f4d527452cba8ebdb"
       advertise-client-urls: "http://$private_ipv4:2379"
       listen-client-urls: "http://0.0.0.0:2379"
       initial-advertise-peer-urls: "http://$private_ipv4:2380"
       listen-peer-urls: "http://$private_ipv4:2380"
```

This will generate the right variables in the `systemd` unit file found at `/run/systemd/system/etcd2.service.d/20-cloudinit.conf`.

```
$ cat /run/systemd/system/etcd2.service.d/20-cloudinit.conf

[Service]

Environment="ETCD_ADVERTISE_CLIENT_URLS=http://172.31.15.59:2379"

Environment="ETCD_DISCOVERY=https://discovery.etcd.io/b8724b9a1456
573f4d527452cba8ebdb"

Environment="ETCD_INITIAL_ADVERTISE_PEER_URLS=http://172.31.15.59:
2380"

Environment="ETCD_LISTEN_CLIENT_URLS=http://0.0.0.0:2379"

Environment="ETCD_LISTEN_PEER_URLS=http://172.31.15.59:2380"
```

When we have our cluster ready, we'll be able to request information as a client on the specified port:

```
$ etcdctl cluster-health

member 7466dcc2053a98a4 is healthy: got healthy result from
http://172.31.15.59:2379

member 8f9bd8a78e0cca38 is healthy: got healthy result from
http://172.31.8.96:2379

member e0f77aacba6888fc is healthy: got healthy result from
http://172.31.1.27:2379

cluster is healthy
```

We can also navigate the etcd key value store to confirm we can access it:

```
$ etcdctl ls

/coreos.com
```

Configuring fleet using cloud-init

Fleet is a distributed init manager based on systemd that we use to schedule services on our CoreOS cluster.

The most important configuration parameters are the following:

- ▸ `public_ip`: This specifies which interface to use to communicate with other hosts. We want the public IP of the host so we can interact with fleet right from our workstation.

- ▸ `metadata`: This is any key value relevant to our needs, so we can schedule units accordingly. We want to store the provider (`aws`), the region (`eu-west-1`), and the name of the cluster (`mycluster`). This is totally arbitrary; adapt keys and values to your own needs.

This is how it looks in the `cloud-config.yml` file:

```
coreos:
  fleet:
    public-ip: "$public_ipv4"
    metadata: "region=eu-west-1,provider=aws,cluster=mycluster"
```

This will generate the right variables in the systemd unit at `/run/systemd/system/fleet.service.d/20-cloudinit.conf`:

```
$ cat /run/systemd/system/fleet.service.d/20-cloudinit.conf
[Service]
Environment="FLEET_METADATA=region=eu-west-1,provider=aws,cluster=myc
luster"
Environment="FLEET_PUBLIC_IP=52.209.159.4"
```

Using fleet is outside of the scope of this book, but we can at least verify the connection to the fleet cluster manager is working from the instance:

```
$ fleetctl list-machines
MACHINE          IP                 METADATA
441bf02a...      52.31.10.18        cluster=mycluster,provider=aws,region
=eu-west-1
b95a5262...      52.209.159.4       cluster=mycluster,provider=aws,region
=eu-west-1
d9fa1d18...      52.31.109.156      cluster=mycluster,provider=aws,region
=eu-west-1
```

We can now submit and start services on our working fleet cluster!

Configuring the update strategy using cloud-init

CoreOS can handle updates in various ways, including rebooting immediately after a new CoreOS version is made available, scheduling with etcd for an ideal time so the cluster never breaks, a mix of both (the default), or even to never reboot. We can also explicitly specify which CoreOS channel to use (stable, beta, or alpha). We want to ensure the cluster never breaks, using the `etcd-lock` strategy, and be sure the stable release is used:

```
coreos:
  update:
    reboot-strategy: "etcd-lock"
    group: "stable"
```

This section generates the `/etc/coreos/update.conf` file:

```
$ cat /etc/coreos/update.conf
GROUP=stable
REBOOT_STRATEGY=etcd-lock
```

We can force an update check to verify it's working (sample taken from a system with an update available):

```
$ sudo update_engine_client -update
[0924/131749:INFO:update_engine_client.cc(243)] Initiating update
check and install.
[0924/131750:INFO:update_engine_client.cc(248)] Waiting for update to
complete.
CURRENT_OP=UPDATE_STATUS_UPDATE_AVAILABLE
[...]
```

Configuring locksmith using cloud-init

Now we're sure the update system is correctly triggered, we are facing a new problem: nodes from our cluster can reboot at any time when an update is available. It's probably less than desirable in a high load environment. So we can configure **locksmith** to allow reboots only during a specific timeframe, such as "every night from Friday to Saturday, between 4 am and 6 am". We're not limited to a single day, so we could also allow reboots any day at 4 am:

```
coreos:
  locksmith:
    window-start: Sat 04:00
    window-length: 2h
```

This generates the following content in `/run/systemd/system/locksmithd.service.d/20-cloudinit.conf`:

```
$ cat /run/systemd/system/locksmithd.service.d/20-cloudinit.conf
[Service]
Environment="REBOOT_WINDOW_START=04:00"
Environment="REBOOT_WINDOW_LENGTH=2h"
```

At any time, we can check for a reboot slot availability using the `locksmithctl` command:

```
$ locksmithctl status
Available: 1
Max: 1
```

If another machine is currently rebooting, its ID is displayed so we know who's rebooting.

Configuring systemd units using cloud-init

We can manage units easily from cloud-init, so critical parts of the system are started right when we need them. For example, we know we want the etcd2 and fleet services to start at every boot:

```
    coreos:
  units:
      - name: etcd2.service
        command: start
      - name: fleet.service
        command: start
```

Configuring flannel using cloud-init

Flannel is used to create an overlay network across all hosts in the cluster, so containers can talk to each other over the network, whatever node they run on. To configure flannel before starting it, we can add more configuration information to the cloud-config file. We know we want our flannel network to work on the 10.1.0.0/16 network, so we can create a drop-in systemd configuration file with its content that will be executed before the `flanneld` service. In this case, setting the flannel network is done by writing the key/value combination to etcd under `/coreos.com/network/config`:

```
    coreos:
      units:
        - name: flanneld.service
          drop-ins:
            - name: 50-network-config.conf
```

```
        content: |
          [Service]
          ExecStartPre=/usr/bin/etcdctl set /coreos.com/network/
config '{ "Network": "10.1.0.0/16" }'
```

This will simply create the file `/etc/systemd/system/flanneld.service.d/50-network-config.conf`:

```
$ cat /etc/systemd/system/flanneld.service.d/50-network-config.conf
[Service]
ExecStartPre=/usr/bin/etcdctl set /coreos.com/network/config '{
"Network": "10.1.0.0/16" }'
```

Verify we have a correct `flannel0` interface in the correct IP network range:

```
$ ifconfig flannel0
flannel0: flags=4305<UP,POINTOPOINT,RUNNING,NOARP,MULTICAST>  mtu 8973
        inet 10.1.19.0  netmask 255.255.0.0  destination 10.1.19.0
[...]
```

Launch a container to verify it's also running in the 10.1.0.0/16 network:

```
$ docker run -it --rm alpine ifconfig eth0
eth0      Link encap:Ethernet  HWaddr 02:42:0A:01:13:02
          inet addr:10.1.19.2  Bcast:0.0.0.0  Mask:255.255.255.0
[...]
```

It's all working great!

 Note that it may take a while to get the interface up, depending on the host Internet connection speed, as flannel is running from a container that needs to be downloaded first (51 MB to date).

We now know the most useful configuration options to bootstrap automatically a CoreOS cluster using cloud-init.

Deploying Chef Client from start to finish using cloud-init

We can deploy Chef using the official **omnibus** installer through cloud-init. This installer embeds everything needed to deploy Chef and all its dependencies. We'll then configure the Chef client to authenticate securely against the Chef Server organization, and finally apply an initial set of cookbooks.

Warning: The current cloud-init version shipped with Ubuntu 16.04 LTS and CentOS 7 is having issues installing Chef. This recipe is using Ubuntu 14.04 LTS waiting for the issue to be fixed.

Getting ready

To step through this recipe, you will need the following:

- Access to a cloud-config enabled infrastructure
- A working Chef Server and organization setup

How to do it...

Everything related to Chef with cloud-init is configured under the directive named `chef`.

Deploying the Chef omnibus installer using cloud-init

As we want to use the official omnibus build (other choices are installing Chef through a Ruby gem—deprecated and too dependent on a locally installed Ruby version and through a package, which is already documented), let's define the installation type to `omnibus`, and ensure it is installed even if, for some reason, the Chef client was found to be already present on the system. Finally, let's explicitly define the installer full URL, so we're sure about what we install (maybe point it to a local version on your own servers).

```
#cloud-config
chef:
  install_type: "omnibus"
  force_install: true
  omnibus_url: "https://www.getchef.com/chef/install.sh"
```

This will output something like the following in the cloud-init logs:

```
Getting information for chef stable  for ubuntu...
downloading https://omnitruck-direct.chef.io/stable/chef/metadata?v=&p
=ubuntu&pv=14.04&m=x86_64
  to file /tmp/install.sh.1294/metadata.txt
[...]
version 12.14.89
[...]
Installing chef
```

```
[...]
Unpacking chef (12.14.89-1) ...
Setting up chef (12.14.89-1) ...
Thank you for installing Chef!
```

At this point, you'll have a valid Chef installation under `/opt/chef`, though not yet configured.

Configuring Chef against a Chef Server organization using cloud-init

Three pieces of information are needed for a chef client to authenticate correctly against a pre-existing Chef Server organization: the URL of the Chef server (`https://api.chef.io/organizations/iacbook`), the private key allowing you to add nodes to the organization, and the name linked to this key (by default, the organization name, such as `iacbook`). This information is mapped like this in the cloud-config file:

```
#cloud-config
chef:
  server_url: "https://api.chef.io/organizations/iacbook"
  validation_name: "iacbook"
  validation_cert: |
    -----BEGIN RSA PRIVATE KEY-----
    MIIEowIBAAKCAQEAuR[...]
    -----END RSA PRIVATE KEY-----
```

With this information, the initial chef-client run will be able to authenticate itself against the Chef organization and add the node. In the cloud-init logs, this step is found at this moment:

```
[...]
Starting Chef Client, version 12.14.89
Creating a new client identity for i-0913e870fb28af4bd using the
validator key.
[...]
```

Applying a Chef cookbook at bootstrap using cloud-init

We certainly want to apply at least an initial cookbook for configuring the instance. In this case, we'll simply apply the starter cookbook shipped with the starter kit, but we can add as many required roles and cookbooks as we want. Refer to the dedicated chapter of this book for more information on obtaining this cookbook:

```
#cloud-config
chef:
  run_list:
  - "recipe[starter]"
```

In the logs, we'll see this being applied like this:

```
[...]
Loading cookbooks [starter@1.0.0]
Storing updated cookbooks/starter/attributes/default.rb in the cache.
Storing updated cookbooks/starter/recipes/default.rb in the cache.
Storing updated cookbooks/starter/templates/default/sample.erb in the
cache.
Storing updated cookbooks/starter/files/default/sample.txt in the
cache.
Storing updated cookbooks/starter/metadata.rb in the cache.
Processing log[Welcome to Chef, Sam Doe!] action write
(starter::default line 4)
Welcome to Chef, Sam Doe!
Chef Run complete in 2.625856409 seconds
```

Our instance is now both registered and configured automatically, as early as possible, with just a few lines in the cloud-config file.

Deploying a remote Docker server using cloud-init

It can be very handy to have a remote Docker server instead of the default local configuration from our workstation because of bandwidth issues, testing a production environment, maybe a customer demonstration, or distant team collaboration. Being able to send the usual Docker commands to a remote server has a multitude of advantages. For speed and comfort, we'll deploy a basic CoreOS system, add one user (Jane) and its public key. Docker will be modified to listen to the network through a socket kind of systemd service, and we'll configure the server time zone to be in New York.

Getting ready

To step through this recipe, you will need:

- Access to a cloud-config enabled infrastructure

How to do it...

Let's start by simply calling this server "docker":

```
#cloud-config
hostname: "docker"
```

In the final system, this will set the hostname to the correct value:

```
$ hostname
docker
$ cat /etc/hostname
docker
```

Now let's create the `Jane` user, so she can log in to the instance to remotely help us. She needs to be in the `docker` group, so she can manipulate the containers, and she gave us her SSH public key. This is how it translates in the cloud-config file:

```
#cloud-config
users:
  - name: "jane"
    gecos: "Jane Docker"
    groups:
      - "docker"
    ssh-authorized-keys:
      - "ssh-rsa AAAAB[...] jane"
```

In the final system, Jane is able to log in using her private key, and interact with the docker daemon as she's a member of the docker group:

```
jane@docker ~ $ docker ps
CONTAINER ID        IMAGE               COMMAND             CREATED
STATUS              PORTS               NAMES
```

The SSH public key ends up in the following file:

```
jane@docker ~ $ cat .ssh/authorized_keys.d/coreos-cloudinit
ssh-rsa AAAAB [..] jane
```

Setting the timezone on CoreOS using cloud-init

CoreOS uses a system built around NTP (short for Network Time Protocol), controlled by the `timedatectl` command. We won't find the usual `/etc/timezone` on CoreOS, so the default `timezone` directive from cloud-init we've seen earlier in this book won't work. To set the time zone to New York on CoreOS, we would set it like this:

```
$ /usr/bin/timedatectl set-timezone America/New_York
```

Easy! So let's launch that command through a systemd unit in the cloud-config file, so we're sure the time zone is set. In-depth knowledge of systemd is out of the scope of this book, but to do that, we'll have to add two options to the unit: one that tells systemd to not think the unit has crashed because the command exited (`RemainAfterExit=yes`), and one that tells the unit type is not executing a long running process, but instead a short one that should exit before continuing (`Type=oneshot`).

Here's the unit in the `cloud-config.yml` file:

```
coreos:
  units:
  - name: settimezone.service
    command: start
    content: |
      [Unit]
      Description=Setting the timezone

      [Service]
      ExecStart=/usr/bin/timedatectl set-timezone America/New_York
      RemainAfterExit=yes
      Type=oneshot
```

Enabling Docker TCP socket for network access

Our final objective is to be able to use a Docker Engine remotely from our workstation. The default Docker configuration is to listen to the Unix socket (`/var/run/docker.sock`)—and we want it to listen to a TCP socket on port 2375 (the default unencrypted port, it's highly recommended to configure TLS encryption; this will use the TCP/2376 by convention). To configure this, we'll use a systemd feature—socket activation. To make it short, this creates a systemd service that listens on port 2375, and spawns the regular `docker.service` unit along with the socket description. This way, this particular Docker Engine will answer to requests on the TCP socket and not on the Unix socket (while keeping the possibility to activate more TCP sockets, or keeping the default `docker.service` clean). Here's how it looks:

```
coreos:
  units:
  - name: docker-tcp.socket
    command: start
    enable: true
    content: |
      [Unit]
      Description=Docker Socket for the API

      [Socket]
      ListenStream=2375
      BindIPv6Only=both
      Service=docker.service

      [Install]
      WantedBy=sockets.target
```

Let's start a remote server with this whole configuration and use it a little for the demonstration (in this example, the Docker remote host is 52.211.117.98, and we'll launch an nginx container with HTTP port forwarding). Refer to the Docker section of this book for more information on the command-line options used:

```
user@workstation $ docker -H 52.211.117.98 run -it --rm -p 80:80 nginx
Unable to find image 'nginx:latest' locally
latest: Pulling from library/nginx
6a5a5368e0c2: Pull complete
4aceccff346f: Pull complete
c8967f302193: Pull complete
Digest: sha256:1ebfe348d131e9657872de9881fe736612b2e8e1630e0508c354ac
b0350a4566
Status: Downloaded newer image for nginx:latest
1.2.3.4 - - [25/Sep/2016:16:06:30 +0000] "GET / HTTP/1.1" 200 612 "-"
"Mozilla/5.0 (Macintosh; Intel Mac OS X 10_11_6) AppleWebKit/537.36
(KHTML, like Gecko) Chrome/53.0.2785.116 Safari/537.36" "-"
```

Make some requests on the remote Docker host HTTP port and it will answer. We now have a full on-demand CoreOS host, capable of giving us control over a Docker Engine remotely, using a nifty systemd configuration feature!

There's more...

When connecting to various remote Docker Engines, we will sooner or later connect to a server not using the same version of the server as our client. In this case, we'll get the following error:

```
Error response from daemon: client is newer than server (client API
version: 1.24, server API version: 1.22)
```

The easy workaround is to override the DOCKER_API_VERSION environment variable and set it to the same value as the server (1.22 in this example):

```
$ DOCKER_API_VERSION=1.22 docker -H 52.211.117.98 ps
```

 Docker 1.13 greatly improved this situation, by managing the version/feature negotiation between the client and the server directly in the CLI.

See also

► For more information about systemd socket activation refer to http://0pointer. de/blog/projects/socket-activation.html.

6

Fundamentals of Managing Servers with Chef and Puppet

In this chapter, we will cover the following recipes:

- ▶ Getting started (notions and tools)
- ▶ Installing the Chef Development kit and Puppet Collections
- ▶ Creating a free hosted server Chef account and a Puppet server
- ▶ Automatically bootstrapping a Chef client and a Puppet agent
- ▶ Installing packages
- ▶ Managing services
- ▶ Managing files, directories, and templates
- ▶ Handling dependencies
- ▶ More dynamic code using notifications
- ▶ Centrally sharing data using a Chef data bag and Hiera with Puppet
- ▶ Creating functional roles
- ▶ Managing external Chef cookbooks and Puppet modules

Introduction

Chef is an open source tool used to automate the configuration of systems and it integrates well with most IaaS such as Amazon Web Services, OpenStack, or Google Cloud. Using Chef, we write infrastructure code in Ruby that describes how every aspect of the system is expected to behave according to a number of conditions, then apply it through various client tools to ensure the defined state is applied.

In this chapter, you'll discover the essentials of managing servers using Chef code with the **Chef Development Kit** (**Chef DK**). You'll learn how to bootstrap a working Chef environment on a new server, how to install packages and manage services, how easy it is to generate dynamic configurations through files and templates, create useful functional roles, centrally share data to dynamically generate content, and show how to articulate dependencies between services while helping them notify each other of their state, so the whole deployment chain works in order. We'll also have an introduction on easily managing those dependencies, that will give an insight of how to deal with more complex infrastructures managed by Chef.

To illustrate all those features, throughout the chapter we will build a classic **LAMP** (**Linux**, **Apache**, **MySQL**, **PHP**) server on CentOS 7.x, from scratch, 100% automated with Chef. This way, we'll go through all the features while progressively building our end project—a working LAMP server with external dependencies on the latest community MySQL 5.7 release, and more features.

All recipes are based on Chef. However, when possible, we'll try to show how things work similarly with Puppet, Chef's direct alternative.

Getting started (notions and tools)

Chef is a very complex system, with a lot of notions and vocabulary that can be very discouraging at first. In this chapter, we'll go through all the most important notions, so it can also serve as a quick cheat sheet or reminder.

Running Chef

Chef can be used in multiple ways, the most important are the following:

- ▶ **Client/server mode**: An agent runs on every managed client, regularly getting updates from the server, and applying them. In this mode, all Chef code is distributed from the Chef server.
- ▶ Chef-Solo: In this mode, the need for a Chef server is removed at the cost of less features, including important ones such as search, API, persistent storage of nodes information, and more. All Chef code needs to be sent over in some way to be applied manually.

Other modes exist, such as Chef Zero, but they are beyond the scope of this book.

The multi-platform client is written in Ruby, while its server counterpart is written in Erlang. The Chef server is open source (Apache License at the time of this writing) and everyone can host it, and the company behind Chef is also proposing their own hosted version, with added features and support.

 A Chef server is a combination of many technologies such as PostgreSQL, RabbitMQ, Redis, Nginx, and so on. Think about maintenance, backup, and performance before deploying your own.

Chef plugins

Chef is also highly modular, with a great number of plugins available either directly from Chef, vendors, or the community. Plugins range from IaaS support such as AWS, OpenStack, VMware, or Digital Ocean to hardware management from Dell, HP, or IPMI interfaces, team workflow integration, or system-related concerns such as logs handling, security, and other similar features.

Chef organizations

At the very top of a Chef hierarchy, we find an *organization*. Nothing can be shared between organizations and this is usually where is defined a *company*, different *business units*, or even deliberately isolated corporate *departments*. It's really up to everyone to know what has to be shared with whom to know what the Chef organization will be.

Chef nodes

A node, in Chef terminology, is anything managed by Chef, be it physical or virtual, and every node has a number of characteristics or parameters that we'll set or change during the lifetime of the node.

Chef environments

Every node runs inside an environment. Environments are usually matching notions such as *development*, *staging*, or *production*, but it's not uncommon to see creative uses to manage different applications or other groups of interest. Environments also have a set of characteristics set.

Chef roles

Roles are usually functional and generic, more than centered around a product. For example, we'll see a *database* role way more often than a *MySQL* role. Other roles can be *monitoring-server* or *loadbalancer*.

Chef resources

This is the single most important notion in Chef: a resource is any part of a system to be set in a desired state. This includes a package to be installed or removed, a service to be enabled or started, a file to be generated from a template, a user to be created or banned, and other expected elements of a system.

Chef recipes

Recipes are simply plain Ruby files including a number of Chef resources describing a coherent desired state, such as a package to be installed, its configuration file written, and a service to be restarted.

Chef cookbooks

Chef cookbooks are used to group many recipes under a coherent set, as well as every other file required to make it work. An example cookbook can be *mysql*, and two recipes from this cookbook can be *mysql::server* to manage the server, and *mysql::client* to manage a client.

Chef run list

A *run list* is a list of roles or recipes that a node has to apply. This is sent by the Chef server by request from the chef client.

There's more...

Puppet is a configuration tool published by Puppet Labs, and is an alternative to Chef.

Puppet can also work in a standalone mode like Chef, but we will focus on a client/server architecture.

The Puppet infrastructure is mainly composed of:

- A Puppet server acting as a main configuration server, which contains all the configuration code
- A Puppet agent running on all infrastructure nodes, applying configurations

Communication between agents and the server is done through HTTPS, and Puppet has its own PKI for the server certificate and for client certificates (client certificates are used to authenticate nodes to the server).

Puppet has its own **Domain Specific Language** (**DSL**). As for Chef, Puppet is using resources for installing packages, managing services, creating files, and more. A Puppet piece of code is called a **manifest**, and is a file with a `.pp` extension. The code is structured using modules. For example, we can imagine an `apache` module containing resources for Apache installation and service management. We can also have a `mysql` module for the MySQL server, with its own resources.

There is also a main manifest, outside any module, which is the list of nodes of the infrastructure. For each node, we can specify which module(s) to use to perform the complete node installation. When a node is requesting its configuration from the server, the server compiles a *catalog* of this node, and the Puppet agent applies this catalog.

We can write our own modules or use existing modules from GitHub of Puppet Forge. Puppet Forge hosts a lot of community modules, and some of them are supported by Puppet Labs.

In this chapter, we will first write our own code in order to learn some basics of the Puppet DSL. We will then use a module from Puppet Forge.

Installing the Chef Development kit and Puppet Collections

The Chef ecosystem is as rich as Chef itself is complex; there's a myriad of tools filling almost every imaginable task we can think of. Chef being written in Ruby, a lot of those tools are also written in Ruby and over the years, the usual dependency hell between tools, plugins, code, and various Ruby versions led to a simple solution—the Chef DK. The Chef DK also brings a nice selection of the best tools and environments that work well together.

We'll see how to install the Chef DK and quickly describe what it includes.

 The current Chef DK version is 1.1.16.

Getting ready

To work through this recipe, you will need the following:

- An Internet connection
- A physical or virtual machine

How to do it...

The Chef DK can be downloaded from `https://downloads.chef.io/chef-dk/`. There're versions for most platforms: Debian, Red Hat-based systems, Ubuntu, and Windows. Simply download the package corresponding to your platform and install it. For example, using a recent Fedora, and installing the Red Hat package, the installation goes like this:

```
$ sudo dnf install chefdk-1.1.16-1.el7.x86_64.rpm
```

Verify the installation worked as expected:

```
$ chef --version
Chef Development Kit Version: 1.1.16
```

That's it! Everything we need to start coding Chef recipes is there.

Chef DK contents

The Chef DK includes a selection of the best tools, including the following:

- ▸ **Chef**: A workflow tool
- ▸ **Berkshelf**: A cookbook dependency manager that does a lot more than that
- ▸ **Test Kitchen**: A full featured integration tests framework
- ▸ **ChefSpec**: easy unit testing of Chef code
- ▸ **FoodCritic**: static code analysis for quality and consistency

The Chef DK also includes all the standard Chef commands (`chef-solo` or `chef-client` to apply cookbooks on nodes, or `knife` to manipulate Chef resources on the developer's workstation, among other tools).

How it works...

The whole Chef environment, as well as its dependencies is deployed under `/opt/chefdk`. The package we installed created symlinks from this directory to `/usr/bin` which is on the `$PATH`:

```
$ ls -al /usr/bin/chef
lrwxrwxrwx. 1 root root 20 Oct  5 16:36 /usr/bin/chef ->
/opt/chefdk/bin/chef
```

This way of packaging software includes all its dependencies, and as Chef relies heavily on Ruby, the Chef DK ships with an embedded version that does not conflict with a Ruby version that might already be installed on your system:

```
$ /opt/chefdk/embedded/bin/ruby --version
ruby 2.3.1p112 (2016-04-26 revision 54768) [x86_64-linux]
```

There's more...

Starting from Puppet 4.x, Puppet Labs is providing repositories for both agent and server packages. These repositories are called **Puppet Collections**. As for Chef, provided packages are shipped with an Embedded Ruby version.

All examples from this book have been developed with Puppet 4.8 (open source edition). Packages can be downloaded from `https://docs.puppet.com/puppet/4.8/puppet_collections.html`.

First of all you need to install the `puppet-agent` package from *Puppet Collections* on your workstation. Even if we won't be managing it using Puppet, these packages will install some commands necessary for upcoming examples.

Once the package is installed, all files are deployed under `/opt/puppetlabs`:

```
$ ls -la /opt/puppetlabs/bin/puppet
lrwxrwxrwx 1 root root 20 Sep 22 18:42 /opt/puppetlabs/bin/puppet ->
../puppet/bin/puppet
$ /opt/puppetlabs/puppet/bin/ruby -version
ruby 2.1.9p490 (2016-03-30 revision 54437) [x86_64-linux]
```

For an easier use of the Embedded Ruby version, you need to add `/opt/puppetlabs/puppet/bin` to the `$PATH` environment variable. For example, on Linux systems, this can be done by appending the following line in the `.bashrc` file located in your home directory:

```
export PATH=/opt/puppetlabs/puppet/bin:$PATH
```

See also

- ▸ The Chef documentation on installing the Chef DK: `https://docs.chef.io/install_dk.html`
- ▸ The Chef documentation on the Chef DK: `https://docs.chef.io/release/devkit/`

Creating a free hosted server Chef account and a Puppet server

In the preferred Chef client/server mode, we need a Chef server to centralize all the information and action. We can build our own, either for testing purposes or for production use (with the maintenance overhead that goes with it), or we can use *Hosted Chef*, the Chef server hosted by the company who wrote Chef. You'll learn here how to create a free Hosted Chef account, so we can start coding with Chef as soon as possible and not worry about the server part. After this first step, we'll download the Chef *Start Kit*, an archive containing a fully working Chef repository, with a sample role and cookbook we can use right away—and that's what we'll do by sending this sample cookbook to the server using our first `knife` command.

Remember: `knife` is the command to use from the developer's workstation to manipulate information and resources on the Chef server. The `knife` command is never used on a Chef node.

Getting ready

To work through this recipe, you will need the following:

▸ An Internet connection

▸ A working Chef DK installation on the workstation

How to do it...

Follow these steps for Creating a free hosted server Chef account and a Puppet server:

1. Go to `https://manage.chef.io/signup`.
2. Fill in the details, use a valid e-mail address, and validate.
3. Click on the link in the e-mail to validate your account.
4. Create a password you remember.
5. Create a new Chef organization.
6. Download the *Starter Kit*.
7. Uncompress the Starter Kit somewhere safe:

```
$ unzip chef-starter.zip
Archive:  chef-starter.zip
   inflating: chef-repo/README.md
   inflating: chef-repo/cookbooks/starter/files/default/sample.txt
   inflating: chef-repo/cookbooks/starter/recipes/default.rb
   inflating: chef-repo/cookbooks/starter/attributes/default.rb
   inflating: chef-repo/cookbooks/starter/metadata.rb
   inflating: chef-repo/cookbooks/starter/templates/default/sample.
erb
   inflating: chef-repo/cookbooks/chefignore
   inflating: chef-repo/.gitignore
   inflating: chef-repo/.chef/knife.rb
   inflating: chef-repo/roles/starter.rb
   inflating: chef-repo/.chef/iacbook.pem
```

8. Verify the connection to Hosted Chef using the `knife` command and request, for example, the list of the users (this will return you user):

```
$ cd chef-repo
$ knife user list
iacbook
```

9. Upload the initial `starter` cookbook, still using the `knife` command:

```
$ knife upload cookbooks/starter
Created cookbooks/starter
```

There's more...

There's no hosted Puppet server offering. We need to deploy our own Puppet server. To simulate a small infrastructure, we will use Vagrant with Ubuntu boxes (for more information about Vagrant, please refer to *Chapter 1, Vagrant Development Environment*). Let's start with a single node infrastructure, with only a Puppet server. Here is our Vagrantfile:

```
vm_memory = 2048
vm_cpus = 2

unless Vagrant.has_plugin?("vagrant-hostmanager")
  raise 'vagrant-hostmanager is not installed!'
end

Vagrant.configure("2") do |config|

    config.hostmanager.enabled = true
    config.hostmanager.manage_guest = true
    config.hostmanager.manage_host = true

    config.vm.define "puppet.pomes.pro" do |puppet|
        puppet.vm.box="bento/ubuntu-16.04"
        puppet.vm.hostname="puppet.pomes.pro"

        puppet.vm.provider :virtualbox do |vb|
                vb.memory = vm_memory
                vb.cpus = vm_cpus
        end

        puppet.vm.network :private_network, ip: "192.168.50.10"
        puppet.hostmanager.aliases = %w(puppet)
        puppet.vm.provision :shell, :path => "puppet_master.sh"
```

```
        puppet.vm.synced_folder "puppetcode", "/etc/puppetlabs/code/
environments/production"
    end
end
```

This Vagrant file relies on the `vagrant-hostmaster` plugin. If you don't already have it, you will need to install it manually using `vagrant plugin install vagrant-hostmanager`. This Vagrant plugin is used to create host entries in `/etc/hosts` in managed boxes and in your workstation. A shared folder will be used to edit code directly from your workstation.

The `puppet_master.sh` provisioning script is as follows:

```bash
#!/usr/bin/env bash

# Exit immediately if a command exits with a non-zero status
set -e

# puppetlabs URL
DEBREPO="https://apt.puppetlabs.com/puppetlabs-release-pc1-xenial.deb"

# Install the PuppetLabs repo
echo "Configuring PuppetLabs repo..."
debrepo=$(mktemp)
wget --output-document=${debrepo} ${DEBREPO}
dpkg -i ${debrepo}
apt-get update

# Install Puppet Server from puppetlabs
# This will remove puppet-common package provided by the
vagrant box (if any)
echo "Installing Puppet..."
apt-get install -y puppetserver

# For tests, limit memory usage. 512m is enough
sed -i 's/2g/512m/g' /etc/default/puppetserver

# For tests, enable autosign for all csr
echo "autosign=true" | tee --append /etc/puppetlabs/puppet/puppet.conf

# Restart puppetserver
service puppetserver restart

# Ensure puppetserver is running and enable it on boot
/opt/puppetlabs/bin/puppet resource service puppetserver
ensure=running enable=true

echo "Puppet server installed!"
```

In this example, we are using a bundled Puppet server from the *Puppet Collections* repository provided by Puppet Labs. For simplicity and following recipes in this chapter, the auto-signing feature has been enabled. This means that when a Puppet node is contacting the server for the first time, a CSR is generated on the node and the Puppet server automatically signs it: subsequent requests will be authenticated and secured.

Let's create the shared folder and start Vagrant:

```
mkdir puppetcode
```

```
vagrant up
```

We now have an Ubuntu Puppet server listening on `192.168.50.10`, with FQDN `puppet.pomes.pro`. A short name puppet is also available, and has been populated by the `vagrant-hostmanager` plugin.

 Depending on your `sudo` configuration, Vagrant may ask you for your password. This is requested by the `vagrant-hostmanager` plugin in order to create entries in the `/etc/hosts` file of your workstation.

Automatically bootstrapping a Chef client and a Puppet agent

The first thing we want to do when working with Chef is to get the Chef client actually bootstrapped on the targeted remote server. For the Chef client to be able to apply Chef code, it first needs to be configured and registered on the Chef server. Thankfully, this can be very easily done.

Getting ready

To work through this recipe, you will need the following:

- A remote server, with a user with SSH access
- A working Chef DK installation on the workstation

How to do it...

Let's say we already have a server running somewhere available with a user. The minimal command line we can build is as follows:

- The IP or FQDN of the host we want to configure (`1.2.3.4`)

- ▸ The name under which to register the node on the Chef server (my_node_hostname)
- ▸ The username to use to connect to the server (sudoer if not root).

Navigate to the Chef repository on your workstation:

```
$ cd chef-repo
```

Now let's remotely install the Chef client on the remote host from your workstation, using an example vagrant user:

```
$ knife bootstrap 1.2.3.4 -N my_node_hostname -x vagrant --sudo
```

This will first download the latest available Chef version and install it. Then it will execute an initial chef-client run to register the node on the Chef server under the specified name. Here it will stop.

If we want to run a cookbook right after bootstrap (and we probably want to), just use the -r option to add cookbooks to the run list, so they are executed right away. Let's use the starter cookbook we uploaded earlier in this chapter, but feel free to use any other cookbook you may have already synchronized on the Chef server.

```
$ knife bootstrap 1.2.3.4 -N my_node_hostname -x vagrant --sudo -r
"starter"
[...]
192.168.146.129 resolving cookbooks for run list: ["starter"]
[...]
192.168.146.129 Recipe: starter::default
192.168.146.129   * log[Welcome to Chef, Sam Doe!] action write
```

There's more...

Using Puppet, we need to install the Puppet agent, once our node is created. Let's add a new node into the Vagrantfile we previously used for the Puppet server:

```
vm_memory = 2048
vm_cpus = 2

unless Vagrant.has_plugin?("vagrant-hostmanager")
  raise 'vagrant-hostmanager is not installed!'
end

Vagrant.configure("2") do |config|

    config.hostmanager.enabled = true
    config.hostmanager.manage_guest = true
```

```
     config.hostmanager.manage_host = true

     config.vm.define "puppet.pomes.pro" do |puppet|
         puppet.vm.box="bento/ubuntu-16.04"
         puppet.vm.hostname="puppet.pomes.pro"

         puppet.vm.provider :virtualbox do |vb|
                 vb.memory = vm_memory
                 vb.cpus = vm_cpus
         end

         puppet.vm.network :private_network, ip: "192.168.50.10"
         puppet.hostmanager.aliases = %w(puppet)
         puppet.vm.provision :shell, :path => "puppet_master.sh"

         puppet.vm.synced_folder "puppetcode",
 "/etc/puppetlabs/code/environments/production"
     end

     config.vm.define "web.pomes.pro" do |web|
         web.vm.box="bento/ubuntu-16.04"
         web.vm.hostname="web.pomes.pro"

         web.vm.network :private_network, ip: "192.168.50.11"

         web.vm.provision :shell, :path => "puppet_node.sh"
     end
 end
```

As you can see, there is now another shell script `puppet_node.sh` used for the provisioning of this new node:

```
#!/usr/bin/env bash

# Exit immediately if a command exits with a non-zero status
set -e

# puppetlabs URL
DEBREPO="https://apt.puppetlabs.com/puppetlabs-release-pc1-xenial.deb"

# Install the PuppetLabs repo
echo "Configuring PuppetLabs repo..."
debrepo=$(mktemp)
wget --output-document=${debrepo} ${DEBREPO}
dpkg -i ${debrepo}
```

```
apt-get update

# Install Puppet Agent from puppetlabs
# This will remove puppet-common package provided by the
vagrant box
echo "Installing Agent..."
apt-get install -y puppet-agent

# Ensure puppet agent is stopped for our tests
/opt/puppetlabs/bin/puppet resource service puppet
ensure=stopped enable=false

echo "Puppet agent installed!"
```

We now also have an Ubuntu Puppet node with FQDN web.pomes.pro with IP 192.168.50.11. By default, the Puppet agent is looking for a server named puppet—that's why this name has been defined as an alias to the puppet server.

 The Puppet agent has been explicitly stopped; during examples, we will start it on demand to see all changes.

Installing packages

We need some packages for our server. Now our server is configured to use Chef and talk to a Chef server, let's install a few packages such as the Apache server, PHP, and MariaDB to build a classic LAMP server on a CentOS 7.2 server.

Getting ready

To work through this recipe, you will need the following:

- A working Chef DK installation on the workstation
- A working Chef client configuration on the remote host

How to do it...

To install a package on a Red Hat-based system, we'd use either yum (until CentOS 7) or dnf (for Fedora after version 22). As we're using a CentOS 7 server, the Apache2 HTTP server package name is httpd, (it's apache2 on Debian-based systems). Manually, we would have typed the following:

```
$ dnf install httpd
$ yum install httpd
```

Let's see how this translates into a repeatable process with a Chef cookbook.

Generating an empty Apache cookbook

Let's start by creating an empty cookbook from inside the Chef repository `cookbooks` folder to install Apache2 using the `chef` command:

```
$ cd chef-repo/cookbooks
$ chef generate cookbook apache
Generating cookbook apache
[...]
Your cookbook is ready. Type `cd apache` to enter it.
[...]
If you'd prefer to dive right in, the default recipe can be found at:
recipes/default.rb
```

Now we need to tell Chef to install a package using the `package` resource.

Open that `apache/recipes/default.rb` file and type in the following:

```
package "httpd"
```

That's the most basic way we can tell Chef to install a package. This will do the `install` action by default. To be a little bit more comprehensive, we can use the full block to do the same:

```
package "httpd" do
  action :install
end
```

Uploading the cookbook

Still from inside the Chef repository, we now need to upload this new `apache` cookbook to the Chef server, so our servers can access it. To do this, we use the `knife` command on our workstation:

```
$ knife cookbook upload apache
Uploading apache         [0.1.0]
Uploaded 1 cookbook.
```

We just uploaded our first cookbook on the Chef server!

Let's confirm the cookbook is available remotely on the Chef server:

```
$ knife cookbook list
apache      0.1.0
starter     1.0.0
```

Applying the cookbook

Now we have the `apache` cookbook remotely available, let's tell the Chef server that our particular node has to run it. Two options here are as follows:

> ▸ From the Chef server UI, select the host and click on **Edit** on the **Run List** box, then drag and drop the correct cookbook name on the **Current Run List** column:

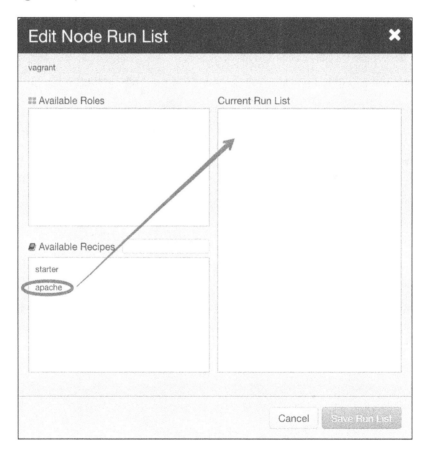

▶ From the `knife` CLI on the workstation, run the following:

```
$ knife node run_list add <nodename> apache
nodename:
  run_list: recipe[apache]
```

Either way, we just told the Chef server to apply the `apache` cookbook on this particular server. Let's launch the Chef client on our remote node:

```
$ sudo chef-client
Starting Chef Client, version 12.15.19
resolving cookbooks for run list: ["apache"]
Synchronizing Cookbooks:
  - apache (0.1.0)
Installing Cookbook Gems:
Compiling Cookbooks...
Converging 1 resources
Recipe: apache::default
  * yum_package[httpd] action install
    - install version 2.4.6-40.el7.centos.4 of package httpd


Running handlers:
Running handlers complete
Chef Client finished, 1/1 resources updated in 32 seconds
```

Chef just installed the Apache HTTP server package for us! If we launch the Chef client, it won't install it again, as it knows it's already there (look at the largely different execution times):

```
$ sudo chef-client
[...]
Recipe: apache::default
  * yum_package[httpd] action install (up to date)
[...]
Chef Client finished, 0/1 resources updated in 04 seconds
```

Verify if the package is really installed:

```
$ which httpd
/usr/sbin/httpd
$ httpd -v
Server version: Apache/2.4.6 (CentOS)
Server built:   Jul 18 2016 15:30:14
```

Creating a MariaDB cookbook

Let's use our knowledge to create a MariaDB cookbook the same way we just deployed Apache, from the Chef repository:

```
$ chef generate cookbook cookbooks/mariadb
```

We want to install two packages: `mariadb` for the client and the libraries, and `mariadb-server` for the server. Add the following on the `mariadb/recipes/default.rb` file:

```
package "mariadb" do
  action :install
end

package "mariadb-server" do
  action :install
end
```

Alternatively, as we're writing plain Ruby, let's rewrite it in a more idiomatic way:

```
%w(mariadb mariadb-server).each do |name|
  package name do
    action :install
  end
end
```

Upload the cookbook from your workstation:

```
$ knife cookbook upload mariadb
```

Add the `mariadb` cookbook to the remote node's run list from your workstation:

```
$ knife node run_list add <nodename> mariadb
```

Run the Chef client on the remote host:

```
$ sudo chef-client
Starting Chef Client, version 12.15.19
```

```
resolving cookbooks for run list: ["apache", "mariadb"]
Synchronizing Cookbooks:
  - apache (0.1.0)
  - mariadb (0.1.0)
[...]
Recipe: mariadb::default
  * yum_package[mariadb] action install
    - install version 5.5.50-1.el7_2 of package mariadb
  * yum_package[mariadb-server] action install
    - install version 5.5.50-1.el7_2 of package mariadb-server
[...]
Chef Client finished, 2/3 resources updated in 25 seconds
```

Verify that the MariaDB package is correctly installed:

```
$ which mysql
/usr/bin/mysql
$ mysql --version
mysql  Ver 15.1 Distrib 5.5.50-MariaDB, for Linux (x86_64) using
readline 5.1
```

Creating a PHP cookbook

Let's reuse our knowledge to create a cookbook that will install the packages needed for PHP support:

```
$ chef generate cookbook cookbooks/php
```

Let's add our Chef code that will install the following three packages: the php, php-cli, and php-mysql packages (respectively for PHP support, command line, and PHP/MySQL support) in the cookbooks/php/recipes/default.rb file:

```
%w(php php-mysql).each do |name|
  package name do
    action :install
  end
end
```

Upload this new php cookbook from your workstation:

```
$ knife cookbook upload php
```

Add the `php` cookbook to the remote node's run list from your workstation:

```
$ knife node run_list add vagrant php
```

Run the Chef client on the remote node:

```
$ sudo chef-client
$ php --version
PHP 5.4.16 (cli) (built: Aug 11 2016 21:24:59)
```

We now know the very basics of deploying cookbooks and installing packages on a remote node, using Chef!

There's more...

Using Puppet, a package installation is done using the `package` resource directive. The following example shows how to install an Apache 2.x server on Ubuntu systems:

```
package {
    'apache2:
        ensure => installed;
}
```

To deploy a LAMP server on the box `web.pomes.pro`, we need Apache2, PHP, and the MariaDB server. In order to do a real example, perform the following steps:

1. Start Vagrant with the Vagrantfile from the previous recipe.
2. Go into the `puppetcode` directory, which is the shared folder between your workstation and the Puppet server: `cd puppetcode`
3. We are about to create three modules (`apache`, `php`, and `mariadb`), so let's create a minimalist module layout for them:

    ```
    mkdir modules/apache
    mkdir modules/apache/manifests
    mkdir modules/apache/templates
    mkdir modules/php
    mkdir modules/php/manifests
    mkdir modules/php/templates
    mkdir modules/mariadb
    mkdir modules/mariadb/manifests
    mkdir modules/mariadb/templates
    ```

4. Create a `module/apache/manifests/init.pp` manifest file with the following content:

```
class apache {
        package {'apache2':
            ensure => present,
        }
}
```

5. Create a `module/php/manifests/init.pp` manifest file with the following content:

```
class php {
        package {['php','php-mysql','libapache2-mod-php']:
            ensure => present,
        }
}
```

6. Create a `module/mariadb/manifests/init.pp` manifest file with the following content:

```
class mariadb {
        package {'mariadb-server':
            ensure => present,
        }
}
```

7. Finally, create the main manifest `manifests/site.pp`, with the following content:

```
node 'web.pomes.pro' {
    class {
        'apache':;
        'php':;
        'mariadb':;
    }
}
```

That's it! With a few lines of code, all necessary binaries will be installed. We can now apply changes, using `puppet agent --test`:

```
$ vagrant ssh web.pomes.pro
Welcome to Ubuntu 16.04.1 LTS (GNU/Linux 4.4.0-51-generic x86_64)
...
...
vagrant@web:~$ sudo -i
root@web:~# puppet agent --test
```

```
Info: Creating a new SSL key for web.pomes.pro

Info: Caching certificate for ca

Info: csr_attributes file loading from /etc/puppetlabs/puppet/csr_
attributes.yaml

Info: Creating a new SSL certificate request for web.pomes.pro

Info: Certificate Request fingerprint (SHA256): 12:9E:DD:E5:85:C9:F2:56:9
2:1B:92:93:0A:3C:7B:00:DE:2A:45:C0:D9:F8:F6:
D0:EC:9D:0B:6E:42:7E:74:33

Info: Caching certificate for web.pomes.pro

Info: Caching certificate_revocation_list for ca

Info: Caching certificate for ca

Info: Using configured environment 'production'

Info: Retrieving pluginfacts

Info: Retrieving plugin

Info: Caching catalog for web.pomes.pro

Info: Applying configuration version '1477085080'

Notice: /Stage[main]/Apache/Package[apache2]/ensure: created

Notice: /Stage[main]/Php/Package[php]/ensure: created

Notice: /Stage[main]/Php/Package[php-mysql]/ensure: created

Notice: /Stage[main]/Php/Package[libapache2-mod-php]/ensure: created

Notice: /Stage[main]/Mariadb/Package[mariadb-server]/ensure: created

Notice: Applied catalog in 59.77 seconds
```

 Unlike what you might think, the --test option does apply changes. This option is used to test code immediately after a change and implies other options such as --no-daemonize, --onetime, and --verbose. If you need to do only a dry-run, you can use the --noop option combined with –test.

See also

▸ The Chef package resource documentation: https://docs.chef.io/
resource_package.html

▸ The Puppet package resource documentation: https://docs.puppet.com/
puppet/4.8/types/package.html

Managing services

We've seen how to install system packages using the `package` resource. In this section, you'll discover how to manage system services, using a resource named `service`. We'll continue to build the LAMP server we started in the previous section by managing the Apache HTTP and MariaDB services right from Chef. This way we'll be able to manage any available service.

Getting ready

To work through this recipe, you will need the following:

- A working Chef DK installation on the workstation
- A working Chef client configuration on the remote host
- The Chef code from the previous recipe

How to do it...

The structure of the service resource is very similar to the `package` resource. We want to do two actions with our services: **enable** them at boot and **start** them right away. This translates into a simple Chef resource with an array of actions:

```
service "service_name" do
  action [:enable, :start]
end
```

Enabling and starting Apache service

Add this `service` resource to the `apache/recipes/default.rb` file, just after the `package` resource:

```
service "httpd" do
  action [:enable, :start]
end
```

Bump the cookbook version number on the `apache/metatada.rb` file:

```
version '0.2.0'
```

This way, the Chef server will always keep version `0.1.0` with only the package installation, and a new version `0.2.0`, with the service support. We'll also be able to easily rollback to a previously running version.

When the Chef client runs, it always downloads and applies the latest version by default. It's advised to fix (or pin) versions where appropriate—especially in production.

Upload the new cookbook version:

```
$ knife cookbook upload apache
```

Now we have both versions of the cookbook available on the Chef server:

```
$ knife cookbook show apache
apache   0.2.0  0.1.0
```

Apply on the remote host:

```
$ sudo chef-client
```

Verify the Apache service is indeed running:

```
$ systemctl status httpd
```

You can also navigate to the site's IP address in HTTP to see the default page displayed.

Enabling and starting the MariaDB service

Do exactly the same for MariaDB's `mariadb` service in `mariadb/recipes/default.rb`:

```
service "mariadb" do
  action [:enable, :start]
end
```

Don't forget to also bump the cookbook version in `mariadb/metadata.rb`:

```
version '0.2.0'
```

Send the updated cookbook to the Chef server:

```
$ knife cookbook upload mariadb
```

Apply the new cookbook:

```
$ sudo chef-client
```

Confirm the MariaDB service is now running:

```
$ systemctl status mariadb
```

Confirm we can access the MariaDB server from the node:

```
$ mysql -e "show databases;"
+--------------------+
| Database           |
+--------------------+
| information_schema |
| test               |
+--------------------+
```

We've just covered how to handle a system service using Chef, so you now know how to easily and repeatedly deploy packages and manage the corresponding service.

There's more...

Using Puppet, services are also managed with a dedicated resource directive. Using the previous example, we now need to ensure that the corresponding services are running.

This resource needs to be added on both Apache and MariaDB modules. The new manifest for the Apache module is:

```
class apache {
        package {'apache2':
            ensure => present,
        }

        service {'apache2':
            ensure => running,
            enable => true
        }
}
```

The new manifest for the MariaDB module is:

```
class mariadb {
        package {'mariadb-server':
            ensure => present,
        }

        service {'mysql':
            ensure => running,
            enable => true
        }
}
```

The `ensure=>running` property is used to check the service is running (and will start it if needed), and `enable=>true` is used to start the service at boot.

 The name of the service used in the service resource is the same as used in a root shell to stop/start/reload the service.

See also

▶ The Chef `service` resource documentation: `https://docs.chef.io/resource_service.html`

▶ The Chef `metadata.rb` resource documentation: `https://docs.chef.io/config_rb_metadata.html`

▶ The Puppet `service` resource documentation: `https://docs.puppet.com/puppet/4.8/types/service.html`

Managing files, directories, and templates

A very useful Chef feature is the ability to manage files right from the Chef code. Either plain files can be copied or dynamic files can be generated through templates. We'll leverage this feature to create an example PHP test file and dynamically generate Apache VirtualHosts for our LAMP server, so you'll know how to reuse it anywhere else.

Getting ready

To work through this recipe, you will need the following:

▶ A working Chef DK installation on the workstation

▶ A working Chef client configuration on the remote host

▶ Optionally, the Chef code from the previous recipes

How to do it...

We'll manage two different kinds of files in two different ways: a static file and a dynamic file generated from a template, so the most common usage is covered.

Managing a simple static file

Let's begin by creating a basic PHP file that will only display the `phpinfo()` result. This is done using the simple `file` resource with the file path as argument, giving its content inline. Other optional properties of the `file` resource include ownership information or the file mode. Add a `file` resource to the `php/recipes/default.rb` recipe:

```
file '/var/www/html/phpinfo.php' do
  content '<?php phpinfo(); ?>'
  mode '0644'
  owner 'root'
  group 'root'
end
```

Don't forget to bump the version in `php/metadata.rb`:

```
version '0.2.0'
```

Upload the new cookbook from your workstation:

```
$ knife cookbook upload php
```

Deploy using the Chef client on the remote node:

```
$ sudo chef-client
```

If you now navigate to `http://node-hostname/phpinfo.php`, you'll see the PHP information displayed.

This is the most static way of shipping a plain file.

Managing dynamic files and directories from a template

Let's now create a generic Apache virtual host to fully control what we'll do with our LAMP server, and not just live with the default configuration shipped with our Linux distribution. We want the website's root folder to be `/var/www/<sitename>` and the configuration file will live under `/etc/httpd/conf.d/<sitename>.conf`. We'll ship a sample HTML index file as well, to validate we're running the correct virtual host.

Start by generating a new recipe in the Apache cookbook using the `chef` command, to manage a default Virtual Host:

```
$ chef generate recipe cookbooks/apache virtualhost
```

A new file named `apache/recipes/virtualhost.rb` is now created.

To store the name of our virtual host, let's create an `attribute`. An attribute is similar to a persisting node setting, declared in a cookbook in a file under the `attribute` directory, and can then be overridden by many mechanisms that we'll later discover. Start by generating an attributes file using the `chef` command:

```
$ chef generate attribute cookbooks/apache default
```

This will create a new file under `apache/attributes/default.rb`. To set the `sitename` attribute with default value of `defaultsite`, add the following in this file:

```
default["sitename"] = "defaultsite"
```

To create a new directory, let's use a resource named `directory` in the `apache/recipes/virtualhost.rb` file, with standard access rights. Note the Ruby `#{node["sitename"]}` syntax to access a node attribute from inside a string that will be recurring from now on:

```
directory "/var/www/#{node["sitename"]}" do
  owner 'root'
  group 'root'
  mode '0755'
  action :create
end
```

Let's reuse the `file` resource to create a basic `index.html` file with a simple string such as `Hello from Chef!` or whatever you find more appealing, in the `apache/recipes/virtualhost.rb` file:

```
file "/var/www/#{node["sitename"]}/index.html" do
  owner 'root'
  group 'root'
  mode '0644'
  content '<html><h1>Hello from Chef!</h1></html>'
end
```

Let's once again use the `chef` generator to create a new template for our Apache virtual host configuration file:

```
$ chef generate template cookbooks/apache virtualhost
```

This will create a template under `apache/templates/` named `virtuahost.erb`. This is a standard **ERB** (short for **Embedded Ruby**) template. This template file will contain the virtual host Apache configuration for our site.

Let's start by populating the content of this ERB with a minimal Apache configuration file, using a new `website` variable that we'll set in a minute.

A variable in an ERB template is prefixed with the @ character.

```
<VirtualHost *:80>
        ServerName <%= @website %>
        DocumentRoot /var/www/<%= @website %>
        ErrorLog /var/log/httpd/error-<%= @website %>.log
        CustomLog /var/log/httpd/access-<%= @website %>.log
combined
        <Directory /var/www/<%= @website %>/ >
           Options Indexes FollowSymLinks MultiViews
           AllowOverride All
           Order allow,deny
           allow from all
        </Directory>
</VirtualHost>
```

This way, the whole configuration is dynamic; we'll be able to instantiate this cookbook for any site name of our choice and it will be dedicated to it.

Now let's use the `template` resource to generate a file from the template we just created, in the `apache/recipes/virtualhost.rb` file. This resource takes a `source` parameter, which is the template file we just created, and the variables to be injected. In our case, we want to inject the value of the `sitename` attribute, so it can be accessed by the template as @website:

```
template "/etc/httpd/conf.d/#{node["sitename"]}.conf" do
  source "virtualhost.erb"
  owner 'root'
  group 'root'
  mode '0644'
  variables(
    :website => "#{node["sitename"]}"
  )
end
```

Don't forget to bump the cookbook version in `apache/metadata.rb`:

```
version '0.3.0'
```

Upload the cookbook to Chef server from the workstation:

```
$ knife cookbook upload apache
```

Add the newly-created recipe to the remote node run list:

```
$ knife node run_list add <node name> apache::virtualhost
```

Apply the new cookbook on the remote host:

```
$ sudo chef-client
```

Restart the Apache server manually to take the changes into account (be sure we'll automate that in the next pages):

```
$ sudo systemctl restart httpd
```

Verify that the served page is the one we added:

```
$ curl http://node_ip_or_hostname/
<html><h1>Hello from Chef!</h1></html>
```

Good job! We've just covered how to manage files, directories, as well as dynamic templates, using pure Ruby code with Chef.

There's more...

Now that we have a LAMP server with Puppet, let's create a virtual host! Our goals are as follows:

- ▶ Removing the default virtual host provided by Ubuntu
- ▶ Creating our own virtual host, with a specific `DocumentRoot` and dedicated log files
- ▶ Deploying a simple PHP page displaying the result of the function `phpinfo()`

These three operations will be done using the `file` directive.

On Ubuntu, we need to remove the default website in order to have virtual hosting up and running. This can be done easily in the Apache manifest; a `file` directive for the deletion of `/etc/apache2/site-enabled/000-default.conf` will remove the symlink and will disable the site:

```
class apache {
    package {'apache2':
        ensure => present,
    }

    service {'apache2':
        ensure => running,
        enable => true,
    }
```

```
file {'/etc/apache2/sites-enabled/000-default.conf':
    ensure => absent,
}
}
```

Now let's create the code for the virtual host generation. The creation of a new virtual host must be done in /etc/apache2/sites-available, and will be generated from a template. Two languages are available:

► ERB for Embedded Ruby.

► EPP for Embedded Puppet (Puppet 4 and higher). Let's choose this one.

Our EPP template will use two parameters: the site name and the document root. Let's create a vhost.epp file in the modules/apache/templates directory:

```
<VirtualHost *:80>
  ServerName <%=$website%>
  DocumentRoot <%=$docroot%>
  <Directory <%=$docroot%>>
    Order deny,allow
    Allow from all
    AllowOverride All
  </Directory>
  ErrorLog /var/log/apache2/error-<%=$website%>.log
  CustomLog /var/log/apache2/access-<%=$website%>.log combined
</VirtualHost>
```

Now we need to instantiate this template. The best way is to think about something we could reuse as many times as needed (in case we would like to add more sites).

We previously used a class statement, but each class in Puppet can be used only once per catalog (remember, a catalog is the result of the compilation for a node). Fortunately, the define statement is used to define a block of code that can be used multiple times.

So let's define a file, module/apache/manifest/vhost.pp that will use such a statement:

```
define apache::vhost (
    $website,
    $docroot
) {

  file { "/etc/apache2/sites-available/$website.conf":
    ensure  => present,
    owner   => 'root',
    group   => 'root',
    mode    => '0640',
    content => epp('apache/vhost.epp',
```

```
                              {'website' => $website,
                               'docroot'=>$docroot}),
        }


    file { "/etc/apache2/sites-enabled/$website.conf":
       ensure  => link,
       target  => "/etc/apache2/sites-available/$website.conf",
       require => File["/etc/apache2/sites-available/$website.conf"],
    }
  }
}
```

The website name and the document root are the two parameters for our `apache::vhost` statement and are passed to the `epp` function along with the template file name in the first `file` directive.

On Ubuntu, to enable a site, a link must be created in `/etc/apache2/site-enabled`; the second `file` directive will handle it.

Finally, we need to deploy our PHP file under the `DocumentRoot` directory. This can be done directly in the main manifest using `file` directives to create the `DocumentRoot` directory and the file itself:

```
node 'web.pomes.pro' {
    $website=$fqdn;
    $docroot="/var/www/$fqdn";

    class {
      'apache':;
      'php':;
      'mariadb':;
    }
    apache::vhost {$website:
        website => $website,
        docroot => $docroot,
    }
    file { $docroot:
      ensure => directory,
      owner  => 'www-data',
      group  => 'www-data',
      mode   => '0755',
    }
    file {"$docroot/index.php":
      ensure  => present,
      owner   => 'www-data',
      group   => 'www-data',
      mode    => '0644',
```

```
            content => "<?php phpinfo() ?>",
        }
    }
}
```

We can now run the Puppet agent again. For now, we need to restart Apache manually in order to have our virtual host running (as for Chef, we'll automate this in the next pages):

root@web:~# service apache2 reload

Now you should see the phpinfo page on http://web.pomes.pro

See also

- ▶ The Chef documentation on attributes: https://docs.chef.io/attributes. html

- ▶ The Chef documentation on the directory resource: https://docs.chef.io/ resource_directory.html

- ▶ The Chef documentation on the file resource: https://docs.chef.io/ resource_file.html

- ▶ The Chef documentation on the template resource: https://docs.chef.io/ resource_template.html

- ▶ The Puppet file resource documentation: https://docs.puppet.com/ puppet/4.8/types/file.html

- ▶ Using templates with Puppet: https://docs.puppet.com/puppet/4.8/lang_ template.html

Handling dependencies

A very nifty feature of Chef is the ability to include recipes from one cookbook with another. This way, we can create cookbooks with a purpose, like a product or an end result. An example of such a cookbook could be an application cookbook named *MyCloudApp*, with calls to, or inclusions of, other cookbooks such as Apache, MySQL, or any other cookbook it might need.

Until now, we added recipe after recipe to the run list of our host. This is not optimal, and less than desirable when managing a lot of nodes. The idea here is to create a new cookbook dedicated to an imaginary MySite application, that will reference and depend on all the other recipes, so we can only load this MySite cookbook and be done with it.

Getting ready

To work through this recipe, you will need the following:

- ▶ A working Chef DK installation on the workstation

> ▸ A working Chef client configuration on the remote host
>
> ▸ Optionally, the Chef code from the previous recipes

How to do it...

We know we want to create a new cookbook named `mysite` so we can centralize everything related to making this application work in the same place. Let's use the `chef` command to do that:

```
$ chef generate cookbook cookbooks/mysite
```

To include a recipe from another cookbook with our default recipe, we'll use the `include_recipe` method in `mysite/recipes/default.rb`:

```
include_recipe "apache"
include_recipe "apache::virtualhost"
include_recipe "mariadb"
include_recipe "php"
```

This is telling Chef to load and execute the content of each recipe.

For Chef to know where this is to be found, we need to create a dependency to those cookbooks. This is done in the `mysite/metadata.rb` file:

```
depends "apache"
depends "mariadb"
depends "php"
```

Now, our MySite cookbook has a nice dependency graph: to fully work, it needs Apache, MariaDB, and PHP. The recipe details what exactly to run.

Since we have a dedicated cookbook for our app, let's try to add some customization to it. Remember the default `sitename` attribute in the `apache` cookbook? Let's override it to match our own value by adding the following at the top of the file, just before the apache recipes inclusion:

```
node.override["sitename"] = "mysite"
```

Upload the cookbook to the Chef server:

```
$ knife cookbook upload mysite
```

Remove previous recipes from our node's run list using `knife node run_list remove <node name> <recipe name>`:

```
$ knife node run_list remove vagrant "recipe[mariadb]" "recipe[php]"
"recipe[apache]" "recipe[apache::virtualhost]"
```

The node's run list is now empty. Simply add the new `mysite` cookbook that includes everything it needs to run:

```
$ knife node run_list add vagrant mysite
```

The next Chef client run won't change anything, but it will be much easier to manage in the future!

There's more...

Using puppet, a module can be used in other modules. Based on previous examples, we could think about a `mysite` module, with the following manifest:

```
class mysite (
    $website,
    $docroot
){
    class {
       'apache'::;
       'php'::;
       'mariadb'::;
    }
    apache::vhost {$website:
       website => $website,
       docroot => $docroot,
    }
    file { $docroot:
      ensure => directory,
      owner    => 'www-data',
      group    => 'www-data',
      mode     => '0755',
    }
    file {"$docroot/index.php":
      ensure => present,
      owner    => 'www-data',
      group    => 'www-data',
      mode     => '0644',
      content => "<?php phpinfo() ?>",
    }
}
```

The main manifest of our node would be as follows:

```
node 'web.pomes.pro' {
    class {
       'mysite':
```

```
        website     => $fqdn,
        docroot     => "/var/www/$fqdn",
    }
}
```

See also

▸ The Chef documentation on attributes: `https://docs.chef.io/attributes.html`

▸ The Chef cookbook `metadata.rb` documentation: `https://docs.chef.io/config_rb_metadata.html`

More dynamic code using notifications

Wouldn't it be great if Chef knew how and what to restart automatically when a change arises? In a previous example, we added a new virtual host to our node, and we had to manually restart Apache to take the change into account. Luckily, there's a mechanism named *notifications* in Chef, that helps trigger an action, when a resource changes. This way, changing a virtual host can trigger a restart of the Apache HTTP server automatically.

Getting ready

To work through this recipe, you will need the following:

▸ A working Chef DK installation on the workstation

▸ A working Chef client configuration on the remote host

▸ The Chef code from the previous recipes

How to do it...

We'll start from the `apache` cookbook we've left in its 0.3.0 version. Bump it right now to `0.4.0` so we're starting fresh in `apache/metadata.rb`:

```
version '0.4.0'
```

Every resource can notify another resource to do something when its state changes, and any resource can also subscribe to a change of state from another resource. In our case, we'd like our `template` resource to notify the `httpd` system service to restart when the Virtual Host template changes, so we're sure the change is automatically taken into account. The httpd service is coming from the default Apache recipe, so it's better to include it right now in the `apache/recipes/virtualhost.rb` file, so we're sure this particular recipe works alone and not by side-effect of a previous inclusion:

include_recipe 'apache::default'

1. In the `apache/recipes/virtualhost.rb` file, add the following highlighted notification section:

```
template "/etc/httpd/conf.d/#{node["sitename"]}.conf" do
  source "virtualhost.erb"
  owner 'root'
  group 'root'
  mode '0644'
  variables(
    :website => "#{node["sitename"]}"
  )
  notifies :restart, resources(:service => "httpd")
end
```

 By default, actions are *delayed* at the end of the Chef run. If we need an action to take place immediately, at the risk of breaking the state of the system, we can add the `:immediately` timer at the end of the line.

2. To validate it's working, we need to change something in our Virtual Host template in `apache/templates/virtualhost.erb`. For this example, I simply set the local IP the node is listening to, but feel free to adapt to your own case:

```
<VirtualHost 192.168.146.129:80>
        ServerName <%= @website %>
        DocumentRoot /var/www/<%= @website %>
        ErrorLog /var/log/httpd/error-<%= @website %>.log
        CustomLog /var/log/httpd/access-<%= @website %>.log
combined
</VirtualHost>
```

3. Now upload the updated cookbook (we've already bumped it):

   ```
   $ knife cookbook upload apache
   ```

4. Run the Chef client on the node and see the magic happen:

   ```
   $ sudo chef-client
   [...]
     * template[/etc/httpd/conf.d/defaultsite.conf] action
   create
       - update content in file /etc/httpd/conf.d/defaultsite.conf
   from 6f4d47 to 05ea5b
       --- /etc/httpd/conf.d/defaultsite.conf    2016-10-17
   01:05:49.243799676 +0000
   ```

```
      +++ /etc/httpd/conf.d/.chef-defaultsite20161017-14052-
1xt951m.conf        2016-10-17 01:10:27.452670052 +0000

      @@ -1,4 +1,4 @@

      -<VirtualHost *:80>

      +<VirtualHost 192.168.146.129:80>

              ServerName defaultsite

              DocumentRoot /var/www/defaultsite

              ErrorLog /var/log/httpd/error-defaultsite.log

  [...]

  Recipe: apache::default

    * service[httpd] action reload

      - reload service service[httpd]
```

The cool thing is we can even see a diff of the change in the logs so we always know what's changed, as well as see the httpd service being reloaded after the change happened.

Our system is now perfectly dynamic and can reload its configuration at will at every change.

There's more...

Puppet has exactly the same feature, using the notify attribute. When the content of /etc/apache2/sites-enabled is modified, Apache configuration needs to be reloaded.

Let's change our Apache manifest to do this.

Apache configuration needs to be reloaded when the default vhost is removed, so we need to modify modules/apache/manifests/init.pp with the corresponding notify attribute:

```
class apache {
    package {'apache2':
        ensure => present,
    }

    service {'apache2':
        ensure => running,
        enable => true
    }

    file {'/etc/apache2/sites-enabled/000-default.conf':
        ensure => absent,
        notify => Service['apache2'],
    }
}
```

The same logic applies for the virtual host creation (`modules/apache/manifests/vhost.pp`):

```
define apache::vhost (
    $website,
    $docroot
) {

    file { "/etc/apache2/sites-available/$website.conf":
        ensure  => present,
        owner   => 'root',
        group   => 'root',
        mode    => '0640',
        content => epp('apache/vhost.epp',
                        {'website' => $website,
                        'docroot'=>$docroot}),
    }

    file { "/etc/apache2/sites-enabled/$website.conf":
        ensure  => link,
        target  => "/etc/apache2/sites-available/$website.conf",
        require => File["/etc/apache2/sites-available/$website.conf"],
        notify  => Service['apache2'],
    }
}
```

Let's try to run the Puppet agent on fresh Vagrant boxes, we will see that the two modifications will schedule a configuration reload, that will be done at the end of the Puppet Agent run. (refer to the lines with `Scheduling refresh of Service[apache2]` and `Triggered 'refresh' from 2 events`):

Notice: /Stage[main]/Apache/File[/etc/apache2/sites-enabled/000-default.conf]/ensure: removed

Info: /Stage[main]/Apache/File[/etc/apache2/sites-enabled/000-default.conf]: Scheduling refresh of Service[apache2]

...

...

Notice: /Stage[main]/Main/Node[web.pomes.pro]/Apache::Vhost[web.pomes.pro]/File[/etc/apache2/sites-enabled/web.pomes.pro.conf]/ensure: created

Info: /Stage[main]/Main/Node[web.pomes.pro]/Apache::Vhost[web.pomes.pro]/File[/etc/apache2/sites-enabled/web.pomes.pro.conf]: Scheduling refresh of Service[apache2]

Notice: /Stage[main]/Apache/Service[apache2]: Triggered 'refresh' from 2 events

`Notice: Applied catalog in 45.46 seconds`

Now we can access the phpinfo page at `http://web.pomes.pro` without manually restarting Apache.

See also

- ▸ The Chef documentation for notifications: `https://docs.chef.io/resource_common.html#notifications`

- ▸ The Chef documentation for subscribes: `https://docs.chef.io/resource_common.html#subscribes`

- ▸ The Puppet notify resource documentation: `https://docs.puppet.com/puppet/4.8/types/notify.html`

Centrally sharing data using a Chef data bag and Hiera with Puppet

Now we have the basics of our LAMP infrastructure up and running, let's secure it a little by creating an `htaccess` file with a few authorized users in it. To achieve this, we could use different techniques, but the *data bag* feature in Chef is pretty convenient for our objective. A data bag is simply data in a JSON file stored on the Chef server, that can be searched from the cookbooks. It's especially useful for storing data that need to be accessed globally from a central point (such as users, service credentials, version numbers, URLs, even feature flags, and other similar features depending on your usage).

Getting ready

To work through this recipe, you will need the following:

- ▸ A working Chef DK installation on the workstation
- ▸ A working Chef client configuration on the remote host
- ▸ The Chef code from the previous recipes

How to do it...

Our objective is to create two users—John and Mary. Here's a table of the required information:

User	Password	Hash
John	p4ssw0rd	$apr1$AUI2Y5pj$0v0PaSlLfc6QxZx1Vx5Se
Mary	s3cur3	$apr1$eR7H0C5r$OrhOQUTXfUEIdvWyeGGGy/

To generate the encrypted passwords, you can use the simple `htpasswd` utility:

```
$ htpasswd -n -b mary s3cur3
mary:$apr1$eR7H0C5r$OrhOQUTXfUEIdvWyeGGGy/
```

We want to store that piece of information (username and password), inside a single entity: this is the data bag. Let's name it `webusers`, and we'll store our users under this directory.

1. Let's create this directory inside our Chef repository for our revision control system (RCS, like git):

    ```
    $ mkdir -p data_bags/webusers
    ```

2. To create the data bag entry on the Chef server, use the following `knife` command:

    ```
    $ knife data bag create webusers
    ```

3. As we know, an entry is simple JSON structured data. Let's write the content of our data bag for our user John, in `data_bags/webusers/john.json`:

    ```
    {
      "id": "john",
      "htpasswd": "$apr1$AUI2Y5pj$0v0PaSlLfc6QxZx1Vx5Se."
    }
    ```

4. Let's do the same for Mary in `data_bags/webusers/mary.json`

    ```
    {
      "id": "mary",
      "htpasswd": "$apr1$eR7H0C5r$OrhOQUTXfUEIdvWyeGGGy/"
    }
    ```

5. Now let's send this data on the Chef server using the `knife` command:

    ```
    $ knife data bag from file webusers mary.json
    Updated data_bag_item[webusers::mary]
    $ knife data bag from file webusers john.json
    Updated data_bag_item[webusers::john]
    ```

You can see the current entries in the data bag using the knife command:

```
$ knife data bag show webusers
john
mary
```

Now the data is globally available from the Chef server, how do we access it dynamically from inside our code? This is where the `search` feature in Chef is useful to create dynamically generated content.

Before starting any work in the `mysite` cookbook, let's bump the version in `mysite/metadata.rb` so we're sure not to break anything:

```
version '0.2.0'
```

1. Let's create a new recipe named `htaccess.rb` under the `mysite` cookbook so we can create both the `htaccess` file under `/etc/httpd/htaccess` (this is an arbitrary location, adaptable to your needs) and the Apache configuration file under the web root:

   ```
   $ chef generate recipe cookbooks/mysite htaccess
   ```

2. To have our entries automatically populated in the `htaccess` file, we'll have to iterate through all existing entries. This is done using the `search` in Chef, specifying the data bag, and the scope to search (in our case, everything). This is simply added in the `mysite/recipes/htaccess.rb` file:

   ```
   users = search(:webusers, "*:*")
   ```

3. This variable, `users`, will then be passed to the template file to generate the content, like we did previously—except this time we have multiple entries, not just one. We're using the `htpasswd.erb` file as a source, that we'll create in a moment:

   ```
   template "/etc/httpd/htpasswd" do
     source "htpasswd.erb"
     owner 'root'
     group 'root'
     mode '0660'
     variables(
       :users => users
     )
   end
   ```

4. Generate a new template for the `htpasswd` file, using the `chef` command:

   ```
   $ chef generate template cookbooks/mysite htpasswd
   ```

5. Inside this ERB file in `mysite/templates/htpasswd.erb`, enter the following:

```
<% @users.each do |user| -%>
<%= user["id"] %>:<%= user["htpasswd"] %>
<% end -%>
```

The `.each` method loops around the `users` variable that we passed through the template, iterates on `user`, and extracts our two values of interest: `id` and `htpasswd`.

While we're at it, let's create the template for the `.htaccess` file under our web root folder:

$ chef generate template cookbooks/mysite htaccess

Its content is the most basic we can find:

```
AuthType Basic
AuthName "Restricted Area"
AuthUserFile /etc/httpd/htpasswd
Require valid-user
```

 There's currently no variable in this template. As I know, files most often end up being dynamic, I always prefer to start them as templates, even if content is currently static. It's very likely that in the near future we'll want to use a variable for `AuthUserFile`.

6. Back to our `mysite/recipes/htaccess.rb` recipe, let's add the template we just created:

```
template "/var/www/mysite/.htaccess" do
  source "htaccess.erb"
  owner 'root'
  group 'root'
  mode '0644'
end
```

Don't forget the last step: we have to call this new recipe from our main, `default.rb` recipe! In `mysite/recipes/default.rb`, include our new recipe, so it gets picked up by the client:

```
include_recipe "mysite::htaccess"
```

Just upload the new version of the cookbook:

$ knife cookbook upload mysite

After you've run `chef-client` on your node, the site will be protected and users `mary` and `john` will be able to use basic HTTP authentication.

There's more...

With Puppet, we can do it using Hiera. Hiera can be seen as datastore keeping site information out of manifests. Hiera can be customized in the way data is stored, but this will be out of the scope of this chapter; we will use default configuration.

First of all, we need to define the data in Hiera. This will be done by creating `web.pomes.pro.yaml` in the Hiera tree:

```
$ cd puppetcode/hieradata
$ mkdir nodes
$ cat > nodes/web.pomes.pro.yaml
webusers:
  - id: john
    htpasswd: $apr1$AUI2Y5pj$0v0PaSlLfc6QxZx1Vx5Se
  - id: mary
    htpasswd: $apr1$eR7H0C5r$OrhOQUTXfUEIdvWyeGGGy/
^D
```

This file now contains an array of hashes for authorized users, for the node `web.pomes.pro`.

From the main manifest, we need to look up our Hiera data using the following code:

```
$users=hiera('webusers');
```

Now it's easy to generate the password file using a new `apache::htpasswd define` statement, that we need to create in `modules/apache/manifests/htpasswd.pp`:

```
define apache::htpasswd (
    $filepath,
    $users
) {

  file { "$filepath":
    ensure  => present,
    owner   => 'root',
    group   => 'root',
    mode    => '0644',
    content => template('apache/htpasswd.erb'),
  }
}
```

For the corresponding template, this time, let's try an ERB template in `modules/apache/templates/htpasswd.erb`:

```
<% @users.each do |user| -%>
<%= user['id'] %>:<%= user['htpasswd'] %>
<% end -%>
```

From the main manifest, we can now create the password file:

```
apache::htpasswd{'htpasswd':
        filepath => '/etc/apache2/htpasswd',
        users    => hiera('webusers'),
}
```

We also need to create a `.htaccess` file. Let's create a new `apache::htaccess` statement in `modules/apache/manifests/htaccess.pp`:

```
define apache::htaccess (
    $filepath,
    $docroot
) {

  file { "$docroot/.htaccess":
    ensure  => present,
    owner   => 'root',
    group   => 'root',
    mode    => '0644',
    content => template('apache/htaccess.erb'),
  }
}
```

The associated template in `modules/apache/templates/htaccess.erb` is:

```
AuthType Basic
AuthName "Restricted Area"
AuthUserFile <%= @filepath %>
Require valid-user
```

From the main manifest, we can now create the `.htaccess` file:

```
apache::htaccess{"$docroot-htaccess":
  filepath => '/etc/apache2/htpasswd',
    docroot  => $docroot,
  }
```

As a result, here is the main manifest of the `web.pomes.pro` node:

```
node 'web.pomes.pro' {
    $website=$fqdn;
    $docroot="/var/www/$fqdn";
    $users=hiera('webusers');

    class {
      'apache'::;
      'php'::;
      'mariadb'::;
    }
    apache::vhost{$website:
      website => $website,
      docroot => $docroot,
    }
    apache::htpasswd{'htpasswd':
      filepath => '/etc/apache2/htpasswd',
      users    => hiera('webusers'),
    }
    apache::htaccess{"$docroot-htaccess":
      filepath => '/etc/apache2/htpasswd',
      docroot  => $docroot,
    }
    file { $docroot:
      ensure => directory,
      owner   => 'www-data',
      group   => 'www-data',
      mode    => '0755',
    }
    file {"$docroot/index.php":
      ensure => present,
      owner   => 'www-data',
      group   => 'www-data',
      mode    => '0644',
      content => "<?php phpinfo() ?>",
    }
}
```

After running the Puppet agent, `http://web.pomes.pro` will now ask you for a login/password.

See also

▶ The Chef documentation on data bags: `https://docs.chef.io/data_bags.html`

▶ Puppet Hiera: `https://docs.puppet.com/hiera/3.2/`

Creating functional roles

Until now, we have created cookbooks based on a particular technology. We created a cookbook for MariaDB, one for Apache HTTPd, and one for our app (including all the dependencies). What about the role of each of those infrastructure elements? A *database* role can include what is now running our database (MariaDB), but maybe tomorrow it can run something else (migrate back to MySQL, or switch to PostgreSQL). As roles in Chef have a dedicated run list, it's common to see a role include the product recipes, and everything related to it, think monitoring for example. Roles can do a lot more, like overriding attributes or have different run lists for each environment. Here, we'll create two generic *database* and *webserver* roles that might be simply reused later for another project that just need those services and a *mysite* role, that will include the two other roles. A role can include other roles as well as recipes. This way, the role for mysite will be enough to run our infrastructure, from a functional point of view.

Getting ready

To work through this recipe, you will need the following:

- ► A working Chef DK installation on the workstation
- ► A working Chef client configuration on the remote host
- ► The Chef code from the previous recipes

How to do it...

Follow these steps for creating functional roles:

1. We can write roles in plain JSON or in Ruby. Let's try Ruby for our `webserver` role in `roles/webserver.rb`. It requires a name, a description, and a run list. That's the bare minimum:

   ```
   name "webserver"
   description "An HTTP server for our application"
   run_list "recipe[apache]"
   ```

2. Let's do the same for our `database` role; we currently want to use our `mariadb` cookbook. So let's write it in `roles/database.rb`:

   ```
   name "database"
   description "A database server for our application"
   run_list "recipe[mariadb]"
   ```

3. Finally, let's write the `mysite` role, that will include a webserver, a database, as well as its own cookbook, in `roles/mysite.rb`:

```
name "mysite"
description "MySite role"
run_list(
  "role[webserver]",
  "role[database]",
  "recipe[mysite]"
)
```

4. Send the roles to the Chef server using the `knife` command:

```
$ knife role from file database.rb
Updated Role database
$ knife role from file webserver.rb
Updated Role webserver
$ knife role from file mysite.rb
Updated Role mysite
```

5. Now, either edit your current node's run list (if you have one) to use only this role (`role[mysite]`), or if you're about to bootstrap the server; adding the `-r "role[mysite]"` option will bootstrap Chef on the node as well as execute Chef with this run list:

```
$ knife bootstrap 192.168.146.129 -N vagrant -x vagrant --
sudo -r "role[mysite]"
```

We'll now be free to add more complex features to our role in the future!

There's more...

Puppet does not provide a role feature. However, this can be done by adding a level of abstraction using the *role and profile* design pattern. In this pattern:

▶ A *role* is a class defining a behavior (For example, a web server). This class needs to include all needed *profiles* to create the role.

▶ A *profile* is a class used to manage the underlying technology (For example, by installing Apache)

▶ In the main manifest, nodes are only using *roles*.

Using this pattern, it is easier to refactor only *profiles* classes when the technology needs to be changed.

See also

▶ The Chef documentation on roles: `https://docs.chef.io/roles.html`

Managing external Chef cookbooks and Puppet modules

Up till now, we've written our own cookbooks, which are fairly simple in their current state. Chances are, we'll expect a lot more complicated setups in our real life infrastructure. To help us, there're two kinds of external cookbooks we can use: community-backed cookbooks and *official* cookbooks, written and maintained by the Chef team directly. To browse available cookbooks, navigate to the Chef Supermarket (think of it as a store for cookbooks): `https://supermarket.chef.io/`.

The thing is, our life will become increasingly complicated with all those cookbooks downloaded here and there, each of them having dependencies of their own. Fortunately, the Chef DK ships with a superb utility for this use case—Berkshelf.

Berkshelf allows us to declare cookbook dependencies, versions and locations in a single file, and in a single command, upload everything needed to run our cookbook.

In this section, we'll migrate away from our distribution's MariaDB default and unconfigured package, to a fully configured MySQL 5.7—and that workflow is pretty close to everyday life using Chef in production.

Getting ready

To work through this recipe, you will need the following:

- A working Chef DK installation on the workstation
- A working Chef client configuration on the remote host
- The Chef code from the previous recipes

How to do it...

Let's start by discovering how Berkshelf works. Under the `cookbooks/mysite/` directory, we find a file named `Berksfile` (if you didn't create the cookbook with the `chef` utility, create the file manually). As Berkshelf works per cookbook, we'll declare all our cookbook dependencies to run this particular cookbook here, which in our case, happens to be currently all local. In this `Berksfile`, enter the following:

```
source 'https://supermarket.chef.io'

metadata

cookbook 'apache', path: '../apache'
cookbook 'php', path: '../php'
cookbook 'mariadb', path: '../mariadb'
```

This tells us three important things:

▶ Where to find unknown cookbooks (on the official supermarket, we can replace with our own internal supermarket if we run one)

▶ Where to find dependencies: in our cookbook's metadata file

▶ Where each of those cookbooks reside: in our case, the local relative path

Bump the `mysite` cookbook version in `metadata.rb` so we don't mess with our previous work, and, from the `mysite` cookbook directory, upload all our cookbook's dependencies at once:

```
$ berks upload
Uploaded apache (0.5.0) to:
'https://api.chef.io:443/organizations/iacbook'
Uploaded mariadb (0.2.0) to:
'https://api.chef.io:443/organizations/iacbook'
Uploaded mysite (0.3.0) to:
'https://api.chef.io:443/organizations/iacbook'
Uploaded php (0.2.0) to:
'https://api.chef.io:443/organizations/iacbook'
```

Now we start to realize how faster it is than manual uploading all the cookbooks one by one!

Using the official MySQL cookbook and its dependencies with Berkshelf

As we already know, we didn't make any special configuration with MariaDB; we just installed it from our distribution's repositories. This needs to change! We want a full-fledged MySQL deployment. Looking at the Chef Supermarket, we notice an official MySQL cookbook maintained by the Chef team, currently at version 8.0.4: `https://supermarket.chef.io/cookbooks/mysql`. It seems to do wonders; there are many configuration options, and many other things. Pages and pages of tested, reliable code ready to use! Good.

By reading the README file, it is stated that it needs two other cookbooks as dependencies—`selinux` and `yum-mysql-community`. The first one to work around SELinux temporarily, and the second one to manage the official MySQL community repository for RHEL. We could solve those dependencies by hand, but we have a better idea: use the `Berksfile`!

Let's start by replacing our dependency on our own `mariadb` cookbook with this cookbook, in `mysite/Berksfile`:

Find the following code:

```
cookbook 'mariadb', path: '../mariadb'
```

Replace the previous code with the following:

```
cookbook 'mysql', '8.0.4'
```

This way, we ensure we'll ever only run this particular cookbook version (8.0.4) and not a new one that might break things in production.

1. Then add the following two dependencies from the `mysql` cookbook:

   ```
   cookbook 'selinux'
   cookbook 'yum-mysql-community', '~> 1.0'
   ```

   In this case, we declared a dependency on any version of the `selinux` cookbook, the latest being the default, and a loose constraint on any minor revision of the `yum-mysql-community` 1.0 cookbook.

2. In the cookbooks `mysite/metadata.rb` file, do the same and replace the `mariadb` dependency with the three new ones:

   ```
   depends "mysql" , '~> 8.0'
   depends "selinux"
   depends "yum-mysql-community", '~> 1.0'
   ```

3. Run the `berks` command from inside the cookbook directory to grab the new cookbook dependencies:

   ```
   $ berks install
   Resolving cookbook dependencies...
   [...]
   Fetching cookbook index from https://supermarket.chef.io...
   Using mysql (8.0.4)
   Using selinux (0.9.0)
   Using yum-mysql-community (1.0.0)
   [...]
   ```

4. Great! It automatically downloaded our dependencies. Upload them all now:

   ```
   $ berks upload
   ```

5. Let's now create a new recipe named `mysql` under our `mysite` cookbook, so we can deploy the MySQL we need for our application. In our case, we want the latest and greatest MySQL 5.7 with the admin password: `super_secure_password`.

6. Start by bumping the cookbook's version in `metadata.rb` to a minor version:

   ```
   version '0.3.1'
   ```

7. Now generate the new `mysql` recipe so we can use it:

   ```
   $ chef generate recipe cookbooks/mysite mysql
   ```

8. In the newly-created `mysite/recipes/mysql.rb` file, start by including the new recipes described as needed by the documentation:

```
include_recipe "selinux::disabled"
include_recipe "yum-mysql-community::mysql57"
```

9. Then, still following the documentation, just add the following block to fully deploy MySQL 5.7 on the default port (TCP/`3306`):

```
mysql_service 'default' do
  port '3306'
  version '5.7'
  initial_root_password 'super_secure_password'
  action [:create, :start]
end
```

 What happened here is that the official `mysql` cookbook didn't make anything inside the cookbooks. It, in fact, extended Chef functionalities by offering a `mysql_service` resource. In Chefspeak, it is called **LWRP** (**Lightweight Resources and Providers**).

10. Finally, remove the reference to the `mariadb` recipe from the default `mysite` recipe in `mysite/recipe/default.rb`, and replace it with a call to the new `mysql` recipe:

```
include_recipe "mysite::mysql"
```

Including dependencies in a role

To fully match our environment with what we just did in the cookbook, let's remove the call to the old `mariadb` cookbook from the `database` role, and as there's no recipe to call (as we said, this cookbook is just extending Chef functionality), let's instead add the two cookbook dependencies as stated in the documentation in `roles/database.rb`:

```
name "database"
description "A database server for our application"
run_list(
  "recipe[selinux::disabled]",
  "recipe[yum-mysql-community::mysql57]"
)
```

Upload the updated role using the `knife` command:

```
$ knife role from file database.rb
Updated Role database
```

Our node running the `mysite` role, calling the database role will be alright. If we did choose to run only nodes with a call to the `mysite::default` recipe, it will also work.

Uploading cookbook dependencies using Berkshelf

Now navigate to the `mysite` cookbook directory and use the `upload` feature from Berkshelf, so it will upload all necessary cookbooks at once:

```
$ berks upload
```

 With Berkshelf, dependencies of the dependencies are uploaded as well!

Testing MySQL deployment

Run the chef-client on the node, and when the process is done, ensure we can connect to the local MySQL server using the supplied password:

```
$ mysql -h 127.0.0.1 -uroot -psuper_secure_password -e "show
databases;"
+--------------------+
| Database           |
+--------------------+
| information_schema |
| mysql              |
| performance_schema |
| sys                |
+--------------------+
```

There's more...

With Puppet, there is also a lot of code ready to use. We can use modules from Puppet Forge or GitHub for example. Modules hosted on Puppet Forge can be searched using the `puppet module search` command:

```
$ puppet module search mysql | head -10
Notice: Searching https://forgeapi.puppetlabs.com ...
NAME                DESCRIPTION        AUTHOR        KEYWORDS
puppetlabs-mysql    Installs, con...   @puppetlabs   mysql
```

example42-mysql	Puppet module...	@example42	mysql
gousto-mysql	Installs, con...	@gousto	
ULHPC-mysql	Configure and...	@ULHPC	mysql
aco-mysql_yumrepo	Puppet module...	@aco	mysql
BoxUpp-mysql	A puppet modu...	@BoxUpp	mysql
rgevaert-mysql	Manage your p...	@rgevaert	mysql
rocha-mysql	Resources to ...	@rocha	mysql

We can install one of them:

```
$ puppet module install puppetlabs-mysql
Notice: Downloading from https://forgeapi.puppetlabs.com ...
Notice: Installing -- do not interrupt ...
/Users/me/.puppetlabs/etc/code/modules
└─┬ puppetlabs-mysql (v3.9.0)
  ├── puppet-staging (v2.0.1)
  └── puppetlabs-stdlib (v4.13.1)
```

By default, installation is done in a hidden folder under the home directory. We can see that the MySQL module from Puppet Labs depends on two other modules.

Several tools can be used to manage packages; r10k is one of them. It can also manage environments (such as staging, development, production), but we will focus on package management in this chapter.

The first thing we need is to install r10k. In previous examples, we edited code directly on our workstation in a shared folder used by Vagrant, so we need to install r10k directly on our workstation:

```
$ sudo puppet resource package r10k  provider=puppet_gem
Notice: /Package[r10k]/ensure: created
package { 'r10k':
  ensure => ['2.5.1'],
}
$ r10k version
r10k 2.5.1
```

r10k is using a file named Puppetfile in which we declare all necessary modules. Here is an example of Puppetfile:

```
    forge 'http://forge.puppetlabs.com'

    mod 'puppetlabs/mysql'
```

Unfortunately at the time of writing, r10k does not support dependencies, so we need to discover and add them in the `Puppetfile`. We can discover dependencies manually by installing modules using `puppet module install` as we did earlier. However, this is not very handy, and fortunately we can use external tools such as `https://github.com/rnelson0/puppet-generate-puppetfile`.

Let's install it:

```
$ sudo puppet resource package generate-puppetfile provider=puppet_gem
Notice: /Package[generate-puppetfile]/ensure: created

package { 'generate-puppetfile':

  ensure => ['0.10.0'],

}
```

So now, let's discover dependencies for the Puppet Labs MySQL module:

```
$ generate-puppetfile puppetlabs/mysql


Installing modules. This may take a few minutes.



Your Puppetfile has been generated. Copy and paste between the
markers:


=========================================================================
forge 'http://forge.puppetlabs.com'


# Modules discovered by generate-puppetfile
mod 'puppet/staging', '2.1.0'
mod 'puppetlabs/mysql', '3.10.0'
mod 'puppetlabs/stdlib', '4.15.0'

=========================================================================
```

We now have all dependencies.

Now suppose we want to use our previous example, using the code we made for Apache, and the official Puppet Labs MySQL package.

To do so, let's adjust the `Puppetfile` in order to download the official Mysql module from Puppet Labs and keep our existing modules. We need to inform r10k which modules are *local*. If we don't, r10k will perform a complete installation after removing all the content in the modules directory. Here is the `Puppetfile`:

```
forge 'http://forge.puppetlabs.com'

# Local modules
mod 'apache', :local =>true
mod 'php', :local =>true
mod 'mariadb', :local =>true

# Modules discovered by generate-puppetfile
mod 'puppet/staging', '2.0.1'
mod 'puppetlabs/mysql', '3.9.0'
mod 'puppetlabs/stdlib', '4.13.1'
```

Now we need to run r10k to install packages:

```
$ ls modules/
apache/  mariadb/ php/
$ r10k puppetfile install
$ ls modules/
apache/  concat/  mariadb/ mysql/   php/       stdlib/
```

Let's modify the main manifest to use the official MySQL package; we need to remove the reference to our MariaDB module, and use the class provided by the official MySQL package:

```
node 'web.pomes.pro' {
    $website=$fqdn;
    $docroot="/var/www/$fqdn";
    $users=hiera('webusers');

    class {
      'apache':;
      'php':;
    }
    class { 'mysql::server':
      root_password => 'super_secure_password',
    }
    apache::vhost{$website:
```

```
            website => $website,
            docroot => $docroot,
      }
      apache::htpasswd{'htpasswd':
          filepath => '/etc/apache2/htpasswd',
          users    => hiera('webusers'),
      }
      apache::htaccess{"$docroot-htaccess":
          filepath => '/etc/apache2/htpasswd',
          docroot  => $docroot,
      }
      file { $docroot:
        ensure => directory,
        owner  => 'www-data',
        group  => 'www-data',
        mode   => '0755',
      }
      file {"$docroot/index.php":
        ensure => present,
        owner  => 'www-data',
        group  => 'www-data',
        mode   => '0644',
        content => "<?php phpinfo() ?>",
      }
   }
}
```

Let's start a fresh Vagrant setup. After applying Puppet, we can now use the MySQL server with the root credentials we specified in the main manifest:

```
vagrant@web:~$ mysql -h 127.0.0.1 -uroot -
psuper_secure_password -e "show databases;"

+--------------------+
| Database           |
+--------------------+
| information_schema |
| mysql              |
| performance_schema |
+--------------------+
```

If needed, you can browse the online documentation of this module to create custom databases and grants.

See also

- ▶ The Chef documentation on roles: `https://docs.chef.io/roles.html`
- ▶ The Chef Supermarket: `https://supermarket.chef.io/`
- ▶ The Berkshelf documentation: `http://berkshelf.com/`
- ▶ MySQL cookbook source on GitHub: `https://github.com/chef-cookbooks/mysql`
- ▶ Puppet r10k: `https://github.com/puppetlabs/r10k`
- ▶ The Puppet Labs MySQL module on Puppet Forge: `https://forge.puppet.com/puppetlabs/mysql`

7
Testing and Writing Better Infrastructure Code with Chef and Puppet

In this chapter, we will cover the following recipes:

- ▸ Linting Chef code with Foodcritic and Puppet code with puppet-lint
- ▸ Unit testing with ChefSpec and rspec-puppet
- ▸ Testing infrastructure with Test Kitchen for Chef and Beaker for Puppet
- ▸ Integration testing with ServerSpec

Introduction

In the development world, good practices of testing software are widespread, such as unit and integration tests. Linters are also used daily for most languages by software developers. These techniques are fortunately brought to the infrastructure world through the tools we use; now as infrastructure is basically code, it can be analyzed, tested, and reported! Combined with CI systems, writing infrastructure code that is thoroughly tested at different levels helps hugely to achieve a very high quality of sustainable code and prevents unexpected regressions that would have otherwise broken things later.

In this chapter, you'll discover various techniques to write cleaner code using linters and styling tools, so our code follows high standards. You'll learn how to unit test infrastructure code such as Chef resources and achieve the highest code coverage possible, so we're sure nothing is there by error or is being modified unintentionally. Then we'll configure the testing environment Test Kitchen, which leverages the use of VMs through Vagrant (or other systems) to apply test suites. This will be our base to then write integration tests so we can make sure we achieve what we intended to achieve with multiple cookbooks and sources of code, really reaching the target and doing the job on a real system.

These tools and techniques are absolutely key to write the best infrastructure code possible, and they are as fun to use as they are powerful!

All recipes are based on Chef. However, when possible, we'll try to show how things work similarly with Puppet, Chef's direct alternative.

Linting Chef code with Foodcritic and Puppet code with puppet-lint

Since we're mainly coding in Ruby, we can use common linters such as Rubocop in the Ruby world. However, Rubocop, is targeted at software development by default and is not really optimized for Chef cookbooks development. So, Chef adapted their own version of Rubocop, named Cookstyle. In the meantime, the Foodcritic tool used in conjunction with rules checks our code for a set of commonly accepted good practices by the community. We'll walk through those tools to end up with a much better and cleaner code.

Getting ready

To step through this recipe, you will need the following:

- A working Chef DK installation on the workstation
- A working Chef client configuration on the remote host
- The Chef code from *Chapter 6, Fundamentals of Managing Servers with Chef and Puppet*, or any custom Chef code.

How to do it...

We'll study and follow suggestions of the two complimentary tools—Cookstyle and Foodcritic. Both give some precious and complementary advice on code quality and portability. Let's start with the quickest and easiest—Cookstyle.

Cookstyle

Navigate to a cookbook root directory and type in the following:

```
$ cookstyle
```

This will output all the suggestions for a cleaner code.

To get more information about the suggestions, including a URL with more information, use the following options:

```
$ cookstyle -DES
```

If you're happy with the propositions and would like to automatically apply them all directly in the code, use the following switch:

```
$ cookstyle -a
```

If we apply `cookstyle` to the *Chapter 6, Fundamentals of Managing Servers with Chef and Puppet*, Chef cookbooks we've written, we'll end up with two good suggestions:

- Single quotes for strings when interpolation is not needed
- Newer Ruby 1.9 syntax for hashes

As these are valuable and recommended changes, let's bump our cookbook versions in all concerned `metadata.rb` files, apply those suggestions, and upload the new minor revision to the Chef server.

Foodcritic

Foodcritic goes much further than Cookstyle and checks the Chef code for things such as incompatible, nonidempotent, repetitive, or deprecated code, and missing templates, files, dependencies, or variables. All the rules are described on the Foodcritic website at `http://www.foodcritic.io`, along with examples and explanations.

Execute `foodcritic` by navigating to the Chef repo and type in the following command:

```
$ foodcritic <cookbook path>
```

For example, for testing our previous `mysite` cookbook (excluding the auto-generated `test` directory, as it's not a cookbook in itself), we type the following command:

```
$ foodcritic --exclude test cookbooks/mysite
FC003: Check whether you are running with chef server before using
server-specific features: cookbooks/mysite/recipes/htaccess.rb:7
FC033: Missing template: cookbooks/mysite/recipes/htaccess.rb:9
FC033: Missing template: cookbooks/mysite/recipes/htaccess.rb:19
FC064: Ensure issues_url is set in metadata:
cookbooks/mysite/metadata.rb:1
FC065: Ensure source_url is set in metadata:
cookbooks/mysite/metadata.rb:1
```

Interesting! Let's start with FC003 (http://www.foodcritic.io/#FC003). Our code is indeed not usable with other Chef modes such as chef-solo, as we're using Chef Search directly in the code and chef-solo can't interact with a Chef server. Two options here are that either we don't care about chef-solo portability and you exclude that rule from the tests, or we care and modify the code accordingly.

To exclude the `FC003` rule, use the `-t` option:

```
$ foodcritic -t ~FC003 --exclude test cookbooks/mysite/
```

FC033: Missing template: cookbooks/mysite/recipes/htaccess.rb:9

FC033: Missing template: cookbooks/mysite/recipes/htaccess.rb:19

FC064: Ensure issues_url is set in metadata: cookbooks/mysite/metadata.rb:1

FC065: Ensure source_url is set in metadata: cookbooks/mysite/metadata.rb:1

Alternatively, if we care about chef-solo compatibility, let's change the code as proposed by the FC003 rule. Bump the `mysite` cookbook in the `mysite/metadata.rb` file, and edit the `users` search in the `mysite/recipes/htaccess.rb` file to include an evaluation of whether we're running chef-solo or not:

```
if Chef::Config[:solo]
  Chef::Log.warn('This recipe uses search. Chef Solo does not
support search.')
else
  users = search(:webusers, '*:*')
end
```

Upload the new version of the cookbook using Berkshelf:

```
$ berks upload
```

Rerun `foodcritic` and the warning is gone:

```
$ foodcritic --exclude test cookbooks/mysite
```

Let's continue our investigation of the suggestions. FC033 (http://www.foodcritic.io/#FC033) is about missing templates. However, our templates are placed under `mysite/templates` by the `chef` workflow command. This is typically why it's important to understand why suggestions are only that—suggestions. The Foodcritic team proposes to enforce in FC033 the presence of default templates in the `templates/default` directory. It is entirely up to you and your team to decide what to follow: the recommended behavior from Chef or from Foodcritic. Let's decide to follow Chef and ignore this warning:

```
$ foodcritic -t ~FC033 --exclude test cookbooks/mysite/
```

FC064: Ensure issues_url is set in metadata: cookbooks/mysite/metadata.rb:1

```
FC065: Ensure source_url is set in metadata:
cookbooks/mysite/metadata.rb:1
```

The previous two warnings (FC064 and FC065) are only about cookbooks released on the Chef Supermarket, which is not our case. Let's exclude globally all supermarket-related warnings using the -t ~supermarket switch:

```
$ foodcritic -t ~FC033 -t ~supermarket --exclude test
cookbooks/mysite/
```

No more warnings now; our cookbook is following the best advice on the planet from both Chef and the Foodcritic community!

It's highly recommended that you add those tests to your automated testing process. Let's say we're using a global Makefile to do that. Create it at the root of the Chef repository:

```
$ cat Makefile

tests:
   foodcritic -t ~FC033 -t ~supermarket --exclude test
cookbooks/mysite
```

Now, you or some CI system can automatically check the code for quality or regression in quality.

There's more...

Using Puppet, puppet-lint will help us to clean code. We need to install puppet-lint using the following command:

```
$ sudo puppet resource package puppet-lint
provider=puppet_gem
```

If you are already familiar with Puppet, you probably saw that the code we wrote in the previous chapter does not conform to standards. Let's discover some issues with puppet-lint based on the latest recipe for our Apache module:

```
$ puppet-lint modules/apache/manifests/init.pp

WARNING: class not documented on line 1

ERROR: two-space soft tabs not used on line 3

...

$ puppet-lint modules/apache/manifests/vhost.pp

WARNING: defined type not documented on line 1

WARNING: variable not enclosed in {} on line 6

...
```

```
ERROR: trailing whitespace found on line 11

...

ERROR: two-space soft tabs not used on line 2

...

WARNING: indentation of => is not properly aligned (expected in
column 34, but found it in column 31) on line 12

...

$ puppet-lint modules/apache/manifests/htpasswd.pp
WARNING: defined type not documented on line 1
WARNING: string containing only a variable on line 6
WARNING: variable not enclosed in {} on line 6
ERROR: two-space soft tabs not used on line 2

...

$ puppet-lint modules/apache/manifests/htaccess.pp
WARNING: defined type not documented on line 1
WARNING: variable not enclosed in {} on line 6
ERROR: two-space soft tabs not used on line 2
```

We can see two error categories:

- Puppet coding style warnings/errors
- Missing documentation

Let's try to fix them!

Puppet coding style

For our concerns here, the basic rules are:

- Tabulation needs to be *two-space* characters
- No trailing whitespaces
- In string interpolation, variables should be enclosed in braces; for example, `"$docroot/.htaccess"` is wrong and must be `"${docroot}/.htaccess"`

Documentation

Documentation should be done using Markdown. If you've never heard about it, Markdown is a language used to format a document in plain text mode, in order to export it in HTML. With Markdown, it becomes easy to add headers, links, bullets and font effects. A short and interactive tutorial can be found on `http://www.markdowntutorial.com`.

A Markdown editor with a *live preview* mode is available at `https://stackedit.io`.

We need to create a `README.md` file at the top-level directory of the module. This file should contain a short description, and some usage examples. For more readability, we will focus only on the installation and the definition of a virtual host. The complete documentation can be found in the code bundle. Here is an extract of `modules/apache/README.md`:

```
# Apache module

## Table of Contents

1. [Description](#description)
1. [Usage](#usage)
    * [Apache installation](#installation)
    * [Defining a vhost](#vhost)

## Description

Sample module for Apache on Ubuntu systems

## Usage

### installation

To install apache2:

```
class {
  'apache':;
}
```


vhost

To create a vhost:

```
apache::vhost{'mysite':
  website    => 'www.example.com',
  docroot    => '/var/www/example',
}
```
```

We also need to document all statements and their parameters, using the `@param` tag inside comments at the top of each manifest. The new code following puppet-lint recommendations, is:

- For `modules/apache/manifests/init.pp`:

```
# See README
class apache {
  package {'apache2':
    ensure => present,
  }

  service {'apache2':
    ensure => running,
    enable => true
  }

  file {'/etc/apache2/sites-enabled/000-default.conf':
    ensure => absent,
    notify => Service['apache2'],
  }
}
```

- For `modules/apache/manifests/htpasswd.pp`:

```
# @param filepath Path of the htpasswd database
# @param users Array of hash containing users
# See README
define apache::htpasswd (
  $filepath,
  $users
) {
  file { $filepath:
    ensure  => present,
    owner   => 'root',
    group   => 'root',
    mode    => '0644',
    content => template('apache/htpasswd.erb'),
  }
}
```

- For `modules/apache/manifests/htaccess.pp`:

```
# @param filepath Path of the htpasswd database
# @param docroot DocumentRoot where the .htaccess should be
generated
# See README
define apache::htaccess (
  $filepath,
  $docroot
) {
  file { "${docroot}/.htaccess":
    ensure  => present,
    owner   => 'root',
    group   => 'root',
    mode    => '0644',
    content => template('apache/htaccess.erb'),
  }
}
```

- For `modules/apache/manifests/vhost.pp`:

```
# @param website Site name
# @param docroot DocumentRoot
# See README
define apache::vhost (
  $website,
  $docroot
) {
  file { "/etc/apache2/sites-available/${website}.conf":
    ensure  => present,
    owner   => 'root',
    group   => 'root',
    mode    => '0644',
    content => epp('apache/vhost.epp', {
      'website'  => $website,
      'docroot' => $docroot}
    ),
  }

  file { "/etc/apache2/sites-enabled/${website}.conf":
    ensure  => link,
    target  => "/etc/apache2/sites-available/${website}.conf",
    require => File["/etc/apache2/sites-available/${website}.
conf"],
    notify  => Service['apache2'],
  }
}
```

The documentation can be automatically generated to a set of HTML pages. To do so, we need to install the `yard` and `puppet-strings` packages:

```
$ sudo puppet resource package yard provider=puppet_gem
```

```
$ sudo puppet resource package puppet-strings provider=puppet_gem
```

Now, from the top-level directory of our module, the documentation can be generated:

```
$ puppet strings
Files:                    4
Modules:                  0 (     0 undocumented)
Classes:                  0 (     0 undocumented)
Constants:                0 (     0 undocumented)
Attributes:               0 (     0 undocumented)
Methods:                  0 (     0 undocumented)
Puppet Classes:           1 (     0 undocumented)
Puppet Defined Types:     3 (     0 undocumented)
Puppet Types:             0 (     0 undocumented)
Puppet Providers:         0 (     0 undocumented)
Puppet Functions:         0 (     0 undocumented)
 100.00% documented
$ ls -1 doc
_index.html
css/
file.README.html
frames.html
index.html
js/
puppet_class_list.html
puppet_classes/
puppet_defined_type_list.html
puppet_defined_types/
top-level-namespace.html
```

The documentation is in the `doc` directory. We can now read it by opening `index.html` in any browser.

See also

The Puppet Language Style:

- ▸ Cookstyle: `https://github.com/chef/cookstyle`
- ▸ Foodcritic: `http://www.foodcritic.io/`

Unit testing with ChefSpec and rspec-puppet

ChefSpec is a Chef cookbook RSpec unit testing framework written by the great Seth Vargo (Opscode Chef, Hashicorp). ChefSpec helps to create a fast feedback loop, locally simulate Chef runs (solo or server) over the code, and issue a code coverage statement for every resource used. It integrates very well with Berkshelf, so cookbook dependencies are easily handled during the testing process.

We'll create unit tests for the cookbooks created in *Chapter 6, Fundamentals of Managing Servers with Chef and Puppet,* that covers the most common tests, such as convergence issues, packages installation, services status check, file and template creation, access rights, recipe inclusion, stubbing data bag searches, or even intercepting expected errors. These tests are so generic, we'll be able to reuse them in all our future recipes and get started on more.

Getting ready

To step through this recipe, you will need the following:

- ▸ A working Chef installation on the workstation
- ▸ A working Chef client configuration on the remote host
- ▸ The Chef code from Chapter 6, *Fundamentals of Managing Servers with Chef and Puppet*, or any custom Chef code

How to do it...

ChefSpec unit tests are found in the `spec/unit/recipes` folder of every Chef cookbook. Depending on how we created our cookbooks, this folder may already exist.

To illustrate, let's start from the `apache` cookbook from *Chapter 6, Fundamentals of Managing Servers with Chef and Puppet,* but any similar custom cookbook is equally good.

If the `spec/unit/recipes` directory doesn't exist, create it by executing the following command:

```
$ mkdir -p spec/unit/recipes
```

In this `recipes` directory in `spec/unit` are found the ChefSpec unit tests, typically:

```
$ tree spec/
spec/
├── spec_helper.rb
└── unit
    └── recipes
        ├── default_spec.rb
        └── virtualhost_spec.rb
```

Each recipe gets its matching ChefSpec file. In this case, our simple cookbook contains two recipes, so we get two specs.

The Spec Helper

It's helpful to have a common set of requirements for all the concerned cookbook tests. The default is to have it named `spec_helper.rb` at the root of the `spec/unit` directory. We suggest to include at least three requirements:

- ChefSpec itself
- The Berkshelf plugin for dependencies management
- Immediately start the code coverage

Here's our sample `spec_helper.rb` file:

```
require 'chefspec'
require 'chefspec/berkshelf'
ChefSpec::Coverage.start!
```

Testing a successful Chef run context

We'll now unit test the default apache cookbook recipe. Our first step is to require the helper created earlier in the `default_spec.rb` file. It will be required in all of our future tests:

```
require 'spec_helper'
```

All unit tests start with a descriptive block, as given here:

```
describe 'cookbook::recipe_name' do
  [...]
end
```

Inside this block, we want to simulate the Chef run in a simulated CentOS 7.2 environment, with the default attributes. This is the context, and we expect this Chef run to not raise any errors:

```
describe 'apache::default' do
  context 'Default attributes on CentOS 7.2' do
    let(:chef_run) do
      runner = ChefSpec::ServerRunner.new(platform: 'centos',
version: '7.2.1511')
      runner.converge(described_recipe)
    end

    it 'converges successfully' do
      expect { chef_run }.to_not raise_error
    end
  end
end
```

To find the exact past or future CentOS version we might need, we can go to the CentOS mirror site, `http://mirror.centos.org/centos/`, or read a full list of available simulated platforms at `https://github.com/customink/fauxhai/tree/master/lib/fauxhai/platforms`.

Execute our first unit test using `chef exec rspec` (it's using the bundled `rspec` from the Chef DK):

```
$ chef exec rspec --color
.....


Finished in 0.82521 seconds (files took 1.87 seconds to load)
5 examples, 0 failures


ChefSpec Coverage report generated...

  Total Resources:   2
  Touched Resources: 0
  Touch Coverage:    0.0%

Untouched Resources:

  yum_package[httpd]                apache/recipes/default.rb:7
  service[httpd]                    apache/recipes/default.rb:11
```

We see the simulated Chef run execution times, as well as a coverage report (0%, as we didn't test anything for now). ChefSpec even shows us what's not unit tested yet!

A nice option is the *documentation* RSpec formatter, so we have descriptions of what's being tested. At the end of this section, we'll have something like this, using this formatter:

```
$ chef exec rspec --format documentation --color


apache::default
  Default attributes on CentOS 7.2
    converges successfully
    installs httpd
    enables and starts httpd service

apache::virtualhost
  Default attributes on CentOS 7.2
    converges successfully
    creates a virtualhost directory
    creates and index.html file
    creates a virtualhost configuration file


Finished in 1.14 seconds (files took 2.56 seconds to load)
7 examples, 0 failures



ChefSpec Coverage report generated...

  Total Resources:    5
  Touched Resources:  5
  Touch Coverage:     100.0%


You are awesome and so is your test coverage! Have a fantastic day!
```

Testing a package installation

Our default recipe starts by installing the `httpd` package. Here's how to test it using ChefSpec, inside the context we created earlier:

```
    it 'installs httpd' do

      expect(chef_run).to install_package('httpd')

    end
```

Execute `rspec` again and see the touch coverage attain 50% as one of the two resources from the default recipe is now tested.

Testing services status

The default recipe enables and starts the `httpd` service. Here's how to test if both actions are handled by the code using ChefSpec, inside the context created earlier:

```
it 'enables and starts httpd service' do
  expect(chef_run).to enable_service('httpd')
  expect(chef_run).to start_service('httpd')
end
```

Our test coverage is now 100% for the default recipe as we tested both declared resources.

Testing another recipe from the same cookbook

As we have two recipes in the apache cookbook, let's create tests for our second recipe—`virtualhost_spec.rb`. Start it exactly like the first one, with a description, context, and an initial test for a valid Chef run:

```
require 'spec_helper'

describe 'apache::virtualhost' do
  context 'Default attributes on CentOS 7.2' do
    let(:chef_run) do
      runner = ChefSpec::ServerRunner.new(platform: 'centos',
version: '7.2.1511')
      runner.converge(described_recipe)
    end

    it 'converges successfully' do
      expect { chef_run }.to_not raise_error
    end
  end
end
```

Execute RSpec and see the coverage fall from 100% to 40%. Three new resources are now untested, from the `apache::virtualhost` recipe:

```
$ chef exec rspec --color
[...]
ChefSpec Coverage report generated...

  Total Resources:   5
  Touched Resources: 2
```

```
Touch Coverage:      40.0%


Untouched Resources:


  directory[/var/www/default]          apache/recipes/virtualhost.rb:8
  file[/var/www/default/index.html]
apache/recipes/virtualhost.rb:15
  template[/etc/httpd/conf.d/default.conf]
apache/recipes/virtualhost.rb:22
```

The good news is that ChefSpec still tells us which resources are not tested!

Testing directory creation

This particular `apache::virtualhost` recipe starts by creating a directory. Here's how we can test for this directory existence, along with its ownership parameters:

```
it 'creates a virtualhost directory' do
  expect(chef_run).to create_directory('/var/www/default').with(
    user: 'root',
    group: 'root'
  )
end
```

Code coverage is now 60%!

Testing file creation

The same recipe then creates an index file. This is how we test it's created with the required ownership:

```
it 'creates and index.html file' do
  expect(chef_run).to
create_file('/var/www/default/index.html').with(
    user: 'root',
    group: 'root'
  )
end
```

Code coverage is now 80%!

Testing templates creation

The recipe ends with the creation of Apache VirtualHost from a template. This is how to test it's in place with the default attributes:

```
it 'creates a virtualhost configuration file' do
  expect(chef_run).to create_template('/etc/httpd/conf.d/default.
conf').with(
    user: 'root',
    group: 'root'
  )
end
```

All in all, we've now covered 100% of our resources!

As the output says:

You are awesome and so is your test coverage! Have a fantastic day!

Stubbing data bags for searches

The mysite cookbook we created earlier contains a search in a data bag to later populate a file with content. The thing is, we're unit testing, and no real Chef server is answering requests. So the tests are failing: the simulated Chef run doesn't end well because a search can't be executed. Fortunately, ChefSpec allows us to stub the data bag with real content. So here's how it looks in spec/unit/recipes/default_spec.rb from the mysite cookbook:

```
describe 'mysite::default' do
  context 'Default attributes on CentOS 7.2' do
    let(:chef_run) do
      runner = ChefSpec::ServerRunner.new(platform: 'centos', version:
'7.2.1511')
      runner.create_data_bag('webusers', {
        'john' => {
          'id' => 'john',
          'htpasswd' => '$apr1$AUI2Y5pj$0v0PaSlLfc6QxZx1Vx5Se.'
        }
      })
      runner.converge(described_recipe)
    end

    it 'converges successfully' do
      expect { chef_run }.to_not raise_error
    end
  end
end
```

Now the simulated Chef run has a `webusers` data bag and some sample data to work with!

Testing recipes inclusion

It's very common to include recipes inside another recipe. Typically, when using notifications for restarting a service from a file change, the concerned service must be included in the recipe where the file resource is located; otherwise, the code most probably works by chance because the required dependent cookbook is included elsewhere! Here's how to test for a cookbook inclusion:

```
it 'includes the `apache` recipes' do
  expect(chef_run).to include_recipe('apache::default')
  expect(chef_run).to include_recipe('apache::virtualhost')
end
```

We now ensure that dependencies are always included.

Intercepting errors in tests

Sometimes we have to work with third-party cookbooks, that may somehow raise errors. It's the case with the official MySQL cookbook, which depends on the SELinux cookbook for the RHEL/CentOS platform. This cookbook, for some reason, doesn't work with ChefSpec, so when converged, it errors out the following string: `chefspec not supported!`. ChefSpec stops there, and say the Chef run is in error. As we don't have any power on why is that, here's a workaround to expect a very specific error from a Chef run, and this will be helpful many times later:

```
it 'converges successfully' do
  # The selinux cookbook raises this error.
  expect { chef_run }.to raise_error(RuntimeError, 'chefspec
not supported!')
end
```

We've seen a selection of the most common and reusable unit tests for Chef cookbooks!

There's more...

Using Puppet, Puppet Labs is providing a repository containing several useful tools we will use in this chapter—the Puppet Labs Spec Helper. Let's install it:

```
$ sudo puppet resource package puppetlabs_spec_helper provider=puppet_gem
```

For unit testing, rspec-puppet is the counterpart of ChefSpec for Puppet, and has been installed as a dependency of `puppetlabs_spec_helper`. We will now add a unit test for each manifest in our Apache module. First of all, we need a `Rakefile` to create the required targets. Fortunately, the `puppetlabs_spec_helper` gem provides such targets. Let's create a `Rakefile` in the top-level directory of our Apache module with the following content:

require 'puppetlabs_spec_helper/rake_tasks'

All unit tests should remain in a `spec` directory. Before writing any test, we also need a helper script that will be common to all tests. Let's create it in `spec/spec_helper.rb`. This file should contain the following line:

require 'puppetlabs_spec_helper/module_spec_helper'

We are now ready to write unit tests. We have four manifests in our module, and we are about to create a unit test for each of them. Here are the goals:

- For the `apache/manifests/init.pp` manifest: The unit test needs to validate the manifest is compiling, the `apache2` package installation is done, and the `apache2` service is running and activated on boot.

- For the `apache/manifests/vhost.pp` manifest: The unit test should ensure the virtual host is created in `/etc/apache2/sites-available` and activated in `/etc/apache2/sites-enabled`.

- For the `apache/manifests/htpasswd.pp` manifest: The unit test should ensure a `htpasswd` file is generated correctly.

- For the `apache/manifests/htaccess.pp` manifest: The unit test should ensure a `.htaccess` file is generated correctly.

Let's try the first one! Since the manifest contains a class declaration, the unit test should be in `spec/classes`. The class name is `apache`; this will be the base name of the file containing the test. Each test file should be suffixed by `_spec.rb`, so let's create `spec/classes/apache_spec.rb` with the following content:

```
require 'spec_helper'

# Description of the "apache" class
describe 'apache' do
  # Assertion list
```

```
it { is_expected.to compile.with_all_deps }
it { is_expected.to contain_package('apache2').with(
    {
      'ensure' => 'present',
    }
) }
it { is_expected.to contain_service('apache2').with(
    {
      'ensure' => 'running',
      'enable' => 'true',
    }
) }
end
```

Unit tests are in descriptive blocks, with a list of assertions. Here, we have the three assertions we mentioned earlier when describing the goal of the test.

Now, let's run the unit test using the `spec` rake target:

$ rake spec

. . .

Finished in 2.42 seconds (files took 1.53 seconds to load)

3 examples, 0 failures

That's it! Our three assertions have been tested successfully!

The three other tests should be placed under `spec/defines`, this is because the corresponding manifests declare a `define` statement. Let's create:

- ▶ `spec/defines/apache_vhost_spec.rb`, with the following content:

    ```
    require 'spec_helper'

    # Description of the "apache::vhost" 'define' resource
    describe 'apache::vhost', :type => :define do

      # As a requirement, we should load the apache class
      let :pre_condition do
        'class {"apache":;}'
      end

      # Define a title for the 'define' resource
      let :title do
    ```

```
      'mysite'
    end

    # Parameters list
    let :params do
      {
        :website => 'www.sample.com' ,
        :docroot => '/var/www/docroot',
      }
    end

    # Assertions list
    it { is_expected.to compile }
    it { is_expected.to contain_class('apache') }
    it { is_expected.to contain_file('/etc/apache2/sites-
  available/www.sample.com.conf')
       .with_content(/DocumentRoot \/var\/www\/docroot/) }
    it { is_expected.to contain_file('/etc/apache2/sites-
  enabled/www.sample.com.conf').with(
      'ensure' => 'link',
      'target' => '/etc/apache2/sites-
  available/www.sample.com.conf'
    ) }
  end
```

▶ `spec/defines/apache_htpasswd_spec.rb`, with the following content:

```
require 'spec_helper'

# Description of the "apache::htpasswd" 'define' resource
describe 'apache::htpasswd', :type => :define do

  # As a requirement, we should load the apache class
  let :pre_condition do
    'class {"apache":;}'
  end

  # Define a title for the 'define' resource
  let :title do
    'myhtpasswd'
  end

  # Parameters list
  let :params do
    {
```

```
            :filepath => '/tmp/htpasswd' ,
            :users => [ { "id" => "user1", "htpasswd" => "hash1"
      } ]
        }
      end

      # Assertion list
      it { is_expected.to compile }
      it { is_expected.to contain_class('apache') }
      it { is_expected.to contain_file('/tmp/htpasswd')
        .with_content(/user1:hash1/) }
    end
```

▶ `spec/defines/apache_htaccess_spec.rb`, with the following content:

```
require 'spec_helper'

# Description of the "apache::htaccess" 'define' resource
describe 'apache::htaccess', :type => :define do

  # As a requirement, we should load the apache class
  let :pre_condition do
    'class {"apache":;}'
  end

  # Define a title for the 'define' resource
  let :title do
    'myhtaccess'
  end

  # Parameters list
  let :params do
    {
      :filepath => '/tmp/htpasswd' ,
      :docroot => '/var/www/docroot',
    }
  end

  # Assertion list
  it { is_expected.to compile }
  it { is_expected.to contain_class('apache') }
  it { is_expected.to contain_file('/var/www/docroot/.htaccess')
    .with_content(/AuthUserFile \/tmp\/htpasswd/) }
end
```

Now we have all our unit tests, and each one validates the initial target we defined earlier. The total number of assertions is 13, and we can now run the complete test suite:

```
$ rake spec

. . . . . . . . . . . . .


Finished in 2.88 seconds (files took 1.52 seconds to load)
13 examples, 0 failures
```

 The Rake targets provided also contain a `lint` target that can be used with `rake lint`. We can use this target directly instead of puppet-lint manually as we did earlier.

See also

▸ ChefSpec: `http://sethvargo.github.io/chefspec`

▸ A wide selection of quality examples is given on the ChefSpec GitHub repository: `https://github.com/sethvargo/chefspec/tree/master/examples`

▸ Puppet RSpec: `http://rspec-puppet.com`

▸ Rspec: `http://rspec.info`

Testing infrastructure with Test Kitchen for Chef and Beaker for Puppet

Test Kitchen is a central tool in the Chef ecosystem as it enables thorough testing of infrastructure code and plays very well with a lot of other tools we already use and know. It takes the strong testing culture from the development world and applies it to an infrastructure-as-code environment. Test Kitchen helps start an isolated system environment, apply Chef cookbooks to it, and then execute tests. Supported test frameworks include RSpec, ServerSpec, or Bats (and more), with a large choice of supported environments such as AWS, Vagrant, Digital Ocean, Docker, and OpenStack. Test Kitchen integrates very well with Berkshelf, so cookbook dependencies aren't an issue while testing complex infrastructures. The best part is, it's already included in the Chef DK, so we just have to use it.

In this section, we'll structure everything needed to properly test our Chef cookbooks code using Vagrant with CentOS 7.2

 The Test Kitchen version in use in the Chef DK at the time of writing is 1.13.2.

Getting ready

To step through this recipe, you will need the following:

- A working Chef DK installation on the workstation
- A working Vagrant installation on the workstation
- The Chef code from *Chapter 6*, *Fundamentals of Managing Servers with Chef and Puppet,* or any custom Chef code

How to do it...

Test Kitchen is configured by a single `.kitchen.yml` file at the root of the cookbook. It contains a lot of information:

- How to test the system (Vagrant, by default)
- How to provision the system (chef-solo, chef-zero, or other modes)
- Which platforms to test (Ubuntu 16.04, CentOS 7.2, or other distributions)
- The test suites (what to apply, where to find information, in what context, and similar information)

Configuring Test Kitchen

Irrespective of whether we already have a `.kitchen.yml` file or not, let's open it and fill in the following details:

- We want to run the tests with **Vagrant** to closely simulate a VM in production
- We want to provision using **Chef Zero** (by simulating a Chef server locally)
- We want to test only on **CentOS 7.2** (our code isn't currently designed to run on something else)
- We want a single suite of tests, with a run list of the `mysite::default` recipe, and a path to the **Data Bags**

This is how our `.kitchen.yml` file looks for the `mysite` cookbook:

```
---
driver:
  name: vagrant

provisioner:
  name: chef_zero
```

```
platforms:
  - name: centos-7.2

suites:
  - name: default
    data_bags_path: "../../data_bags"
    run_list:
      - recipe[mysite::default]
    attributes:
```

Testing with Test Kitchen

To simply launch Test Kitchen with the specified configuration, execute the following command:

```
$ kitchen test
-----> Testing <default-centos-72>
-----> Creating <default-centos-72>...
[...]
       Finished creating <default-centos-72> (1m1.51s).
-----> Converging <default-centos-72>...
[...]
-----> Installing Chef Omnibus (install only if missing)
[...]
       resolving cookbooks for run list: ["mysite::default"]
       Synchronizing Cookbooks:
         - apache (0.5.0)
         - php (0.2.0)
         - selinux (0.9.0)
         - yum-mysql-community (1.0.0)
         - mysite (0.3.1)
         - mysql (8.0.4)
         - yum (4.0.0)
[...]
       Chef Client finished, 41/56 resources updated in 02 minutes 47
seconds
       Finished converging <default-centos-72> (3m18.96s).
-----> Setting up <default-centos-72>...
       Finished setting up <default-centos-72> (0m0.00s).
-----> Verifying <default-centos-72>...
       Preparing files for transfer
       Transferring files to <default-centos-72>
       Finished verifying <default-centos-72> (0m0.00s).
```

```
-----> Destroying <default-centos-72>...
        ==> default: Stopping the VMware VM...
        ==> default: Deleting the VM...
        Vagrant instance <default-centos-72> destroyed.
        Finished destroying <default-centos-72> (0m28.38s).
        Finished testing <default-centos-72> (4m48.86s).
-----> Kitchen is finished. (4m50.01s)
```

What happened here is the following:

- ▸ Test Kitchen read the `.kitchen.yml` file
- ▸ Test Kitchen created the Vagrant VM with the specified image
- ▸ Test Kitchen installed Chef, synchronized the cookbooks, solved dependencies with Berkshelf, and applied the `run_list` content
- ▸ Test Kitchen launched tests (we don't have any for now)
- ▸ Test Kitchen destroyed the VM as everything went smoothly

How it works...

When we execute the simple `kitchen test` command, we are in fact running through five steps:

1. `kitchen create`: This creates the virtual testing environment (in our case, through Vagrant and an hypervisor), but does not provision it.
2. `kitchen converge`: This provisions the instance with the suite information from the `.kitchen.yml` we created. As we're using Test Kitchen with Chef, it starts by installing Chef and then resolves cookbook dependencies for us. Then it applies `run_list` with the requested Chef mode (chef-zero in our case).
3. `kitchen setup`: This installs any additional plugin we might need.
4. `kitchen verify`: This first installs everything needed to run the tests—in our case, this will be ServerSpec.
5. `kitchen destroy`: If all tests pass, this step destroys the testing environment.

We highly recommend that you use each command sequentially for debugging purposes.

For reference, as this will all be discussed in the next section, all tests are located in the `test/integration/<suite_name>/<plugin_name>` folder. In other words, the `test/integration/default/serverspec/virtualhost_spec.rb` file will match the Chef cookbook recipe named `virtualhost`, executed from the `default` Kitchen test suite, and tested with the `serverspec` plugin.

There's more...

The counterpart for Puppet is Beaker. The development of Beaker is very active, and the current version (6.x) needs at least Ruby 2.2.5. In order to use the Embedded Ruby provided by Puppet Collections, let's stay on the 5.x branch:

```
$ sudo puppet resource package beaker-rspec
provider=puppet_gem ensure=5.6.0
```

 A C/C++ compiler is needed to install Beaker, so install gcc/g++ or clang before trying to install beaker-rspec. The Zlib library is also needed (binaries and headers).

We also need another gem containing helpers: beaker-puppet_install_helper. This gem is mainly used to install Puppet in boxes during tests:

```
$ sudo puppet resource package beaker-
puppet_install_helper provider=puppet_gem
```

We first need to define a list of supported platforms for running test acceptances. Each platform must be defined in a YAML file in spec/acceptance/nodesets. Since our code only works on Ubuntu, let's define a single platform in spec/acceptance/nodesets/default.yml:

```
HOSTS:
  ubuntu-1604-x64:
    roles:
      - agent
      - default
    platform: ubuntu-16.04-amd64
    hypervisor: vagrant
    box: bento/ubuntu-16.04
CONFIG:
  type: foss
```

As you can see, we will use Vagrant as hypervisor, with an Ubuntu Xenial box.

 type: foss means that the open source edition of Puppet will be used.

Now we can run Beaker:

```
$ rake beaker
/opt/puppetlabs/puppet/bin/ruby -
I/opt/puppetlabs/puppet/lib/ruby/gems/2.1.0/gems/rspec-support-
3.6.0.beta1/lib:/opt/puppetlabs/puppet/lib/ruby/gems/2.1.0/gems/rspec-
core-3.6.0.beta1/lib
/opt/puppetlabs/puppet/lib/ruby/gems/2.1.0/gems/rspec-core-
3.6.0.beta1/exe/rspec --pattern spec/acceptance --color
No examples found.
Finished in 0.00081 seconds (files took 0.14125 seconds to load)
0 examples, 0 failures
```

No acceptance test has been defined yet, but we will see how to write one in the next pages.

See also

> ► Bats testing framework: `https://github.com/sstephenson/bats`
> ► RSpec: `http://rspec.info/`
> ► ServerSpec: `http://serverspec.org/`
> ► Test Kitchen drivers: `https://rubygems.org/search?query=kitchen-`

Integration testing with ServerSpec

Integration testing comes after unit testing: we're now testing the actual functionality on a real black box system. We're probably using many cookbooks that are doing a lot of things, each unit tested in an early stage, but how are they playing together for real? Everything assembled together, intentions might match, but reality can be very different. Overrides might overlap, a forgotten recipe can change behavior, a service might not start and then changes will happen, regression can be introduced, or newer systems or updates can break; there are countless reasons why things can go wrong at a certain point on a real system. That's the reason we need integration testing; testing the outcome of the combination of all our cookbooks applied to a real test system, and now.

In the case of Chef, we have a great tool to help us for this matter named Test Kitchen, which we previously installed and configured to run and execute tests. Let's now write these tests!

We'll write integrations tests for the `mysite` cookbook written in *Chapter 6, Fundamentals of Managing Servers with Chef and Puppet,* for demonstration purposes, but those are completely generic and can be reused anywhere. We'll test for services, files, directories, yum repositories, packages, ports, and injected content. This way, we'll be certain that the code we're writing actually does what it's expected to do in the (simulated) real world!

 We strongly suggest that you add those integrations tests to an automated CI system. So that after a change in the code, tests can be automatically launched and as time go by, complexity soars with many cases added, so you just don't have to think about it: it's all going to be tested, and if your change breaks something you missed, you'll know it in seconds. Nobody wants to manually verify that nothing breaks on three versions of four operating systems at each change.

Getting ready

To step through this recipe, you will need the following:

- A working Chef DK installation on the workstation
- A working Vagrant installation on the workstation
- The Chef code from *Chapter 6, Fundamentals of Managing Servers with Chef and Puppet,* or any custom Chef code

How to do it...

Depending on how the cookbooks we test are created, a `test` folder can be created with some sample content under it. We don't need it, so be sure to get rid of everything under the `test` folder to start fresh. We'll use the `mysite` cookbook from *Chapter 6, Fundamentals of Managing Servers with Chef and Puppet,* as the base cookbook to build our ServerSpec tests on, but obviously those tests can be used anywhere:

```
$ cd cookbooks/mysite
$ rm -rf test/*
```

Test Kitchen works with *test suites*, and consequently expects a folder hierarchy with the same name as the suite name, in an `integration` folder. The final folder hierarchy for a `default` test suite will then be `mysite/test/integration/default/serverspec`.

```
$ mkdir -p test/integration/default/serverspec
```

Creating a ServerSpec helper script

ServerSpec needs a minimum of two lines of configuration that must be repeated on each test. Instead of repeating ourselves, let's create a helper script in `test/integration/default/serverspec/spec_helper.rb`:

```
require 'serverspec'
# Required by serverspec
set :backend, :exec
```

Now all our tests will just need to include the following at the top of the file:

```
require 'spec_helper'
```

Testing a package installation

Our cookbooks are doing a lot of things, and among the most important things is package installation. These things were unit tested previously, but now we're in integration. Are those packages really installed? Let's find out by writing the test for the `httpd` package in `apache_spec.rb`:

```
require 'spec_helper'

describe package('httpd') do
  it { should be_installed }
end
```

We can now fire up Test Kitchen and see if this specific package is really installed!

 While writing integration tests, we strongly suggest that you use Test Kitchen to create/converge/set up/verify the sequence and not the simple `kitchen test` command that does everything at once—the manual way is much faster!

Similarly, testing for the `php` packages in a `php_spec.rb` file will look exactly the same:

```
require 'spec_helper'

describe package('php') do
  it { should be_installed }
end

describe package('php-cli') do
  it { should be_installed }
end

describe package('php-mysql') do
  it { should be_installed }
end
```

Testing for service status

ServerSpec allows us to test the actual process status. In the recipe to install the Apache HTTPD server, we requested it to be enabled and running. Let's find out if it's really the case by adding the following to the `apache_spec.rb` file:

```
describe service('httpd') do
  it { should be_enabled }
  it { should be_running }
end
```

In the case of our MySQL installation, the documentation from the official cookbook indicates the service is by default named `mysql-default` (and not the usual `mysqld`). In a `mysql_spec.rb` file, add the following:

```
describe service('mysql-default') do
  it { should be_enabled }
  it { should be_running }
end
```

Testing for listening ports

ServerSpec is a great tool to test listening ports. In our case, we expect Apache to listen on port `80` (HTTP) and we configured MySQL to listen to `3306`. Add the following to the `apache_spec.rb` file:

```
describe port('80') do
  it { should be_listening }
end
```

Similarly, add the following for MySQL in the `mysql_spec.rb` file:

```
describe port('3306') do
  it { should be_listening }
end
```

Testing for files existence and content

We previously unit tested the intention to create all those files in our cookbooks, such as a VirtualHost with a custom name, impacting both filename and content (that's what the `mysite` cookbook from *Chapter 6, Fundamentals of Managing Servers with Chef and Puppet,* does, override the defaults from the custom apache cookbook). Is it really working? Let's find out by testing our virtual hosting configuration with `vhost_spec.rb`:

```
describe file('/etc/httpd/conf.d/mysite.conf') do
  it { should exist }
  it { should be_mode 644 }
  its(:content) { should match /ServerName mysite/ }
  it { should be_owned_by 'root' }
  it { should be_grouped_into 'root' }
end
```

This actually proves the default attribute really got overridden by the `mysite` value, and the content of the virtual host configuration file also matches this value. The cookbook really works.

A directory can similarly be tested like this in the same `vhost_spec.rb` file:

```
describe file('/var/www/mysite') do
  it { should be_directory }
end
```

Another interesting test to be done is to check the content of the `htpasswd` file; in *Chapter 6, Fundamentals of Managing Servers with Chef and Puppet,* we wrote a recipe making a request to the Chef server for authorized users in a data bag. We unit tested the feature by stubbing the data bag, and then using Test Kitchen, we configured it to simulate the availability of those data bags. Is this Chef Server-specific code really working and adding the `john` user in the `htpasswd` file while restricting access to it? Let's find out by adding the following to an `htaccess_spec.rb` file:

```
describe file('/etc/httpd/htpasswd') do
  it { should exist }
  it { should be_mode 660 }
  its(:content) { should match /john/ }
  it { should be_owned_by 'root' }
  it { should be_grouped_into 'root' }
end
```

Testing for repository existence

Our `mysite` cookbook example from *Chapter 6, Fundamentals of Managing Servers with Chef and Puppet,* is using the official Chef cookbook to deploy MySQL, and that includes adding a yum repository. As it's now an important part of the system, we'd better test for its existence and status! To test a yum repository, add the following to the `mysql_spec.rb` file:

```
describe yumrepo('mysql57-community') do
    it { should be_exist   }
    it { should be_enabled }
end
```

Many other parts of a system can be tested using ServerSpec, notably in networking (routing tables, gateways, and interfaces), Unix users and groups, real commands, cron jobs, and many more.

There's more...

Using Puppet and Beaker, let's try to write acceptance tests for our Apache module. Acceptance tests needs to be placed in the `spec/acceptance` directory.

We need to define a helper file that will be shared by all acceptance tests. Let's create a spec/`spec_helper_acceptance.rb` file with the following content:

```
require 'beaker-rspec'
require 'beaker/puppet_install_helper'

# Install puppet
run_puppet_install_helper

RSpec.configure do |c|
  # Project root
  proj_root = File.expand_path(File.join(File.dirname(__FILE__),
'..'))

  # Output should contain test descriptions
  c.formatter = :documentation

  # Configure nodes
  c.before :suite do
    # Install module
    puppet_module_install(:source => proj_root, :module_name =>
'apache')
  end
end
```

This helper file will be used to install Puppet on the test box, and populate the module directory with our apache module.

As a first basic acceptance test for the main apache class, let's create spec/acceptances/classes/apache_spec.rb, with the following content:

```
require 'spec_helper_acceptance'

describe 'Apache' do
  describe 'Puppet code' do
    it 'should compile and work with no error' do
      pp = <<-EOS
        class { 'apache': }
      EOS

      apply_manifest(pp, :catch_failures => true)
      apply_manifest(pp, :catch_changes => true)
    end
  end
end
```

The goals of this test are as follows:

- ▸ Installing Apache using our class.
- ▸ Verifying Puppet applies properly.
- ▸ Verifying that a second run of Puppet does not change anything: we want to prove the code is idempotent.

Let's try the test!

```
$ rake beaker
...
...
Beaker::Hypervisor, found some vagrant boxes to create
Bringing machine 'ubuntu-1604-x64' up with 'virtualbox' provider...
...
...
Apache
  Puppet code
localhost $ scp /var/folders/k9/7sp85p796qx7c22btk7_tgym0000gn/T/
beaker20161101-75828-1of1g5j ubuntu-1604-x64:/tmp/apply_manifest.
pp.cZK277 {:ignore
=> }
localhost $ scp /var/folders/k9/7sp85p796qx7c22btk7_tgym0000gn/T/
beaker20161101-75828-1128bth ubuntu-1604-x64:/tmp/apply_manifest.
pp.q2Z81Z {:ignore
=> }
    should compile and work with no error
Destroying vagrant boxes
==> ubuntu-1604-x64: Forcing shutdown of VM...
==> ubuntu-1604-x64: Destroying VM and associated drives...


Finished in 19.68 seconds (files took 1 minute 20.11 seconds to load)
1 example, 0 failures
```

In this example, Beaker created the box, installed Puppet, uploaded our code, applied Puppet twice to validate our test, and destroyed the box.

To have more logs regarding Puppet agent installation and execution, we can add a line `log_level: verbose` in the `nodeset` file:

```
HOSTS:
  ubuntu-1604-x64:
    roles:
      - agent
      - default
```

```
      platform: ubuntu-16.04-amd64
      hypervisor: vagrant
      box: bento/ubuntu-16.04
  CONFIG:
    type: foss
    log_level: verbose
```

Now let's extend our test to use all code contained in the apache module. We want to update the manifest at the top of the file in order to do the following:

- Install apache
- Define a virtual host
- Create the root directory of the virtual host
- Create a htpasswd file with a test user
- Create a .htaccess file in the root directory, using the previous htpasswd file

Regarding tests, we want to:

- Verify Puppet applies
- Verify the code is idempotent
- Verify apache is running and activated at boot
- Verify apache is listening
- Verify the virtual host is deployed and activated with the correct DocumentRoot
- Verify the htpasswd file is deployed with a correct content
- Verify the .htaccess file is deployed with a correct content

The updated acceptance test code is now as follows:

```
require 'spec_helper_acceptance'

describe 'Apache' do
  describe 'Puppet code' do
    it 'should compile and work with no error' do
      pp = <<-EOS
        class { 'apache': }
        apache::vhost{'mysite':
          website   => 'www.sample.com',
          docroot   => '/var/www/docroot',
        }
        apache::htpasswd{'htpasswd':
          filepath => '/etc/apache2/htpasswd',
          users    => [ { "id" => "user1", "htpasswd" =>
"hash1" } ],
        }
```

```
        file { '/var/www/docroot':
          ensure => directory,
          owner  => 'www-data',
          group  => 'www-data',
          mode   => '0755',
        }
        apache::htaccess{'myhtaccess':
          filepath => '/etc/apache2/htpasswd',
          docroot  => '/var/www/docroot',
        }
      EOS

      apply_manifest(pp, :catch_failures => true)
      apply_manifest(pp, :catch_changes => true)
    end
  end

  # Apache running and enabled at boot ?
  describe service('apache2') do
    it { is_expected.to be_enabled }
    it { is_expected.to be_running }
  end

  # Apache listening ?
  describe port(80) do
    it { is_expected.to be_listening }
  end

  # Vhost deployed ?
  describe file ('/etc/apache2/sites-available/www.sample.com.conf')
do
    its(:content) { should match /DocumentRoot \/var\/www\/docroot/ }
  end

  describe file ('/etc/apache2/sites-enabled/www.sample.com.conf') do
    it { is_expected.to be_symlink }
  end

  # htpasswd file deployed ?
  describe file ('/etc/apache2/htpasswd') do
    its(:content) { should match /user1:hash1/ }
  end

  # htaccess file deployed ?
  describe file ('/var/www/docroot/.htaccess') do
    its(:content) { should match /AuthUserFile \/etc\/apache2\/
```

```
    htpasswd/ }
      end

  end
```

Now, let's try to run Beaker again:

```
$ rake beaker

…

…

Beaker::Hypervisor, found some vagrant boxes to create

Bringing machine 'ubuntu-1604-x64' up with 'virtualbox'
provider...

…

…

Apache
  Puppet code
localhost $ scp /var/folders/k9/7sp85p796qx7c22btk7_tgym0000gn/T/
beaker20161103-41882-1twwbr2 ubuntu-1604-x64:/tmp/apply_manifest.
pp.nWPdZJ {:ignore => }

localhost $ scp /var/folders/k9/7sp85p796qx7c22btk7_tgym0000gn/T/
beaker20161103-41882-73vqlb ubuntu-1604-x64:/tmp/apply_manifest.pp.0Jht7j
{:ignore => }
    should compile and work with no error
  Service "apache2"
    should be enabled
    should be running
  Port "80"
    should be listening
  File "/etc/apache2/sites-available/www.sample.com.conf"
    content
      should match /DocumentRoot \/var\/www\/docroot/
  File "/etc/apache2/sites-enabled/www.sample.com.conf"
    should be symlink
  File "/etc/apache2/htpasswd"
    content
      should match /user1:hash1/
  File "/var/www/docroot/.htaccess"
    content
```

```
    should match /AuthUserFile \/etc\/apache2\/htpasswd/
Destroying vagrant boxes
==> ubuntu-1604-x64: Forcing shutdown of VM...
==> ubuntu-1604-x64: Destroying VM and associated drives...


Finished in 20.22 seconds (files took 1 minute 24.54 seconds
to load)
8 examples, 0 failures
```

We now have a complete acceptance test suite for our Apache module!

See also

- ▸ ServerSpec GitHub: `https://github.com/serverspec/`
- ▸ ServerSpec Homepage: `http://serverspec.org/`
- ▸ Test Kitchen Homepage: `http://kitchen.ci/`
- ▸ A sample skeleton for Puppet module with Beaker enabled: `https://gitlab.com/joshbeard/puppet-module-test`

8

Maintaining Systems Using Chef and Puppet

In this chapter, we will cover the following recipes:

- Maintaining consistent systems using scheduled convergence
- Creating environments
- Using Chef encrypted data bags and Hiera-eyaml with Puppet
- Using Chef Vault encryption
- Accessing and manipulating system information with Ohai
- Automating application deployment (a WordPress example)
- Using a TDD workflow
- Planning for the worse – train to rebuild working systems

Introduction

We've previously seen how to automate systems with code and how to properly test this code. Now we're ready for prime time; there's a whole set of features, constraints, and objectives to be properly set. We'll want to isolate environments such as dev, staging, and production. We'll need our infrastructure code to stay consistent without our intervention. Security and confidentiality will start becoming an issue, and maybe those passwords and secret keys should not be stored in clear text at all. After a few months, our automated infrastructure will grow into a large number of managed nodes, and it will become critical to have coherent behaviour according to systems profiles—we'll need to gather and process system information. We'll eventually end up deploying web applications directly from Chef. To keep a high level of quality while our code base gets more and more complex, we'll switch to the **Test-Driven Development** (**TDD**) approach for our workflow. And finally, we'll make sure we're always ready to redeploy any part of the infrastructure at any time (think of a disaster).

All recipes are based on Chef. However, when possible, we'll try to show how things work similarly with Puppet, Chef's direct alternative.

Maintaining consistent systems using scheduled convergence

Once initially deployed and configured, it's hardly imaginable to let our systems be manually updated afterwards by logging in to each host and launching the `chef-client` command. Systems maintained with Chef have the opportunity to be converged at a predetermined time, either through a `chef-client` daemon or a cron job. We'll go through both these options.

Getting ready

To step through this recipe, you will need:

- A working Chef DK installation on the workstation
- A working Vagrant installation on the workstation
- The Chef code (optionally) from either *Chapter 6, Fundamentals of Managing Servers with Chef and Puppet, Chapter 7, Testing and Writing Better Infrastructure Code with Chef and Puppet*, or any custom Chef code

How to do it...

We recommend that you create a cookbook, different from other cookbooks, dedicated to configuring the underlying host. Let's call this cookbook `common`:

```
$ cd chef-repo/cookbooks
$ chef generate cookbook common
$ cd common
```

To configure the Chef client, there's an official cookbook aptly named `chef-client`. Let's declare a `cookbook` requirement to it, specifically to `Berksfile`:

```
cookbook 'chef-client', '~> 7.0.0'
```

To the `common/metadata.rb` file, add the dependency:

```
depends 'chef-client'
```

Using the Chef client as a daemon

The documentation tells us that including the default recipe will automatically detect the host platform and configure `chef-client` accordingly to run as a daemon. Here are the steps to enable `chef-client`:

1. Add the following to `recipes/default.rb`:

   ```
   include_recipe 'chef-client'
   ```

2. Install the dependencies using Berkshelf:

   ```
   $ berks install
   ```

3. Now upload the `common` cookbook with all its dependencies:

   ```
   $ berks upload
   ```

4. Add the `common` cookbook to the host `run-list`:

   ```
   $ knife node run_list add vagrant common
   ```

5. On the target host, launch the Chef client one last time to make it deploy itself as a service:

   ```
   $ chef-client
   Recipe: chef-client::systemd_service
   [...]
     * service[chef-client] action enable
       - enable service service[chef-client]
     * service[chef-client] action start
       - start service service[chef-client]
     * service[chef-client] action restart
       - restart service service[chef-client]
   ```

6. The logs seem pretty optimistic, but let's double-check the daemon is really running on the host:

   ```
   $ systemctl status chef-client
   • chef-client.service - Chef Client daemon
      Loaded: loaded (/etc/systemd/system/chef-client.service;
   enabled; vendor preset: disabled)
      Active: active (running) since Mon 2016-11-07 01:35:05 UTC; 57s
   ago
    Main PID: 12943 (chef-client)
      CGroup: /system.slice/chef-client.service
           └─12943 /opt/chef/embedded/bin/ruby /usr/bin/chef-
   client -c /etc/chef/client.rb -i 1800 -s 300
   ```

The `chef-client` service is indeed enabled and running!

Tweaking the convergence interval time

Interesting enough, we see that the interval is introduced every 1,800 seconds (30 minutes). What if we want a different convergence interval, say, every 900 seconds (15 minutes)? Let's transform the `default.rb` recipe:

```
node.override['chef_client']['interval'] = '900'
include_recipe 'chef-client'
```

Bump the version in `metadata.rb`, upload the new version, wait for the new `chef-client` execution, or launch it yourself to save some time. The `systemd` unit is now updated:

```
$ systemctl status chef-client
• chef-client.service - Chef Client daemon
[...]
        └─13316 /opt/chef/embedded/bin/ruby /usr/bin/chef-client -c /
etc/chef/client.rb -i 900 -s 300
```

Our system is now configured to converge every 15 minutes with a controlled variation of 300 seconds.

> We highly suggest that you include this `common` cookbook in every new host deployment process so they could all be automatically configured to converge at a predetermined interval.

Running the Chef client as a cron

Under certain circumstances, we might not want to run the Chef client as a daemon (such as memory or security requirements). So luckily, we can simply fall back to a simple method that is based on a cron. Let's transform the default `recipe.rb` recipe to match this:

```
node.override['chef_client']['init_style'] = 'none'
include_recipe 'chef-client::cron'
```

Upload this cookbook version using Berkshelf and execute `chef-client` on the target host. See root's `crontab` file:

```
$ sudo crontab -l
# Chef Name: chef-client
0 0,4,8,12,16,20 * * * /bin/sleep 69;  /usr/bin/chef-client > /dev/null
2>&1
```

By default, it's executing `chef-client` every four hours with, in this case, a 69 seconds delay to avoid every node from hammering the Chef server at the same time.

Tweaking the Chef cron job

If converging every four hours is not enough for you and you would like to converge every 15 minutes, like we did with the daemon in the `default.rb` recipe, here's what you need to do:

```
node.override['chef_client']['init_style'] = 'none'
node.override['chef_client']['cron']['minute'] = '*/15'
node.override['chef_client']['cron']['hour'] = '*'

include_recipe 'chef-client::cron'
```

Upload the cookbook and run `chef-client` (or wait for the next scheduled run). The interval is now set to run every 15 minutes:

```
$ sudo crontab -l
# Chef Name: chef-client
*/15 * * * * /bin/sleep 69;  /usr/bin/chef-client > /dev/null 2>&1
```

There's more...

With Puppet, the agent can also run as a service or a cron.

The following command is used to enable the service mode:

```
# puppet resource service puppet ensure=running enable=true
```

In this mode, the Puppet agent will apply the configuration every 30 minutes by default. This delay can be changed in `/etc/puppetlabs/puppet.conf`. Here is an example to reduce this delay to five minutes:

```
[agent]
  runinterval = 5m
```

To run the Puppet agent as a cron, we need to declare a Puppet cron resource as follows:

```
# puppet resource cron puppet-agent ensure=present user=root minute=0
command='/opt/puppet/bin/puppet agent --onetime --no-daemonize --splay
--splaylimit 60'
```

The generated `crontab` file is:

```
$ sudo crontab -l
0 * * * * /opt/puppet/bin/puppet agent --onetime --no-daemonize --splay
--splaylimit 60
```

In this example, the Puppet agent will run every hour. The `splay` option is used to introduce a random delay before the run itself, and this delay cannot exceed 60 minutes (the value of the `splaylimit` option). This is particularly useful when a lot of nodes are connected to the same Puppet server in order to spread the Puppet agent's requests in time.

Of course, if there are many nodes in your infrastructure, you should create a module containing these Puppet resources and include it for each node. Based on our previous Vagrant-based LAMP setup, let's create a local module with a single file, namely `module/baseconfig/manifests/init.pp`, with:

```
# @param agentmode Agent type: service or cron. If anything else,
agent will be disabled. Default value: service
class baseconfig (
  $agentmode='service'
) {
  case $agentmode {
    'service': {
      $ensureservice='running';
      $enableservice=true;
      $ensurecron='absent'
    }
    'cron': {
      $ensureservice='stopped';
      $enableservice=false;
      $ensurecron='present'
    }
    default: {
      $ensureservice='stopped';
      $enableservice=false;
      $ensurecron='absent'
    }
  }
  service {'puppet':
    ensure => $ensureservice,
    enable => $enableservice,
  }
  cron {'puppet-agent':
    ensure  => $ensurecron,
    user    => root,
    minute  => 0,
    command => '/opt/puppet/bin/puppet agent --onetime
    --no-daemonize --splay --splaylimit 60',
  }
}
```

Now we can define the requested mode from the main manifest:

```
node 'web.pomes.pro' {
...
  class { 'baseconfig':
    agentmode => 'cron';
  }
...
}
```

If there is any future change between `service` versus `cron`, our `baseconfig` module will remove the configuration for the previous mode.

See also

▶ The `chef-client` cookbook source at `https://github.com/chef-cookbooks/chef-client`

▶ The Puppet cron resource at `https://docs.puppet.com/puppet/4.8/types/cron.html`

Creating environments

A classic organization has a minimum of two environments in which the infrastructure is run: development and production. Very often, a lot of environments are seen, such as staging, testing, alpha or beta. It's entirely up to the organization to model the infrastructure according to its needs, and the complexity can grow very quickly. The good news is that Chef helps a lot in mapping this model to the infrastructure. There's a set of information that will be different in two distinct environments, such as cookbook versions or attributes, and Chef makes it as easy as possible to manage these environments. By default, nodes without an environment set will run in a `_default` environment.

In this section, we'll see how to create different environments, how to set nodes (both existing and new) in a dedicated environment, how to set cookbook constraints, and finally how to override the attributes in each environment.

Getting ready

To step through this recipe, you will need:

▶ A working Chef DK installation on the workstation

▶ A working Vagrant installation on the workstation

▶ The Chef code (optionally) from *Chapter 6, Fundamentals of Managing Servers with Chef and Puppet, Chapter 7, Testing and Writing Better Infrastructure Code with Chef and Puppet,* or any custom Chef code

How to do it...

Chef environments live in a folder named `environments` at the root of `chef-repo`. If the folder doesn't exist, create it:

```
$ mkdir environments
```

Creating a production environment

To create a production environment, follow these steps:

1. Let's start by creating a `production` environment in a `production.rb` file:

    ```
    name 'production'
    description 'The production environment'
    ```

2. This is the simplest environment possible; it does nothing. Upload it to the Chef server:

    ```
    $ knife environment from file environments/production.rb
    Updated Environment production
    ```

3. List the available remote environments:

    ```
    $ knife environment list
    _default
    production
    ```

We see we have two environments available: `production` and `_default`.

Setting an environment to a node

To set an already existing node to this new `production` environment, execute the following command:

```
$ knife node environment set my_node_name production
my_node_name:
  chef_environment: production
```

Bootstrapping a node with an environment

If we're bootstrapping a node with the `knife bootstrap` command, we can start in the required environment right from the beginning (using an user named `vagrant` like the previous examples):

```
$ knife bootstrap a.b.c.d -N vagrant -x vagrant --sudo --environment
production --run-list 'recipe[mysite]'
```

Fixing cookbook versions for an environment

Let's say our production systems are running a perfectly stable `mysite` cookbook in version 0.3.1, but we want to try a new feature in the development infrastructure in the 0.4.0 version of the same cookbook. As every cookbook version can live together, each environment can call its own version. The `production.rb` file would contain the following for the `production` environment:

```
cookbook_versions  'mysite' => '= 0.3.1'
```

The `development.rb` file would contain the following for the development environment:

```
cookbook_versions  'mysite' => '= 0.4.0'
```

A Chef environment file may contain many cookbook constraints, as follows:

```
cookbook_versions: {
    'mysite': '= 0.4.0',
    'apache': '= 0.6.0'
}
```

Overriding attributes for an environment

Each environment can override any value, and, in Chef, it's the highest level of override. Nothing else can override a value set for an environment. So, if we simply want to override the value of the `sitename` attribute to `production.rb`, it will look like this:

```
override_attributes 'sitename' => 'mysite_production'
```

Accessing the environment from a recipe

The node's environment is available from any recipe through the `node.chef_environment` attribute.

So if our wish is to create a file that would display the environment inside which the node is running, we would need to create a template like this:

```
Running in <%= @node.chef_environment %> mode.
```

There's more...

With Puppet, environments are located in distinct directories on the Puppet server. You probably noticed this in *Chapter 6, Fundamentals of Managing Servers with Chef and Puppet*; we created the code in the `/etc/puppetlabs/code/environments/production` directory.

This is because the default Puppet environment is `production`. Other environments, for example `test`, should be created under `/etc/puppetlabs/code/environments/`.

Manual environment creation in the Puppet server

Let's start with samples from *Chapter 6, Fundamentals of Managing Servers with Chef and Puppet*, and try creating a new environment, namely `test`. On the Puppet server, we just need to do this:

```
$ sudo -s
# cd /etc/puppetlabs/code/environments/
# cp -a production test
```

Node environment selection

On the node side, the environment to use can be controlled using `--environment`:

```
# puppet agent --test --environment test
```

To use this environment as the default one, without using `--environment`, we can configure it in `/etc/puppetlabs/puppet/puppet.conf` with the following:

```
[agent]
environment = test
```

Getting the environment from manifests

As for Chef, we can get the name of the running environment from any manifest. This is done by using the `$environment` variable, which is set by the Puppet server.

To illustrate this, let's modify our `index.php` file (`manifests/site.pp`), both in `production` and `test`:

```
file {"${docroot}/index.php":
    ensure  => present,
    owner   => 'www-data',
    group   => 'www-data',
    mode    => '0644',
    content => "<?php echo \"Running from ${environment}\" ?>"
}
```

We can now switch between `test` and `production` and see the changes:

```
# puppet agent --test
Info: Using configured environment 'production'
...
@@ -1 +1 @@
-<?php echo "Running from test" ?>
+<?php echo "Running from production" ?>
...
```

```
# puppet agent --test --environment test
Info: Using configured environment 'test'
@@ -1 +1 @@
-<?php echo "Running from production" ?>
+<?php echo "Running from test" ?>
```

The dynamic way – r10k

We edited the environments and code directly in the Puppet master, which is not recommended. Fortunately, r10k (which we already used in *Chapter 6, Fundamentals of Managing Servers with Chef and Puppet*, to install modules) can be used to create environments from a Git repository. Each branch from the Git repository will be checked out into a distinct directory and will be available as an environment. This feature is dynamic: each new branch added to the Git repository will be deployed by r10k.

Let's try it from our workstation. Until now, the job of the shared folder of our Vagrant setup was to map the relative directory `puppetcode` to `/etc/puppetlabs/code/environments/production` in the `puppet.pomes.pro` box. We are about to use multiple environments, so we need to change the mapping to `/etc/puppetlabs/code/`.

We need a Git repository with two branches, `production` and `test`, with all of the previous code. An example is available at `https://github.com/ppomes/r10k_sample.git`.

The r10k tool needs a global configuration file, which must be created at the same level as our Vagrantfile, with the following content:

```
:sources:
  :my-repos:
    remote: 'https://github.com/ppomes/r10k_sample.git'
    basedir: 'puppetcode/environments'
```

Now let's use r10k:

```
$ r10k -c ./r10k.yaml deploy environment -p
$ ls -l puppetcode/environments/
total 0
drwxr-xr-x  8 ppomes  staff   272B 26 Nov 16:40 production/
drwxr-xr-x  8 ppomes  staff   272B 26 Nov 16:40 test/
```

Both branches from the Git repository have been deployed, and we can now fire up Vagrant and play with our boxes and branches.

> The r10k tool also takes care of the `Puppetfile` file in each branch, as we already saw in *Chapter 6, Fundamentals of Managing Servers with Chef and Puppet*, and deploys external modules, if any.

See also

▶ The Chef environment documentation at `https://docs.chef.io/environments.html`

▶ Puppet's r10k at `https://github.com/puppetlabs/r10k`

Using Chef encrypted data bags and Hiera-eyaml with Puppet

Some information in data bags can be safely stored in the Chef server in plain text, but under some circumstances, sensitive information might be safer if encrypted. Companies might not like production API keys, private keys, or similar sensitive content to be stored in plain text on the Chef server or on third-party services, such as GitHub. We'll see how to encrypt and decrypt data in the command line and from inside a Chef recipe.

Getting ready

To step through this recipe, you will need:

▶ A working Chef DK installation on the workstation

▶ A working Vagrant installation on the workstation

▶ The Chef code (optionally) from *Chapter 6*, *Fundamentals of Managing Servers with Chef and Puppet*, *Chapter 7*, *Testing and Writing Better Infrastructure Code with Chef and Puppet*, or any custom Chef code

How to do it...

Our goal is to create a configuration file containing our AWS credentials for the `us-east-1` region, and it's not acceptable that you store the credentials in clear text on the Chef server. We'd like to use a data bag, as it can be encrypted:

1. Create a data bag folder `aws` to store the credentials for the `us-east-1` region:

   ```
   $ mkdir data_bags/aws
   ```

2. Create the data bag on the Chef server while we're at it:

   ```
   $ knife data bag create aws
   Created data_bag[aws]
   ```

3. Inside this `aws` data bag folder, create a sample `us-east-1.json` file containing the credentials:

```json
{
  "id": "us-east-1",
  "aws_access_key": "AKIAJWTIBGE3NFDB4HOB",
  "aws_secret_key":
  "h77/xZt/5NUafuE+q5Mte2RhGcjY4zbJ3V0cTnAc"
}
```

This is the standard procedure for a normal data bag. If we upload it now as is, it won't be encrypted.

Encrypting data bags with a shared secret

The solution to use an encrypted data bag is to send it encrypted from our workstation. The encryption is done through a shared secret, the secret being either a file or a string. Let's use the string `s3cr3t` as an encryption key (weak). To simply send the encrypted version of the data bag, let's use the encryption feature of the `knife` command:

```
$ knife data bag from file --encrypt --secret s3cr3t aws us-east-1.json
Updated data_bag_item[aws::us-east-1]
```

If we request the data without providing a decryption key, we'll get the encrypted data from the Chef server:

```
$ knife data bag show aws us-east-1
WARNING: Encrypted data bag detected, but no secret provided for
decoding. Displaying encrypted data.
aws_access_key:
  cipher:         aes-256-cbc
  encrypted_data: RwbfsWgKk16sSCkMD38tXKGHmT1AHFGHRm/7fyzppye7wSS0kk19Zml
0VuhQ
  XxxI

  iv:             iRRgrKfz6Ou2qdpYLkUA+w==

  version:        1
aws_secret_key:
  cipher:         aes-256-cbc
  encrypted_data: uSppKMYrRbEYn/njDYo3CIGC5tY+pptN1Z7LiARtNIU/
zsllBNdSVENC1XwX
  QksifE6g00sdcHTGlHlVU0WJ0Q==
```

```
    iv:                 ppjeAJcegZ9Yyn9rXgHRBQ==


    version:            1
id:                     us-east-1
```

It looks like we got what we wanted: data is stored encrypted on the Chef server!

As it may not be a secure move to store unencrypted data bags on version control systems, such as Git, we can ask for a JSON-formatted encrypted version, such as the following, and redirect the output to a JSON file for storage purposes:

```
$ knife data bag show aws us-east-1 -Fj
{
  "id": "us-east-1",
  "aws_access_key": {
    "encrypted_data": "RwbfsWgKk16sSCkMD38tXKGHmT1AHFGHRm/7fyzppye7wSS0kk
19Zml0VuhQ\nXxxI\n",
    "iv": "iRRgrKfz6Ou2qdpYLkUA+w==\n",
    "version": 1,
    "cipher": "aes-256-cbc"
  },
  "aws_secret_key": {
    "encrypted_data": "uSppKMYrRbEYn/njDYo3CIGC5tY+pptN1Z7LiARtNIU/
zsllBNdSVENC1XwX\nQksifE6g00sdcHTGlHlVU0WJ0Q==\n",
    "iv": "ppjeAJcegZ9Yyn9rXgHRBQ==\n",
    "version": 1,
    "cipher": "aes-256-cbc"
  }
}
```

This might be the content you'd like to store on Git!

Accessing an encrypted data bag in the CLI

To access unencrypted data from the knife CLI, the process is as easy as encrypting data—pass the shared secret as an argument:

```
$ knife data bag show aws us-east-1 --secret s3cr3t
Encrypted data bag detected, decrypting with provided secret.
aws_access_key: AKIAJWTIBGE3NFDB4HOB
aws_secret_key: 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
id:                 us-east-1
```

Now we have access to our data but in an unencrypted form.

Using an encrypted data bag from a recipe

Now that the data is safely stored on the Chef server, how do we access it from inside a Chef recipe? Let's say our objective is to create a file named `/etc/aws/credentials` that will contain the unencrypted value from the encrypted version on the Chef server. The final file should look like this:

```
[region_name]
aws_access_key_id = the_access_key
aws_secret_access_key = the_secret_key
```

1. To do so, create a new recipe named `aws` inside the `mysite` cookbook:

    ```
    $ chef generate recipe aws
    ```

     Don't forget to bump the cookbook version and environment constraints accordingly.

2. Start by creating the `/etc/aws` folder using the `directory` resource:

    ```
    directory "/etc/aws" do
      owner 'root'
      group 'root'
      mode '0755'
      action :create
    end
    ```

3. Here's a `templates/aws.erb` ERB template file for our destination, namely `/etc/aws/credentials`:

    ```
    [<%= @aws_region %>]
    aws_access_key_id = <%= @aws_access_key %>
    aws_secret_access_key = <%= @aws_secret_key %>
    ```

    We see the template is expecting the `aws_region`, `aws_access_key`, and `aws_secret_key` variables. Let's write the code to inject these values to the `aws.rb` recipe. To begin with, let's access our encrypted data bag item `us-east-1` from the `aws` data bag, using the inline shared secret `s3cr3t`:

    ```
    aws = Chef::EncryptedDataBagItem.load("aws", "us-east-1",
    's3cr3t')
    ```

     All of this information can be set as attributes if we like. If the file method is chosen for the shared secret, the final argument will be the path to the secret key file to decrypt the data.

4. Now let's create the template, writing the decrypted credentials to the /etc/aws/credentials file:

```
template "/etc/aws/credentials" do
  source 'aws.erb'
  owner 'root'
  group 'root'
  mode '0600'
  variables(
    aws_region: aws['id'],
    aws_access_key: aws['aws_access_key'],
    aws_secret_key: aws['aws_secret_key']
  )
end
```

Here we are! The Chef server is now safely storing encrypted data. For added security, it's better to not hardcode the shared key—use the key file that is sent separately (but this creates an added layer of complexity in the deployment system).

There's more...

While using Puppet, it is a good practice to store the credentials and site information in Hiera, as we saw in *Chapter 6, Fundamentals of Managing Servers with Chef and Puppet*. Using hiera-eyaml, it is possible to encrypt sensitive data. Using our previous LAMP setup with Vagrant, let's try to encrypt the root password for MySQL.

Preparing the Puppet server

We need to install a new backend for Hiera. We have not discussed a lot about Hiera yet, and it's time to do so. Hiera is used to store data out of manifests, and is based on a hierarchy to look up data. A default configuration is provided with the Puppet server installation and is located at /etc/puppetlabs/puppet/hiera.yaml:

```
---
:backends:
  - yaml
:hierarchy:
  - "nodes/%{::trusted.certname}"
  - common

:yaml:
:datadir:
```

Here, a `yaml` backend is defined, allowing us to use `yaml` files in the `hieradata` directory of our environments. Then, a hierarchy is defined. Puppet will first try to look up data in a `yaml` file with the name matching the name of the client certificate (that is, the FQDN node) and located under the `nodes` subdirectory. If no data is found, Puppet will try to look up a `common.yaml` file.

With `hiera-eyaml`, we need to declare a new backend to look up data in encrypted files. This backend is `eyaml`, and by default, we will look for files with the `.eyaml` extension. This backend relies on a key pair to read data, so we need to generate these keys.

Fortunately, a Puppet module, named `puppet/hiera`, exists to handle all of this for us. So we just need to add it to `Puppetfile` with its dependencies (do not forget to run `r10k puppetfile install`):

```
mod 'puppetlabs/inifile'
mod 'puppet/hiera'
mod 'puppetlabs/puppetserver_gem'
```

With this module, it is now very easy to prepare the Puppet server using the following:

```
node 'puppet.pomes.pro' {

  # Create a service resource for the puppetserver
  # This is needed by the hiera module, in order
  # to restart the server once hiera-eyaml is installed
  service {'puppetserver':
    ensure => running,
  }
  # Configure hiera
  class { 'hiera':
    hierarchy => [
      'nodes/%{::trusted.certname}',
    ],
    eyaml          => true,
    manage_package => true,
    provider       => 'puppetserver_gem',
    master_service => 'puppetserver',
  }
}
```

This piece of code will:

▸ Declare a service resource for the Puppet server. This is needed by the `puppet/hiera` module (see parameter `master_service`)

▸ Install the `eyaml` backend in the Puppet server

▸ Update the Hiera configuration in order to use this backend

▸ Generate the private and public keys

▸ Restart the Puppet server

Private and public keys will be respectively placed in `/etc/puppetlabs/puppet/keys/private_key.pkcs7.pem` and `/etc/puppetlabs/puppet/keys/public_key.pkcs7.pem`.

Preparing the workstation

To prepare the workstation, follow these steps:

1. To create and edit encrypted data, we need `eyaml`. Let's install it using the following:

   ```
   $ sudo puppet resource package hiera-eyaml provider=puppet_gem
   ```

2. Let's copy the keys from the Puppet server and store them in a `keys` folder under `$HOME`:

   ```
   $ ls ~/keys/
   private_key.pkcs7.pem  public_key.pkcs7.pem
   ```

3. For security reasons, it is a good idea to restrict access to the private key:

   ```
   $ chmod 500 keys
   $ chmod 400 keys/private_key.pkcs7.pem
   ```

4. We also need an `eyaml` configuration file, located in `~/.eyaml/config.yaml`, with this content (do not forget to adjust the path of your `$HOME` directory):

   ```
   ---
   pkcs7_public_key: "/Users/me/keys/public_key.pkcs7.pem"
   pkcs7_private_key: "/Users/me/keys/private_key.pkcs7.pem"
   ```

We are now ready to encrypt sensitive data.

Securing the MySQL root password

From the command line, `eyaml` can encrypt values. Here is a session example:

```
$ eyaml encrypt -s 'super_secure_password'
[hiera-eyaml-core] Loaded config from /Users/me/.eyaml/config.yaml
string: ENC[PKCS7,MIIBiQYJKoZIhvcNAQcDoIIBejCCAXYCAQAxggEhMIIBHQIBADAFMA
ACAQEwDQYJKoZIhvcNAQEBBQAEggEALjJ2a9uZO41k2V5xKqEd0n3BtA4OLe1B6rA2iVru
JRKxWJdevuGvJ55DDedRwBMZmqbvSMO1cgMUyPbfEy54i3SXw4x3LEuxc1R31ILoOspBgz
U4OLuepCotuhBASA/pI/xu40y66AZAcCQ4CtD9SZJYjiWNtUA91rcARy/xYQGK39Qievx
T2eq5De89qIn2w/5fIRIkJBRyNqnwyYCWKcKSRwaiLbimpwmarOP+dxGHEFRrD/
FiM4NfoV1WNNVr1UkPEFuNrWBzwBpvyZUnMbGHN676Rg5vq9sS6aWI6zPxTrJyLtss
Zm1f4GsfhmE+anFmuxrcWtEH6C82wKMOoTBMBgkqhkiG9w0BBwEwHQYJYIZIAWUDBAEq
BBC3MhSP09yUw8XTj0XdlG1VgCCDCGhqIFdUmORYK1q0Pn5CE/cDZKTO+bhHxdBw5amAGQ==]
```

OR

```
block: >
    ENC[PKCS7,MIIBiQYJKoZIhvcNAQcDoIIBejCCAXYCAQAxggEhMIIBHQIBADADAFMAACAQEw
    DQYJKoZIhvcNAQEBBQAEggEALjJ2a9uZO4lk2V5xKqEd0n3BtA4OLe1B6rA2
    iVruJRKxWJdevuGvJ55DDedRwBMZmqbvSMO1cgMUyPbfEy54i3SXw4x3LEux
    c1R31ILoOspBgzU4OLuepCotuhBASA/pI/xu4Oy66AZAcCQ4CtD9SZJYjiWN
    tUA91rcARy/xYQGK39QievxT2eq5De89qIn2w/5fIRIkJBRyNqnwyYCWKcKS
    RwaiLbimpwmarOP+dxGHEFRrD/FiM4NfoV1WNNVr1UkPEFuNrWBzwBpvyZUn
    MbGHN676Rg5vq9sS6aWI6zPxTrJyLtssZm1f4GsfhmE+anFmuxrcWtEH6C82
    wKMOoTBMBgkqhkiG9w0BBwEwHQYJYIZIAWUDBAEqBBC3MhSP09yUw8XTj0Xd
    1G1VgCCDCGhqIFdUmORYK1q0Pn5CE/cDZKTO+bhHxdBw5amAGQ==]
```

Since the `eyaml` backend is looking for files with the `.eyaml` extension, we just need to create a `hieradata/nodes/web.pomes.pro.eyaml` file with the following content:

```
---

root_password: >
    ENC[PKCS7,MIIBiQYJKoZIhvcNAQcDoIIBejCCAXYCAQAxggEhMIIBHQIBADADAFMAACAQEw
    DQYJKoZIhvcNAQEBBQAEggEALjJ2a9uZO4lk2V5xKqEd0n3BtA4OLe1B6rA2
    iVruJRKxWJdevuGvJ55DDedRwBMZmqbvSMO1cgMUyPbfEy54i3SXw4x3LEux
    c1R31ILoOspBgzU4OLuepCotuhBASA/pI/xu4Oy66AZAcCQ4CtD9SZJYjiWN
    tUA91rcARy/xYQGK39QievxT2eq5De89qIn2w/5fIRIkJBRyNqnwyYCWKcKS
    RwaiLbimpwmarOP+dxGHEFRrD/FiM4NfoV1WNNVr1UkPEFuNrWBzwBpvyZUn
    MbGHN676Rg5vq9sS6aWI6zPxTrJyLtssZm1f4GsfhmE+anFmuxrcWtEH6C82
    wKMOoTBMBgkqhkiG9w0BBwEwHQYJYIZIAWUDBAEqBBC3MhSP09yUw8XTj0Xd
    1G1VgCCDCGhqIFdUmORYK1q0Pn5CE/cDZKTO+bhHxdBw5amAGQ==]
```

However, `eyaml` has a very handy feature—the `edit` mode—allowing us to create and edit encrypted values in plain text, based on the keys stored in the `$HOME` directory:

```
$ eyaml edit hieradata/nodes/web.pomes.pro.eyaml
```

This command will launch an editor, and we just need to enter the following content:

```
---

root_password: >
  DEC::PKCS7[super_secure_password]!
```

While saving, `eyaml` will write the file with the encrypted content for `root_password`. If needed, we can edit the file again and all the encrypted values will be automatically decrypted.

 When editing with `eyaml edit`, all the new values should be contained in a `DEC::PKCS7[value]!` block. For existing values, `eyaml` will add an index called `num` to `DEC(<num>)::PKCS7[value]!` blocks. This index must remain unchanged.

As our last step, we need to modify the main manifest to do a Hiera lookup in order to get the password:

```
node 'web.pomes.pro' {
...
    $pass=hiera('root_password');
...
    class { 'mysql::server':
      root_password => $pass;
    }
...
}
```

Now the root password is encrypted in Hiera, and only people having the keys can recover it.

See also

- ▸ The `hiera-eyaml` GitHub repository with its documentation at `https://github.com/TomPoulton/hiera-eyaml`

- ▸ The `puppet-hiera` GitHub repository with its documentation at `https://github.com/voxpupuli/puppet-hiera`

Using Chef Vault encryption

A different way of encrypting data is proposed through Chef Vault, and this does not require you to include the key somewhere in the code. The concept is elegant and simple: shared key encryption is done for each and every existing Chef node through their already existing client keys. This way, only the nodes allowed to access the data can decrypt it—each with their own private key—ensuring no clear-text shared keys are being sent, like with the classic encrypted data bag scheme.

Getting ready

To step through this recipe, you will need:

- A working Chef DK installation on the workstation
- A working Vagrant installation on the workstation
- The Chef code (optionally) from *Chapter 6, Fundamentals of Managing Servers with Chef and Puppet, Chapter 7, Testing and Writing Better Infrastructure Code with Chef and Puppet*, or any custom Chef code

How to do it...

We'll build on the previous, already existing, `mysite` cookbook; however, any other situation will work similarly. Instead of using the `us-east-1` item from the `aws` data bag, let's create a new `eu-west-1` item, very similar to the other item for `us-east-1` in `data_bags/aws/eu-west-1.json`:

```
{
  "id": "eu-west-1",
  "aws_access_key": "an_access_key",
  "aws_secret_key": "a_secret_key"
}
```

As we know, the data will be encrypted for each and every running node's public key. It means we have to filter hosts based on a search. I propose, that you search for every node using `search(*:*)`; however, feel free to limit to whatever is more secure or appropriate for you, such as tags or roles, like `search(tags:aws)` or `search(role:mysite)`:

```
$ knife vault create aws eu-west-1 --json data_bags/aws/eu-west-1.json
--search "*:*" --mode "client"
```

 Don't forget the `--mode "client"` option when executing with a Chef server like we do!

Accessing the encrypted vault from a cookbook

The companion to `knife vault` is the `chef-vault` cookbook. We'll use it to easily access encrypted data in our recipe. If you're using Berkshelf to manage dependencies, don't forget to add the cookbook where required (either `metadata.rb` or `Berksfile`). In the `aws.rb` file, include the `chef-vault` recipe and set `aws` to the result of the `chef_vault_item` helper search:

```
include_recipe 'chef-vault'
aws = chef_vault_item('aws', 'eu-west-1')
```

If the node making the request isn't allowed to decrypt the data with its private key, we'll get an error. If the node can decrypt it, like we did previously with traditional data bags, the data will be available for use:

```
template "/etc/aws/credentials" do
  source 'aws.erb'
  owner 'root'
  group 'root'
  mode '0600'
  variables(
    aws_region: aws['id'],
    aws_access_key: aws['aws_access_key'],
    aws_secret_key: aws['aws_secret_key']
  )
end
```

In the end, the `/etc/aws/credentials` file is populated with valid unencrypted data:

```
$ sudo cat /etc/aws/credentials
[eu-west-1]
aws_access_key_id = an_access_key
aws_secret_access_key = a_secret_key
```

Using Chef Vault, no shared key has ever transited in clear text, and only filtered and existing nodes can decrypt data that has been encrypted specifically for them. Much more can be done with this tool!

See also

- ▶ The Chef Vault gem at `https://github.com/chef/chef-vault`
- ▶ The Chef Vault cookbook at `https://github.com/chef-cookbooks/chef-vault`

Accessing and manipulating system information with Ohai

A vast amount of information from a given system is available to Chef through Ohai. This program is executed during each Chef run and stores all of the gathered information in the Chef database to make it available right from the cookbooks. The kind of information gathered by default is quite large.

It ranges from networking details—such as link speed, MTU, or addresses—to all the memory usage details you'd find on a utility such as `top`, all of the imaginable data regarding filesystems or virtualization systems, or the list of every single installed package and logged-in users.

On top of this, Ohai is a modular system with a lot of community plugins to integrate Dell DRAC information with support information related to a KVM, LXC, or XenServer.

It can even be used to retrieve some specific data related to **Windows Management Instrumentation** (**WMI**). We obviously can write our own plugins, but that's way beyond the scope of this book.

Getting ready

To step through this recipe, you will need:

▸ A working Chef DK installation on the workstation

▸ A working Vagrant installation on the workstation

▸ The Chef code (optionally) from *Chapter 6*, *Fundamentals of Managing Servers with Chef and Puppet*, *Chapter 7*, *Testing and Writing Better Infrastructure Code with Chef and Puppet*, or any custom Chef code

How to do it...

In a fresh and minimal installation of a CentOS 7.2 virtual machine, the `ohai` output is 5,292 lines long, which is full of information. To see it bit by bit, refer to the following:

```
$ ohai | more
{
  "cpu": {
    "0": {
      "vendor_id": "GenuineIntel",
      "family": "6",
      "model": "69",
      "model_name": "Intel(R) Core(TM) i7-4578U CPU @ 3.00GHz",
      "stepping": "1",
      "mhz": "2999.991",
      "cache_size": "4096 KB",
      "physical_id": "0",
      "core_id": "0",
      "cores": "1",
```

Alternatively, another solution is to redirect its content to a file so it's easier to process with a dedicated tool:

```
$ ohai > ohai.json
```

All of this information is also graphically available on the Chef interface when you select a node in the **Attributes** tab:

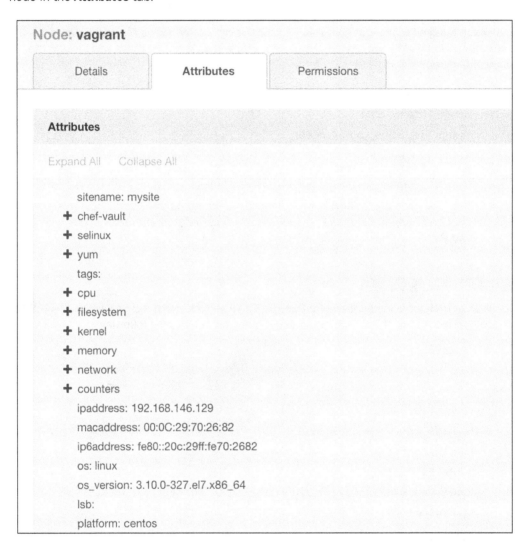

Accessing Ohai information from a Chef recipe

Now let's access this information from a recipe. We'd like an `index.html` page with some of this information, so let's edit the one we already have from the `apache` cookbook; however, you can start from scratch as well. We'd like this page to dynamically display something like this:

This centos 7.2.1511 linux system version 3.10.0-327.el7.x86_64 listening on 192.168.146.129 is up since 25 minutes 55 seconds

All the information we need is stored somewhere in ohai: `platform`, `platform_version`, `os`, `os_version`, `ipaddress`, or `uptime` are all valid values. Let's use them.

In `apache/templates/index.html.erb`, add the following:

```
This <%= node['platform'] %> <%= node['platform_version'] %> <%=
node['os'] %> system version <%= node['os_version'] %> listening on
<%= node['ipaddress'] %> is up since <%= node['uptime'] %>
```

To build something more interesting, as the platform name is available, let's make our `apache` cookbook a bit more portable across Linux distributions. When running on Ubuntu, install the `apache2` package; else, install the `httpd` package. (This will have to be more precise to handle all the real cases.) In the `apache::default` recipe, make the following change so the `httpd` variable is set to `apache2` when running Ubuntu and to the default `httpd` elsewhere:

```
if node['platform'] == 'ubuntu'
  httpd = 'apache2'
else
  httpd = 'httpd'
end

package httpd do
  action :install
end

service httpd do
  action [:enable, :start]
end
```

This is how we can start leveraging the use of the powerful `ohai` command in our Chef infrastructure.

There's more...

The counterpart for Puppet is `facter`, which is installed with the Puppet agent. Like `ohai`, `facter` is a command-line tool:

```
$ facter | more
aio_agent_version => 1.8.0
augeas => {
  version => "1.4.0"
}
disks => {
  sda => {
    model => "VBOX HARDDISK",
    size => "40.00 GiB",
    size_bytes => 42949672960,
    vendor => "ATA"
  }
}
dmi => {
  bios => {
    release_date => "12/01/2006",
    vendor => "innotek GmbH",
    version => "VirtualBox"
  },
  board => {
    manufacturer => "Oracle Corporation",
    product => "VirtualBox"
  },
...
```

As for Chef, the `facter` information can be accessed from a Puppet manifest. Such information in the Puppet world is named **facts**.

Starting from Puppet 4.x, facts can be accessed from manifests using the `$facts` hash. Let's try to create more portable lines of code for the `apache` module:

```
if $facts['os']['family'] == 'debian' {
  $packagename='apache2'
} else {
  $packagename='httpd'
```

```
}

package{'apache2':
  ensure => present,
  name    => $packagename,
}

service{'apache2':
  ensure => running,
  enable => true,
  name    => $packagename,
}
```

 You may find pieces of codes that are accessing facts using variables, such as $osfamily instead of $facts['os']['family']. This method works with previous versions of Puppet, but it is not obvious here that a fact is being used.

See also

▸ Ohai plugins at `https://docs.chef.io/plugin_community.html#ohai`

▸ Ohai documentation at `https://docs.chef.io/ohai.html`

▸ Puppet facts at `https://docs.puppet.com/puppet/4.8/lang_facts_and_builtin_vars.html`

Automating application deployment (a WordPress example)

Chef can also be used to deploy applications from code repositories. It combines one of the most complete, feature rich, and complicated Chef resources available—the `deploy` resource—and the various powerful and popular cookbooks, such as the `database` cookbook. We'll show you how to deploy a simple WordPress application right from the GitHub repository, creating a dedicated database and user as well as all the required dependencies. This builds on what has already been done previously, but the resources and cookbook shown here are made to be reusable anywhere.

Getting ready

To step through this recipe, you will need:

▸ A working Chef DK installation on the workstation

▸ A working Vagrant installation on the workstation

▸ The Chef code (optionally) from *Chapter 6, Fundamentals of Managing Servers with Chef and Puppet, Chapter 7, Testing and Writing Better Infrastructure Code with Chef and Puppet*, or any custom Chef code

How to do it...

As we're going to deploy an application for MySite (maybe an engineering blog for the MySite company), let's call this recipe `mysite::deploy`. Create the recipe like this from `chef-repo`:

```
$ chef generate recipe cookbooks/mysite deploy
```

Our next steps will be to include the Apache and MySQL dependencies, configure everything on MySQL so that WordPress can be installed, and finally deploy the WordPress code from GitHub.

Including dependencies

A WordPress installation needs at least an HTTP server and a database. Start by including the known dependencies to the service we already have: an Apache virtual host and MySQL. Include them in `deploy.rb`:

```
include_recipe 'apache::virtualhost'
include_recipe 'mysite::mysql'
```

Creating the application's database

Before we deploy anything, we need to create a database on our already running MySQL server with a dedicated WordPress user. There's a wonderful cookbook meant just for this: the `database` cookbook. We'll reuse this one very often. It gives access to many helpers for most use cases and most types of databases. According to the documentation, we'll need to deploy a gem named `mysql2_chef_gem`, which fortunately comes with a dedicated cookbook as well. And finally, as we're using MySQL, let's make sure we depend on its official cookbook. Let's include all of this information in our `mysite` cookbook's `metadata.rb`:

```
depends 'database'
depends 'mysql2_chef_gem', '~> 1.1'
depends 'mysql', '~> 8.1'
```

To build the `mysql2` gem using the cookbook's new `mysql2_chef_gem` resource, we'll need the MySQL development package named `mysql-community-devel`. Let's add the following to our `deploy.rb` recipe:

```
package 'mysql-community-devel'

mysql2_chef_gem 'default' do
  action :install
end
```

The database cookbook created, among others, two useful resources for us: `mysql_database` and `mysql_database_user`. As we can guess by their names, they respectively help create MySQL databases and MySQL users. Let's create the MySQL connection information variable so it can be reused in our two resources:

```
mysql_connection_info = {
  host: '127.0.0.1',
  username: 'root',
  password: 'super_secure_password'
}
```

 In a proper `production` environment, we should use encrypted data bags for this matter, as seen in this chapter. We're trying to keep the code simple here.

Now we can create our database named `wordpress` using the `mysql_database` resource:

```
mysql_database 'wordpress' do
  connection  mysql_connection_info
  action      :create
end
```

Also, create a `wordpress_user` MySQL user with the password `changeme`. This will create the user and grant all the privileges to it:

```
mysql_database_user 'wordpress_user' do
  connection     mysql_connection_info
  password       'changeme'
  database_name  'wordpress'
  host           '%'
  privileges     [:all]
  action         [:create, :grant]
end
```

At this point, we should have everything we need related to the database.

Deploying an application from git or GitHub

Now on to application deployment! We know we want to deploy from `git`. Let's make sure `git` is installed:

```
package 'git'
```

The `deploy_revision` resource is the most complex of all. It has a multitude of options, and a full chapter about it wouldn't be enough. Let's keep it simple here and refer to the complete online documentation for more complex uses. Let's keep it simple here, and please refer to the very complete online documentation for more complex uses—because this resource is absolutely powerful and does wonders when properly manipulated. We know the following:

- ▶ Our code is available at `https://github.com/WordPress/WordPress`
- ▶ We want to try the latest revision (`HEAD`) and keep the last five revisions to allow rollbacks
- ▶ Our HTTP web server runs under the `apache` user
- ▶ The virtual host folder is inherited from an attribute set earlier (`/var/www/#{node['sitename']}`)
- ▶ There's no database migrations to execute with WordPress

The `deploy_revision` resource is modeled after Capistrano and therefore comes from the Ruby on Rails world. But the concepts still apply to most languages, and it's a good practice in production to create shared folders and symlinks for long-lasting configurations and files. It includes certificates, database configuration files, local assets, and so on. However, to keep the current deployment simple, we won't use these right now, even though you'll probably start looking into it as soon as you'll need it. We'll include the symlinks configuration and initialize them to nothing so the code is already present when the time arises. Here's how all this ties together:

```
deploy_revision 'wordpress' do
  repo 'https://github.com/WordPress/WordPress'
  revision 'HEAD'
  user 'apache'
  deploy_to "/var/www/#{node['sitename']}"
  keep_releases 5
  symlinks({})
  symlink_before_migrate({})
  migrate false
  action :deploy
end
```

Once the code is applied, the `/var/www/mysite` (or whatever name you may have overridden) structure will change a little:

```
$ ls /var/www/mysite/
current  index.html  releases  shared
```

There's a `current`, `releases`, and `shared` folder. The `shared` folder contains everything that will last through the releases, including a cached copy of the current code. The `releases` folder contains all the stored releases. The `current` folder is itself a symlink to a specific release, which is the git commit SHA on GitHub (`72606bed348e61b6f98318cf920684765aa08b37`). Each subsequent release will be identified by its SHA indicating its unique identification and symlinked to `current` at the end of the deployment process. The number of kept releases is set by the `keep_releases` integer:

```
$ ls -ld /var/www/mysite/current
```

```
lrwxrwxrwx. 1 apache root 65 Nov 17 02:18 /var/www/mysite/current -> /var/www/mysite/releases/72606bed348e61b6f98318cf920684765aa08b37
```

Once this code is applied to our node, if we navigate to `http://<node_ip>/current/`, we'll see the WordPress setup page:

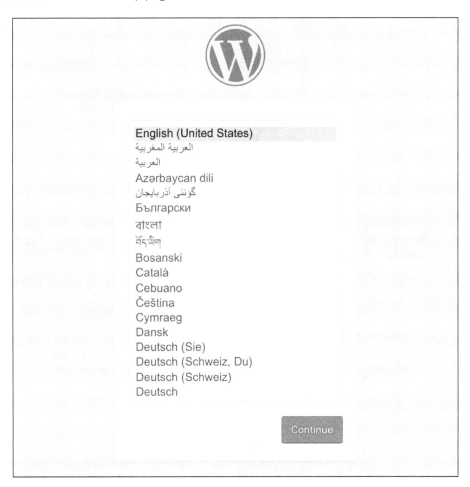

To check whether the connection to the database is working correctly, type in all of the information from our Chef code:

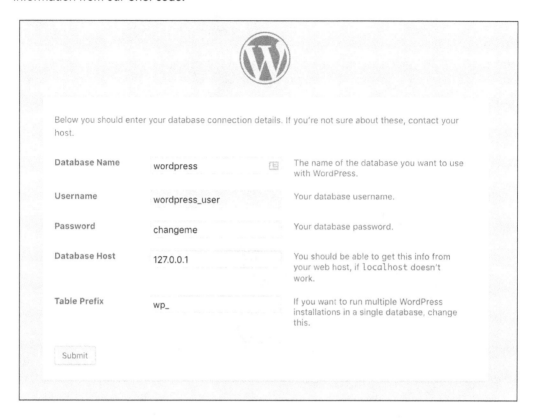

And, job done! The WordPress installer says, **All right, sparky! You've made it through this part of the installation. WordPress can now communicate with your database. If you are ready, time now to... run the installer!**.

We're now basically able to deploy any WordPress installation from scratch, at will, and in seconds, again and again.

Let's insist again:
Once you're comfortable with this, refer to the deploy resource documentation to discover everything this resource has to offer. It works wonders.

There's more...

With Puppet, there is no deploy resource. However, Puppet Labs is providing a useful module—vcsrepo. With this module, we will be able to deploy a WordPress site from git.

Let's reuse our Vagrant LAMP example in *Chapter 6, Fundamentals of Managing Servers with Chef and Puppet.* We just need to add the `vcsrepo` module to `Puppetfile` (do not forget to run `r10k puppetfile install`):

```
mod 'puppetlabs/vcsrepo', '1.4.0'
```

Now we are ready to modify the main manifest of the box, namely `web.pomes.pro`, to include the WordPress deployment. First, install the `git` package:

```
package {'git':
  ensure => installed,
}
```

Then, create a database for WordPress:

```
mysql::db {'wordpress':
  user     => 'wordpress_user',
  password => 'changeme',
  host     => '%',
  grant    => 'ALL',
}
```

Also, update our virtual definition to change `DocumentRoot`:

```
apache::vhost { 'web.pomes.pro':
  website => 'web.pomes.pro',
  docroot => '/var/www/wordpress',
}
```

And finally, install WordPress from `git` and give rights to Apache:

```
vcsrepo {'/var/www/wordpress':
  ensure   => latest,
  provider => git,
  source   => 'https://github.com/WordPress/WordPress',
  revision => 'master',
}

file {'/var/www/wordpress':
  ensure  => directory,
  owner   => 'www-data',
  group   => 'www-data',
  recurse => true,
}
```

See also

- The `deploy` resource documentation at `https://docs.chef.io/resource_deploy.html`
- The PuppetLabs `vcsrepo` module at `https://forge.puppet.com/puppetlabs/vcsrepo`
- The WordPress hardening guide at `https://codex.wordpress.org/Hardening_WordPress`

Using a TDD workflow

TDD is a popular technique in development teams that consists of this: you begin by writing tests that will fail because no code is actually written and then write the code that will make these tests pass. This way, we ensure that the code we write is already tested, that it really covers the tested area; if some regression was to happen someday, it would be immediately noticed. Here, we'll show a whole workflow, from development to production, where we deploy Docker on CentOS 7 and Ubuntu 16.04 using the TDD technique. Using Git branches, Chef tools, Test Kitchen, linting, and ServerSpec, we'll go through each and every step of a small project led by TDD principles. We'll do this to achieve maximum code quality among teams, from the development phase in the beginning to the final production environment.

Getting ready

To step through this recipe, you will need:

- A working Chef DK installation on the workstation
- A working Vagrant installation on the workstation
- The Chef code (optionally) from *Chapter 6*, *Fundamentals of Managing Servers with Chef and Puppet*, *Chapter 7*, *Testing and Writing Better Infrastructure Code with Chef and Puppet*, or any custom Chef code

How to do it...

Our goal is to start a new platform based on Docker. To do this, follow these steps:

1. Start by creating the `platform` cookbook:

   ```
   $ cd chef-repo
   $ chef generate cookbook cookbooks/platform
   ```

2. Now create the empty `platform::docker` recipe:

   ```
   $ chef generate recipe cookbooks/platform docker
   ```

3. Initialize a `git` repo if it's not already done:

   ```
   $ git init
   ```

4. Add and commit whatever work is in the repository right now, if any:

   ```
   $ git add .
   $ git commit -m "initial chef repo state"
   ```

5. Create a feature branch for we're about to work on supporting `docker` in our platform:

   ```
   $ git checkout -b docker_support
   ```

Infrastructure TDD – writing tests first

Let's write our tests first so they will fail for sure, and we'll know we're building from there correctly.

Create the ServerSpec integration folder inside the platform cookbook:

```
$ mkdir -p test/integration/default/serverspec
```

Create `.kitchen.yml` at the root of the `platform` cookbook file with the following content. We'll use Vagrant and simulate a Chef server with the `chef_zero` provisioner. We'd like our platform to work on both Ubuntu 16.04 and CentOS 7.2, and we want the entry point for our cookbook as its default recipe:

```
---
driver:
  name: vagrant

provisioner:
  name: chef_zero
  always_update_cookbooks: true

platforms:
  - name: centos-7.2

suites:
  - name: default
    run_list:
      - recipe[platform::default]
    attributes:
```

As we've seen earlier in this book, create a helper script in the `serverspec` folder named `spec_helper.rb`:

```
require 'serverspec'
# Required by serverspec
set :backend, :exec
```

Let's start our test and see what is it we want to do according to our needs:

- We want the `docker-engine` package to be installed
- We want the `docker` service to be enabled and started
- We want a specific `docker` image to be pulled (that is, `sjourdan/terraform:0.7.10`)

let's write these tests in `docker_spec.rb`, in the `serverspec` folder:

```
require 'spec_helper'

describe package('docker-engine') do
  it { should be_installed }
end

describe service('docker') do
  it { should be_enabled }
  it { should be_running }
end

describe command('docker images') do
  its(:exit_status) { should eq 0 }
  its(:stdout) { should match(%r{^sjourdan/terraform\s.*0.7.10}) }
end
```

This is good enough for our needs! Let's launch our test environment by firing up `kitchen`:

```
$ kitchen create
$ kitchen converge
$ kitchen verify
[...]
        Package "docker-engine"
          should be installed (FAILED - 1)

        Service "docker"
          should be enabled (FAILED - 2)
          should be running (FAILED - 3)

        Command "docker images"
          exit_status
```

```
        should eq 0 (FAILED - 4)
    stdout
        should match /^sjourdan\/terraform\s.*0.7.10/ (FAILED - 5)
[...]
```

We've failed successfully! Docker is neither installed, enabled, nor started, and no `docker` image is there.

Let's get to work.

Deploying Docker with Chef

There's a very nice cookbook, which is extremely well-documented, that does everything we need (`https://github.com/chef-cookbooks/docker`). Let's add it to `metadata.rb` so we depend on it:

```
depends 'docker', '~> 2.0'
```

Add it to Berkshelf as well if you plan to use it in `Berksfile`:

```
cookbook 'docker', '~> 2.0'
```

As we'll be writing our Docker code in the `platform::docker` recipe, let's start by including it in the `default.rb` recipe:

```
include_recipe 'platform::docker'
```

The `docker` cookbook provides us with a new resource named `docker_installation` that does just this: install `docker`. There's a myriad of installation options you can toy around with. Let's keep it simple and install the current stable Docker version from Docker repositories (not from our Linux distribution). Add the following to the `docker.rb` recipe:

```
docker_installation 'default' do
  repo 'main'
  action :create
end
```

Execute `kitchen` again to apply our code and see whether the tests are passing or failing:

```
$ kitchen converge
$ kitchen verify
[...]
        Package "docker-engine"
          should be installed
[...]
        Finished in 0.18797 seconds (files took 0.43908 seconds to load)
        5 examples, 4 failures
```

Good! What was failing a few minutes ago is now passing. It proves our action has fixed the problem, and we're on the right track. However, other tests are still failing, though.

Let's create the Docker service and start it using the `docker_service` resource the cookbook is offering us:

```
docker_service 'default' do
  action [:create, :start]
end
```

Execute `kitchen` again to apply our code and see what the tests say:

```
$ kitchen converge
$ kitchen verify
[...]
        Package "docker-engine"
          should be installed

        Service "docker"
          should be enabled
          should be running
[...]
        Finished in 0.12301 seconds (files took 0.28237 seconds to load)
        5 examples, 1 failure
```

Good! The service is now tested and enabled and it is running. Let's add this little requirement to have an image pulled right from the beginning, and we've chosen the Docker image `sjourdan/terraform` in its version 0.7.10:

```
docker_image 'sjourdan/terraform' do
  tag '0.7.10'
  action :pull
end
```

Execute `kitchen` again to apply our new code and check whether the tests pass:

```
$ kitchen converge
$ kitchen verify
[...]
        Finished in 0.23526 seconds (files took 0.44015 seconds to load)
        5 examples, 0 failures
```

Our code seems to do exactly what our tests expected! Let's destroy our testing environment:

```
$ kitchen destroy
```

Linting the code

Let's not forget to check how clean our code is with `cookstyle` from inside the `platform` cookbook:

```
$ cookstyle
Inspecting 6 files
......

6 files inspected, no offenses detected
```

No offenses! Our code is clean. Let's move on.

Supporting another platform

Let's check whether this code would work on Ubuntu 16.04 as well. Wouldn't it be awesome to have it working on both the current platforms with long-term support? Simply add the platform to the cookbook's `kitchen.yml` file:

```
    - name: ubuntu-16.04
```

Launch `kitchen` again and check whether it works with Ubuntu 16.04 as well:

```
$ kitchen test
[...]

        Package "docker-engine"
          should be installed

        Service "docker"
          should be enabled
          should be running

        Command "docker images"
          exit_status
            should eq 0
          stdout
            should match /^sjourdan\/terraform\s.*0.7.10/

        Finished in 0.27516 seconds (files took 0.43079 seconds to load)
        5 examples, 0 failures

        Finished verifying <default-ubuntu-1604> (5m9.12s).
```

We're now sure that our code supports Ubuntu 16.04 as well!

Team working using Chef and git

Now that our `platform` cookbook works pretty well in our `docker_support` git branch, let's commit that work. Start by verifying what's not tracked:

```
$ git status
On branch docker_support
Untracked files:
  (use "git add <file>..." to include in what will be committed)


        cookbooks/platform/
```

Commit that work:

```
$ git add cookbooks/platform
$ git commit -m "added docker support to the platform"
```

Is our `git` tree clean so that we can ship it to our team? Check this using the following code:

```
$ git status
On branch docker_support
nothing to commit, working tree clean
```

Then, let's push it to our `git` repository (supposedly GitHub, but it might be anything):

```
$ git push
```

Now one of our coworkers can peer review the code and eventually merge `docker_support` with the `master` branch:

```
$ git merge docker_support master
```

Our new cookbook is now ready for prime time and can be deployed to staging.

> In a more complex setup, it's highly recommended that you run those integration tests in a continuous integration system, such as Jenkins. These systems can integrate very well with services such as GitHub or GitLab and launch tests automatically after a push or pull request. This is an added value, ensuring quality in the process before shipping.

Deploying to staging

Now let's deploy this new platform cookbook to our staging environment. Let's begin by making sure we have all the required cookbook dependencies:

```
$ cd cookbooks/platform
$ berks
```

Then, upload all the required cookbooks:

```
$ berks upload
```

Use already existing environments, such as `staging`, and add our new `platform` cookbook version constraint to `environments/staging.rb` or any similar environment you're using:

```
name 'staging'
description 'The staging environment'
cookbook_versions  'platform' => '= 0.1.0'
```

Update that environment using the `knife` command:

```
$ knife environment from file environments/staging.rb
Updated Environment staging
```

Check this code into `git`:

```
$ git add .
$ git commit -m "added platform::docker to staging"
```

Add the platform cookbook to the target node's run_list:

```
$ knife node run_list add my_node_name 'recipe[platform]'
```

Wait for the next Chef run or run it yourself and Docker will be available on any node, including this recipe.

Deploying to production

Deploying to production at this stage is totally similar to shipping to staging; there's no difference. The `environments/production.rb` file should now look like this:

```
name 'production'
description 'The production environment'
cookbook_versions  'platform' => '= 0.1.0'
```

Don't forget to upload it to the Chef server:

```
$ knife environment from file environments/production.rb
Updated Environment production
```

Commit the changes to `git`:

```
$ git add .
$ git commit -m "updated production env with platform::docker"
```

Wait for the next Chef run or execute it yourself, and from now on, we'll have a nice four-step workflow:

1. Storing the TDD infrastructure code locally
2. Peer reviewing and merging
3. Deployment to staging
4. Deployment to production

Now, each time we're interested in testing or staging a new version of the cookbook that has passed steps 1 and 2, we just bump the cookbook's version number constraint, validating the results in the staging environment without impacting production, and finally deploy it in production whenever possible.

There's more...

With Puppet, the same logic applies. In *Chapter 7, Testing and Writing Better Infrastructure Code with Chef and Puppet*, we introduced Beaker as an acceptance test tool. In a TDD workflow, we can first write acceptance tests in the `specs/acceptance` subdirectory of any module and then write the code itself.

Using multiple `nodesets`, we can also ensure tests can be validated on multiple platforms. In *Chapter 7, Testing and Writing Better Infrastructure Code with Chef and Puppet*, we used only one platform (Ubuntu) in `spec/acceptance/nodesets/default.yml`. However, we can create as many as needed. Here is an example of a CentOS node that should be defined in `spec/acceptance/nodesets/centos-7-x64.yml`:

```
HOSTS:
  centos-7-x64:
    roles:
      - agent
      - default
    platform: redhat-7-x86_64
    hypervisor: vagrant
    box: puppetlabs/centos-7.2-64-nocm
CONFIG:
  type: foss
```

Using the environment variable `BEAKER_set`, it is then possible to specify on which platform the test needs to be run:

```
$ BEAKER_set=centos-7-x64 rake beaker
```

And using git and r10k, the same team workflow applies. We first develop in a `test` branch. When all the tests have passed successfully, we merge them into the `production` branch and use r10k to deploy the code.

See also

▶ The Docker chef cookbook at `https://github.com/chef-cookbooks/docker`

Planning for the worse – train to rebuild working systems

It's one thing to get a full infrastructure finally managed by Chef—block by block, weeks after weeks, modification after modification—keeping the Chef run always smooth and working. However, it's something quite different to be able to rebootstrap a working system from scratch. What if the current setup that works perfectly well is in fact working because there's a script or a binary somewhere left from last year, which does the thing that makes it work? What if the application servers get corrupted tonight? If this happens, will we be able to rebuild it from scratch? If tomorrow our IaaS cloud provider crashes, in what timeframe will we be able to rebuild systems somewhere else (provided the backups are working; well, that's another story)?

Now our systems are as much as possible automated, hopefully 100 percent. It's important to know whether we'd be able to fully rebootstrap these systems in case of a disaster; if yes, how long it would take. You may be surprised when you collect some data and discover that many systems can be recovered in minutes. Compare this with the time it might take to find an outdated documentation, apply untested manual processes, and finally do whatever it takes to get something up and running under the pressure of an emergency. We'll all spend better nights and weekends if we know that all the system profiles are being continuously rebootstrapped successfully; in fact, why not use the CI system every night so every morning we would know whether the previous day's changes have impacted something. We, as a team, always know that we're ready to redeploy a system if required.

Getting ready

To step through this recipe, you will need:

▶ A working Chef DK installation on the workstation

▶ A working Vagrant installation on the workstation

▶ The Chef code (optionally) from *Chapter 6*, *Fundamentals of Managing Servers with Chef and Puppet*, *Chapter 7*, *Testing and Writing Better Infrastructure Code with Chef and Puppet*, or any custom Chef code

How to do it...

There is no single way to achieve our goal. We've already covered Test Kitchen, and this might be a good solution, especially if we have written extensive tests. Integrate this in the company's **Continuous Integration** (**CI**) system and this will do the job.

A simpler and quicker solution can also be to just launch Vagrant boxes with the right Chef-provisioning profiles for each use case: `docker`, `webserver`, database server, or full deployment.

 Refer to the Vagrant chapter of this book for more information about the Vagrant tool!

Our production servers are configured by the application of some Chef code, and currently, it does this job pretty well. Are we able to easily rebootstrap a similar CentOS 7.2 server from scratch to the point that it is similarly installed without any Chef or system error? Let's find this out by including `Vagrantfile` at the root of the infrastructure repository, using the previous project code for deploying Docker (but the idea is the same for any kind of Chef repo). The minimum we can do is boot a fresh CentOS 7.2:

```
Vagrant.configure("2") do |config|
  config.vm.box = "bento/centos-7.2"
end
```

We'd like to automatically install Chef on our temporary node, so let's use the `vagrant-omnibus` plugin (remember, installing it is easy: `vagrant plugin install vagrant-omnibus`). Here's the code to do this:

```
config.omnibus.chef_version = :latest
```

Let's configure the Vagrant provisioning system to use Chef Zero in order to simulate a Chef server. We can also directly use a real Chef server; if we have one behind the firewall, it can be handy. We have to specify where is everything placed (cookbooks, environments, roles, and so on) with the added subtlety of a `nodes` folder that will be left empty in our case. Our virtual machine will run in the `production` environment and apply the `docker` role:

```
config.vm.provision "chef_zero" do |chef|
  chef.cookbooks_path = "cookbooks"
  chef.environments_path = "environments"
  chef.roles_path = "roles"
  chef.nodes_path = "nodes"
  chef.environment = "production"
  chef.add_role "docker"
end
```

We're almost done! We need to tell the Vagrant Berkshelf plugin where to look for `Berksfile` and whether to enable it (installing the Berkshelf plugin is easy: `vagrant plugin install vagrant-berkshelf`). Here's the code to do this:

```
config.berkshelf.berksfile_path = "cookbooks/platform/Berksfile"
config.berkshelf.enabled = true
```

Starting Vagrant at this point will just deploy everything from scratch:

```
$ vagrant up
[...]
# Chef Client finished, 17/45 resources updated in 03 minutes 30 seconds
```

If the run succeeds, meaning the code from the Docker role is applied, we're safe. Let's destroy the VM:

```
$ vagrant destroy -f
```

Including this Vagrant command in our CI system will ensure this particular role will run flawlessly in this particular environment and with this particular system, and that potentially, it's a matter of three minutes and 30 seconds to recover from nothing to a working state.

Multi-machine recovery

Let's move to a more complicated setup. Vagrant supports multi-machine setups, letting us define profiles for each one of them. In a previous example of this chapter, we deployed a WordPress installation with a database configured and the Apache web server configured as well, all with encrypted data bags and templates. We'll implement the same idea, except that `Vagrantfile` will include multiple machine profiles: one to start a virtual machine only with the `webserver` role, another to deploy only the database part, and the third one to launch everything together, including the web application. So we'll make sure all the parts of the final product can be redeployed from scratch (which is the main point).

All VM definitions will live inside the main Vagrant configuration:

```
Vagrant.configure('2') do |config|
  config.vm.define 'whatever_vm', autostart: false do |node|
    [...]
  end
end
```

 We suggest disabling the automatic start of VMs so we don't make the mistake of launching dozens of VMs by error.

To make sure our code is capable of bootstrapping only the webserver role from scratch, we will need to do the following—setting paths for everything, including the specific Berksfile for the job:

```
config.vm.define 'webserver', autostart: false do |ws|
  ws.vm.box = 'bento/centos-7.2'

  ws.vm.provision :chef_zero do |chef|
    chef.cookbooks_path = 'cookbooks'
    chef.environments_path = 'environments'
    chef.roles_path = 'roles'
    chef.nodes_path = 'nodes'
    chef.environment = 'production'
    chef.add_role 'webserver'
  end

  ws.berkshelf.berksfile_path = 'cookbooks/apache/Berksfile'
  ws.berkshelf.enabled = true
end
```

To launch only this box in order to make sure the webserver role can be deployed from scratch, use the following command:

```
$ vagrant up webserver
```

To make sure our code is capable of bootstrapping only the database part of this platform from scratch, just execute the mysite::mysql recipe in a similar context:

```
config.vm.define 'db', autostart: false do |db|
  db.vm.box = 'bento/centos-7.2'

  db.vm.provision :chef_zero do |chef|
    chef.cookbooks_path = 'cookbooks'
    chef.environments_path = 'environments'
    chef.roles_path = 'roles'
    chef.nodes_path = 'nodes'
    chef.environment = 'production'
    chef.add_recipe 'mysite::mysql'
  end

  db.berkshelf.berksfile_path = 'cookbooks/mysite/Berksfile'
  db.berkshelf.enabled = true
end
```

To launch only this box in order to make sure the database recipe can be deployed from scratch, use the following command:

```
$ vagrant up db
[...]
Chef Client finished, 29/43 resources updated in 01 minutes 28 seconds
```

To make sure our code is capable of bootstrapping the whole platform from scratch, we'll have to simply execute the whole `mysite::default` recipe with one more step. One of the included recipes uses an encrypted data bag. It's stored encrypted on the Chef server, but locally, our `./data_bags/` directory currently includes only the unencrypted JSON versions. We have to make sure another folder hosts the encrypted versions (maybe you already have one to store them on GitHub for example). Otherwise, import the encrypted version from the Chef server to a new directory, say, in JSON (using `-Fj`):

```
$ mkdir data_bags_encrypted
$ knife data bag show aws us-east-1 -Fj > data_bags_encrypted/us-east-1.json
```

Now we can define the full VM like the others with the modified data bag path for the encrypted version:

```
config.vm.define 'mysite', autostart: false do |mysite|
  mysite.vm.box = 'bento/centos-7.2'

  mysite.vm.provision :chef_zero do |chef|
    chef.cookbooks_path = 'cookbooks'
    chef.environments_path = 'environments'
    chef.data_bags_path = 'data_bags_encrypted'
    chef.roles_path = 'roles'
    chef.nodes_path = 'nodes'
    chef.environment = 'production'
    chef.add_recipe 'mysite::default'
  end

  mysite.berkshelf.berksfile_path = 'cookbooks/mysite/Berksfile'
  mysite.berkshelf.enabled = true
end
```

To launch only this box in order to make sure the whole recipe is deployed from scratch, use the following command:

```
$ vagrant up mysite
```

Put these commands (with their destroy counterparts) in the CI or whatever system you prefer at a regular interval, like daily or weekly, for each and every automated part of the infrastructure. With this, you'll always be certain you can redeploy the system when a disaster comes.

There's more...

Using Puppet, all the examples we used were based on Vagrant, and it is easy to rebuild nodes from scratch. But, in the real word, you probably won't deploy and maintain a production system running from Vagrant on your workstation.

However, these examples show that it is possible to simulate a complete infrastructure using a simple `vagrant up` command, and therefore, it is easy to put it into any CI system to ensure you will be able to rebuild your production system easily.

9
Working with Docker

In this chapter, we will cover the following recipes:

- Docker usage overview
- Choosing the right Docker base image
- Optimizing the Docker image size
- Versioning Docker images with tags
- Deploying a Ruby-on-Rails web application in Docker
- Building and using Golang applications with Docker
- Networking with Docker
- Creating more dynamic containers
- Auto-configuring dynamic containers
- Better security with unprivileged users
- Orchestrating with Docker Compose
- Linting a Dockerfile
- Deploying a private Docker registry with S3 storage

Introduction

In this chapter, we'll discover the best bits of using Docker in a development environment: from Docker image optimizations to versioning, security, and networking, tips on how to choose the right base Docker image and how to make them dynamic and self-configurable, and how to leverage Docker to cross-compile Go programs or deploy Ruby-on-Rails web applications. Still with a focus on developers and achieving the highest code quality possible, we'll spend some time linting our code, and finally deploy our own Docker Registry to store our own images internally—both on local storage and on AWS S3 for infinite space.

Docker usage overview

This section is an introduction to Docker for newcomers, and can be used as a refresher for others. We'll see how to quickly use Docker to achieve some tasks such as executing an Ubuntu container or networked webserver, sharing data with a container, building an image, and accessing a registry other than the default one.

Getting ready

To step through this recipe, you will need a working Docker installation.

How to do it...

We'll quickly manipulate Docker, so we're up and running with some basic usage.

Running Bash in an Ubuntu 16.04 container

To execute /bin/bash in an Ubuntu container, tag 16.04 (ubuntu:16.04). Our environment will be interactive (use -i) and we want a pseudo-terminal to be allocated (use -t). We want the container to be destroyed afterwards (use --rm):

```
$ docker run -it --rm ubuntu:16.04 /bin/bash
root@d372dba0ab90:/# hostname
d372dba0ab90
```

We've run our first container! Now do whatever you want with it. Quitting it destroys it and its content is lost forever as we specified the --rm option.

Running Nginx in a container

Nginx is officially packaged as a Docker container. We want to access port 80 from the container on port 80 of our host using the -p option, with the latest Nginx version available:

```
$ docker run --rm -p 80:80 nginx
```

Make some HTTP requests such as a curl:

```
$ curl -IL http://localhost
HTTP/1.1 200 OK
Server: nginx/1.11.5
[...]
```

The logs on the Docker stdout are displaying the logs as follows:

```
172.17.0.1 - - [21/Nov/2016:21:21:15 +0000] "HEAD / HTTP/1.1" 200 0
"-" "curl/7.43.0" "-"
```

Maybe for some reason we need to launch a specific Nginx version, like this:

```
$ docker run --rm -p 80:80 nginx:1.10
```

The HTTP headers will reflect that we're now running the current stable version:

```
$ curl -IL http://localhost
HTTP/1.1 200 OK
Server: nginx/1.10.2
```

Sharing data with a container

We want our own content to be displayed instead of the default Nginx page. Let's create an index.html file in the www directory, with some custom content such as the following:

```
<html>
  <h1>Hello from Docker!</h1>
</html>
```

Nginx is serving content by default in /usr/share/nginx/html; let's use the -v option to share our own directory with the container:

```
$ docker run --rm -p 80:80 -v ${PWD}/www:/usr/share/nginx/html
nginx:1.10
```

Let's see our new content served:

```
$ curl -L http://localhost
<html>
  <h1>Hello from Docker!</h1>
</html>
```

Building a container with utilities

Let's create our own Ubuntu 16.04 image with some utilities such as curl, dig, and netcat in it, so that whatever machine we're using, we can always have our tools at hand. To build our container, we need a file named Dockerfile, acting like a script, executed line by line, to build the final container. We know we want to start from an Ubuntu 16.04, then update the APT base, and finally install our utilities. Let's do just that using the FROM and RUN instructions:

```
FROM ubuntu:16.04
RUN apt-get -yq update
RUN apt-get install -yq dnsutils curl netcat
```

Now build using the `docker build` command, passing it the name of the container with the
`-t` option:

```
$ docker build -t utils .
Step 1 : FROM ubuntu:16.04
 ---> 2fa927b5cdd3
Step 2 : RUN apt-get update -yq
 ---> Running in 0d8f8e01bde8
[...]
Step 3 : RUN apt-get install ruby -yq
 ---> Running in 425bfb1e8ee1
[...]
Removing intermediate container 425bfb1e8ee1
Successfully built c86310e48731
```

We can see each line of our `Dockerfile` is a *step* in the build process, each step being a
container itself (hence the different ID each time).

Let's now execute our container to make a DNS request using `dig`:

```
$ docker run -it --rm utils dig +short google.com
172.217.5.14
```

Alternatively, we may use `curl` as follows:

```
$ docker run -it --rm utils curl -I google.com
HTTP/1.1 302 Found
Cache-Control: private
Content-Type: text/html; charset=UTF-8
Location: http://www.google.ca/?gfe_rd=cr&ei=UgA1VMLPRUvF9gfJ_riACg
Content-Length: 258
Date: Wed, 23 Nov 2016 02:34:58 GMT
```

Using a private registry

When not specifying anything else than the container name, Docker is looking for it locally,
then on Docker Hub (`https://hub.docker.com`). However, we can run our own registry
or use an alternative registry such as `https://quay.io/`. Here's how it works: instead of
specifying only the container name, or the combo `username/container_name`, we prefix
both by the DNS name of the registry, for example, `https://quay.io/`. Here, we'll launch
the HTTP/2 Caddy webserver hosted in the CoreOS account on the Quay.io registry:

```
$ docker run -it --rm -p 80:2015 quay.io/coreos/caddy
Activating privacy features... done.
http://0.0.0.0:2015
```

Here's for this quick introduction on how to use Docker.

See also

- ▸ Docker run reference: https://docs.docker.com/engine/reference/run/
- ▸ Dockerfile reference: https://docs.docker.com/engine/reference/builder/
- ▸ Quay.io alternative registry: https://quay.io/
- ▸ Docker Hub: https://hub.docker.com/
- ▸ Docker Store: https://store.docker.com/

Choosing the right Docker base image

Depending on our end goal, using the image of our favorite Linux distribution might or might not be the best solution. Starting with a full CentOS container image might be a waste of resources, while an Alpine Linux image might not contain the most complete libc for our usage. In other cases, using the image from our favorite programming language might also be a good idea, or not. Let's see this in depth and learn when to choose what source.

Getting ready

To step through this recipe, you will need a working Docker installation.

How to do it...

Most common distributions are available as a container form.

Starting from an Ubuntu image

Ubuntu ships official images that are all tagged with both their release version and name: `ubuntu:16.04` is equivalent to `ubuntu:xenial`. At the time of writing, the supported Ubuntu releases are 12.04 (precise), 14.04 (trusty), 16.04 (xenial), and 16.10 (yakkety).

To start with an Ubuntu image in a Dockerfile, execute the following:

```
FROM ubuntu:16.04
ENTRYPOINT ["/bin/bash"]
```

Starting from a CentOS image

The CentOS team ships official container images, all tagged with versions. It's highly recommended that you stick with the *rolling builds* that are continuously updated because these are tagged only with major versions such as `centos:7`. At the time of writing, the supported CentOS releases are CentOS 7, 6, and 5. If for some compliance reason we were to use a specific CentOS 7 release, specific tags such as `centos:7.3.1611`, `centos:7.2.1511`, `centos:7.1.1503`, and `centos:7.0.1406` are available.

To start with the latest CentOS 7 available, in a Dockerfile execute the following:

```
FROM centos:7
ENTRYPOINT ["/bin/bash"]
```

Starting from a Red Hat Enterprise Linux (RHEL) image

Red Hat also ships containers for RHEL. At the time of writing, images are hosted on Red Hat's Docker registry servers (`https://access.redhat.com/containers/`). These images aren't tagged with release versions, but directly with their name: `rhel7` for RHEL 7 and `rhel6` for RHEL 6. Similarly, subversions are also directly in the name of the image: RHEL 7.3 has the image named `rhel7.3`.

To start with the latest RHEL 7, in a Dockerfile execute the following:

```
FROM registry.access.redhat.com/rhel7
ENTRYPOINT ["/bin/bash"]
```

Starting from a Fedora image

Fedora is officially built for Docker and each release is simply tagged with its version number. Fedora 25 has `fedora:25`, and it goes back to `fedora:20` at the time of writing.

To start a with the latest Fedora release, use the following in a Dockerfile:

```
FROM fedora:latest
ENTRYPOINT ["/bin/bash"]
```

Starting from an Alpine Linux image

Alpine Linux is a very popular and secure lightweight Linux distribution in the container world. It's dozens of times smaller in size than other main distributions: less than 5 MB. It became so popular that Docker (the company) is now using it as a base for all its official images—and the Alpine founder is now working at Docker. Alpine versions are found in the image tags: Alpine 3.1 is `alpine:3.1`, and similarly, Alpine 3.4 is `alpine:3.4`.

To start with the 3.4 release of Alpine Linux, use this in a Dockerfile:

```
FROM alpine:3.4
ENTRYPOINT ["/bin/sh"]
```

Starting from a Debian image

The Debian distribution is present as well, with many different tags: we can find the usual `debian:stable`, `debian:unstable`, and `debian:sid` we're used to, and also some other tags, such as `debian:oldstable`. Release names are tagged like the corresponding versions, so the image `debian:8` is the same as `debian:jessie`. Debian ships *slim* images for each release: debian:jessie-slim is 30% smaller than the main one (80 MB compared to 126 MB at the time of writing).

To start with the Debian 8 (Jessie) release, use the following in a Dockerfile:

```
FROM debian:jessie
ENTRYPOINT ["/bin/bash"]
```

Linux distributions container image size table

Here's a table with the current size for each referenced image:

Linux distribution image	Size
Alpine 3.4	4.799 MB
Debian 8 (slim)	80 MB
Debian 8	123 MB
Ubuntu 16.04	126.6 MB
RHEL 7.3	192.5 MB
CentOS 7.3	191.8 MB
Fedora 25	199.9 MB

With this information in hand, we can now decide to go for any one of these.

That being said, many popular programming languages (Go, Node, Java, Python, Ruby, PHP, and more) are also shipping their own container images. They are all very often based on the images from the operating system container images in the preceding table. It will be interesting to use them if our product is definitely going to use the corresponding language as they often offer custom versions and features.

Starting from a Node JS image

The official repository for the Node Docker image includes many tagged versions with many base images: `node:7` is based on Debian Jessie, while `node:7-alpine` is based on Alpine 3.4. `node:7-slim` will be based on the slim Debian Jessie, and there's even `node:7-wheezy` if we feel like running Node 7 on Debian Wheezy. Also available are Node 6, 4, and below.

To start from the latest Node 7 image version, use this in a Dockerfile:

```
FROM node:7
ENTRYPOINT ["/bin/bash"]
```

For the record, a `node:7` image will be around 650 MB, while `node:4-slim` will be around 205 MB.

Starting from a Golang image

Go is well distributed as a Docker image. Its releases are tagged by release (such as `golang:1.7`) and with alternatives such as one based on Alpine (`golang:1.7-alpine`) or even for Windows Server (`golang:1.7-windowsservercore` and `golang:1.7-nanoserver`).

To start from the Go image, use the following in a Dockerfile:

```
FROM golang:1.7
ENTRYPOINT ["/bin/bash"]
```

The main Go `1.7` image is 672 MB.

Starting from a Ruby image

Ruby is also distributed as an official Docker image: all the latest releases are found tagged like `ruby:2.3`. Alternative builds from Alpine Linux and Debian Jessie slim images are also available.

 A distinct Ruby-on-Rails Docker image used to exist, but is now deprecated in favor of the main Ruby Docker image.

To start from the Ruby `2.3` image, use the following to start a Dockerfile:

```
FROM ruby:2.3
ENTRYPOINT ["/bin/bash"]
```

The main Ruby `2.3` image is 725 MB.

Starting from a Python image

Python is officially distributed and many of its versions are supported as tagged Docker images. We can find versions 2.7, 3.3, 3.4, 3.5, and current beta versions based on Debian Jessie or Wheezy, Alpine, and Windows Server.

To start our project using the Python `3.5` image, add the following in a Dockerfile:

```
FROM python:3.5
ENTRYPOINT ["/bin/bash"]
```

The main `python:3.5` image is around 683 MB.

Starting from a Java image

Java users are also getting official releases on Docker. Both OpenJDK and JRE are available, for versions 6, 7, 8, and 9, based on Debian Jessie or Alpine.

To start using the OpenJDK 9 image, use the following in a Dockerfile:

```
FROM openjdk:9
ENTRYPOINT ["/bin/bash"]
```

The main `openjdk:9` image is 548 MB—one of the smallest programming language images available.

Starting from a PHP image

The PHP Docker image is very popular, and available in many different flavors. It's one of the easiest ways of easily testing newer and older releases of PHP on a platform. PHP 5.6 and 7.0 (and all beta versions) are available, and each is also available with a different flavor, that is, based on Alpine (`php:7-alpine`), Debian Jessie with Apache (`php:7-apache`), or Debian Jessie with FPM (`php:7-fpm`), but if we still like FPM with Alpine, it's also ok (`php:7-fpm-alpine`).

To start using a classic PHP 7 Docker image, start with the following in a Dockerfile:

```
FROM php:7
ENTRYPOINT ["/bin/bash"]
```

The main `php:7` image is 363 MB—this is the smallest programming language image available.

See also

- ▸ Images on the Docker Hub: `https://hub.docker.com/explore/`
- ▸ Red Hat Container catalog: `https://access.redhat.com/containers`

Optimizing the Docker image size

Docker images are generated instruction by instruction from the Dockerfile. Though perfectly correct, many images are sub-optimized when we're talking about size. Let's see what we can do about it by building an Apache Docker container on Ubuntu 16.04.

Getting ready

To step through this recipe, you will need a working Docker installation.

How to do it...

Take the following `Dockerfile`, which updates the Ubuntu image, installs the `apache2` package, and then removes the `/var/lib/apt` cache folder. It's perfectly correct, and if you build it, the image size is around 260 MB:

```
FROM ubuntu:16.04
RUN apt-get update -y
RUN apt-get install -y apache2
RUN rm -rf /var/lib/apt
ENTRYPOINT ["/usr/sbin/apache2ctl", "-D", "FOREGROUND"]
```

Now, each layer is added on top of the previous. So, what's written during the `apt-get update` layer is written forever, even if we remove it in the last `RUN`.

Let's rewrite this `Dockerfile` using a one-liner, to save some space:

```
FROM ubuntu:16.04
RUN apt-get update -y && \
    apt-get install -y apache2 && \
    rm -rf /var/lib/apt/
ENTRYPOINT ["/usr/sbin/apache2ctl", "-D", "FOREGROUND"]
```

This image is exactly the same, but is only around 220 MB. That's 15% space saved!

Replacing the `ubuntu:16.04` image with the `debian:stable-slim` image gets the same result, but with a size of 135 MB (a 48% reduction in size!):

```
FROM debian:stable-slim
RUN apt-get update -y && \
    apt-get install -y apache2 && \
    rm -rf /var/lib/apt/
ENTRYPOINT ["/usr/sbin/apache2ctl", "-D", "FOREGROUND"]
```

How it works...

Each layer is added to its predecessor. By combining all the related commands from download to deletion, we keep a clean state on this particular layer. Another good example is when the Dockerfile downloads a compressed archive; downloading it, uncompressing it, and then removing the archive uses a lot of added layer space when done separately. The same in one line does everything at once, so instead of having the cumulated space taken from the archive and its uncompressed content, the space taken is only from the uncompressed content alone. Often, there's a very nice gain in size!

Versioning Docker images with tags

A very common need is to quickly identify what version of the software a Docker image is running and optionally stick to it, or to be sure to always run a stable version. This is a perfect use for the Docker tags. We'll build a Terraform container, with both a stable and an unstable tag, so multiple versions can coexist—one for production and one for testing.

 Docker *tags* are not to be mistaken with Docker *labels*. Labels are purely informative when tags can be requested directly to make images distinct from an operational point of view.

Getting ready

To step through this recipe, you will need a working Docker installation.

How to do it...

Here's a simple Dockerfile to create a Terraform container (Terraform was covered earlier in this book):

```
FROM alpine:latest
ENV TERRAFORM_VERSION=0.7.12
VOLUME ["/data"]
WORKDIR /data
RUN apk --update --no-cache add ca-certificates openssl && \
  wget -O terraform.zip
"https://releases.hashicorp.com/terraform/${TERRAFORM_VERSION}/ter
raform_${TERRAFORM_VERSION}_linux_amd64.zip" && \
  unzip terraform.zip -d /bin && \
  rm -rf terraform.zip /var/cache/apk/*
ENTRYPOINT ["/bin/terraform"]
CMD [ "--help" ]
```

This is the current, stable, and latest version, and it's 0.7.12 as well. We'd like our users to be able to request one of the following:

▶   `terraform:latest` (for those of our users who always want the latest version available)

▶   `terraform:stable` (for those of our users who always want the stable version, opposed to a beta version)

▶   `terraform:0.7.12` (for those of our users who always want a very specific version, such as for compatibility issues)

This is easily achievable by building directly with all these different tags:

```
$ docker build -t terraform:latest -t terraform:stable -t
terraform:0.7.12 .
```

Now when requesting which images are available, we can see they all have the same image ID, but with different tags. This is what we wanted, since it's the same image that shares all those tags:

```
$ docker images terraform
```

REPOSITORY SIZE	TAG	IMAGE ID	CREATED
terraform minute ago 83.61 MB	0.7.12	9d53a0811d63	About a
terraform minute ago 83.61 MB	latest	9d53a0811d63	About a
terraform minute ago 83.61 MB	stable	9d53a0811d63	About a

Some days later, we release a new version of the software as a Docker container for our team to test it out. This time it's an unstable, 0.8.0-rc1 version. We'd like our users to request this image as one of the following:

▸ terraform:latest (it's still the latest version available, even unstable)

▸ terraform:unstable (it's a release candidate, not a stable version)

▸ terraform:0.8.0-rc1 (it's this specific version)

Change the TERRAFORM_VERSION variable in the Dockerfile, and build the image with the following tags:

```
$ docker build -t terraform:latest -t terraform:unstable -t
terraform:0.8.0-rc1 .
```

Now, if we look at the available Terraform images, we can confirm that it's the same image ID shared by the latest, unstable, and 0.8.0-rc1 tags, while our users preferring the stable version are not impacted by our changes:

```
$ docker images terraform
```

REPOSITORY SIZE	TAG	IMAGE ID	CREATED
terraform seconds ago 86.77 MB	0.8.0-rc1	44609fa7c016	18
terraform seconds ago 86.77 MB	latest	44609fa7c016	18
terraform seconds ago 86.77 MB	unstable	44609fa7c016	18

| terraform | 0.7.12 | 9d53a0811d63 | 9 minutes ago | 83.61 MB |
| terraform | stable | 9d53a0811d63 | 9 minutes ago | 83.61 MB |

 This leads to a very important question: as the latest tag is by default when not specifying any, should it be also used for unstable releases? This is something you have to answer according to your needs and environment.

Deploying a Ruby-on-Rails web application in Docker

The great thing with Docker is that, as developers, we can ship whatever is working on this particular container on one environment (such as development or staging) and be sure it will run similarly in another environment (such as production). Deploys are less stressful, and rollbacks are easier. However, to achieve this peace of mind, we need more than a Ruby-on-Rails application, for example, we need to ship a Dockerfile containing everything to build a self-sufficient container so anyone can run it. Here's how to do it.

Getting ready

To step through this recipe, you will need the following:

- A working Docker installation
- A Rails application

How to do it...

Here are our standard requirements:

- This Rails application needs Ruby 2.3
- All dependencies are handled by Bundler, and need to be installed in the container
- Node 5 is also needed
- We want assets to be precompiled in the image (putting them somewhere else is out of scope)

Here's how we'll proceed. To match our main requirement, we'll start with the ruby:2.3 image:

```
FROM ruby:2.3
```

One way to enable the official Node 5 repositories is to download and execute a setup script. Let's do it:

```
RUN curl -sL https://deb.nodesource.com/setup_5.x | bash -
```

Now we need to install Node 5 (`apt-get install nodejs`) and remove all the cache files:

```
RUN apt-get install -qy nodejs && \
    rm -rf /var/lib/apt/* && \
    rm -rf /var/lib/cache/* && \
    rm -rf /var/lib/log/* && \
    rm -rf /tmp/*
```

The Ruby image documentation suggests using `/usr/src/app` as a destination folder for our code. Let's ensure it's created and switch to it until the rest of the process:

```
RUN mkdir -p /usr/src/app
WORKDIR /usr/src/app
```

To install all the declared dependencies, we need to send both `Gemfile` and `Gemfile.lock` to the destination folder, `/usr/src/app`. We include it as a distinct step, so we can optionally customize this step later. Then we execute Bundler (without the test and development sections if we have them). If you're a Ruby developer, customize accordingly!

```
COPY Gemfile /usr/src/app/
COPY Gemfile.lock /usr/src/app/
RUN bundle install --without test development --jobs 20 --retry 5
```

It's now time to copy the application code itself to the destination folder, `/usr/src/app` (in this case, it's the current folder):

```
COPY . /usr/src/app
```

The next step is to precompile the assets, with a `RAILS_ENV` set to production, but feel free to adapt, including the compilation command:

```
RUN RAILS_ENV=production rake assets:precompile
```

Finally, run the Rails server on all interfaces through bundler (by default, it listens on TCP/`3000`):

```
CMD ["bundle", "exec", "rails", "server", "-b", "0.0.0.0"]
```

We can now build this Dockerfile and have our complete, standalone, and fully working Ruby-on-Rails application ready on Docker.

 It is a good practice to plug the build process in CI and execute tests against running this new image!

Building and using Golang applications with Docker

Golang is a great language able to create statically linked binaries for different platforms such as Linux (ELF binaries) or Mac OS (Mach-O binaries). These binaries are often very small in size, and the language is getting increasingly popular in the microservices world because of their portability and the speed of deployment it enables: deploying a self-sufficient 10 MB Docker image on dozens of servers is just more convenient and fast than a 1.5 GB image full of libs. Golang and containers are two technologies that go perfectly well together, and shipping or managing infrastructures using Go programs is a breeze.

Getting ready

To step through this recipe, you will need the following:

- A working Docker installation
- A Golang application source code

How to do it...

Let's say our application code is checked in `src/hello`. We'd like to begin by at least compiling the program, either for the Linux platform or for the Mac operating system.

Using the golang Docker image to cross-compile a Go program

We can compile our program sharing the code folder, and setting the work directory to it:

```
$ docker run --rm -v "${PWD}/src/hello":/usr/src/hello -w
/usr/src/hello golang:1.7 go build -v
```

This way, even on a Mac OS system, we can generate a proper ELF binary:

```
$ file src/hello/hello
src/hello/hello: ELF 64-bit LSB executable, x86-64, version 1 (SYSV),
statically linked, not stripped
```

That said, if we explicitly want a Mac binary, we can pass the standard Go environment variables GOOS and GOARCH so even a Linux machine can build a Mac binary:

```
$ docker run --rm -v "${PWD}/src/hello":/usr/src/hello -w
/usr/src/hello -e GOOS=darwin -e GOARCH=amd64 golang:1.7 go build -v
```

Confirm we have a Mach-O executable and not an ELF binary:

```
$ file src/hello/hello
src/hello/hello: Mach-O 64-bit executable x86_64
```

Using the golang Docker image to build and ship a Go program

Now if we want to build our program right from a Dockerfile and generate a Docker image out of it, that would translate like the following:

```
FROM golang:1.7
COPY src/hello /go/src/hello
RUN go install hello
ENTRYPOINT ["/go/bin/hello"]
```

Just build that image and execute it:

```
$ docker build -t hello .
$ docker run -it --rm hello
```

Using the scratch Docker image

Now, it's a bit of a waste of space to have a 675 MB+ image for the very often small Golang application that often is only a few MB, and it takes time to deploy on servers. Here comes the scratch image: it just doesn't exist. We start from nothing, copy the binary, and execute it. Our build process (Makefile, build process, and CI) builds the app with the golang image, but does not ship the compiled application with it, saving usually 95–99% of the space, depending on the size of our binary:

```
FROM scratch
COPY src/hello/hello /hello
ENTRYPOINT ["/hello"]
```

This generates the smallest image imaginable. Think only a few megabytes.

Using the Alpine Linux alternative for a Go program

The main problem with the scratch image solution is the impossibility to debug it easily from inside the container, and the impossibility to rely on external libraries or dependencies such as SSL and certificates. Alpine Linux is this small image (~5 MB) that can greatly help us if we'd like to access a shell (/bin/sh is available) and a package manager to debug our application. This is how we'd do it:

```
FROM alpine:latest
RUN apk --update --no-cache add ca-certificates openssl && \
    rm -rf /var/cache/apk/*
COPY src/hello/hello /bin/hello
ENTRYPOINT ["/bin/hello"]
```

Such an image usually is only a handful of megabytes more than the application binary, but helps greatly for debugging.

Networking with Docker

Docker has some pretty nice networking options, from choosing which ports to expose to concurrently running isolated or bridged networks. It's pretty useful to quickly and easily simulate production environments, create better architectures, and increase container exposure on the network front. We'll see different ways to expose ports, create new networks, execute Docker containers inside them, and even have multiple networks per container.

Getting ready

To step through this recipe, you will need the following:

- A working Docker installation
- A sample HTTP server binary (sample code included)

How to do it...

To make a container network port available to others, it first needs to be *exposed*. Consider any service listening on a port not reachable unless properly exposed in the 3:

```
FROM debian:jessie-slim
COPY src/hello/hello /hello
EXPOSE 8000
ENTRYPOINT ["/hello"]
```

This service is listening on port 8000, and any other Docker container running on the host can access it, by default on the same network:

```
# curl -I http://172.17.0.2:8000/
HTTP/1.1 200 OK
```

However, this service is not available to the host system:

```
$ curl http://localhost:8000
curl: (7) Failed to connect to localhost port 8000: Connection
refused
```

To make it available to the host system, the container has to be run with an explicit port redirection. It can be option -P to map exposed ports randomly (the port 8000 can be mapped to 32768 on the local machine), or the other option -p 8000:8000 to make it fixed:

```
$ docker run -ti --rm -P --name hello hello
```

On another terminal, find the port redirection:

```
$ docker port hello
8000/tcp -> 0.0.0.0:32771
```

Also, try to connect to it:

```
$ curl -I http://localhost:32771/
HTTP/1.1 200 OK
```

These are the basics of networking with Docker containers.

Docker networks

Containers can also live inside dedicated networks for added security and isolation. To create a new Docker network, just give it a name:

```
$ docker network create hello_network
d01a3784dec1ade72b813d87c1e6fff14dc1b55fdf6067d6ed8dbe42a3af96c2
```

Grab some information about this network using the docker network inspect command:

```
$ docker network inspect hello_network -f '{{json .IPAM.Config }}'
[{"Subnet":"172.18.0.0/16","Gateway":"172.18.0.1/16"}]
```

This is a new subnet: 172.18.0.0/16 (in this case).

To execute a container in this specific Docker network, use the --network <docker_network_name> option like this:

```
$ docker run -it --rm --name hello --network hello_network hello
```

Confirm this container is in the 172.18.0.0/16 network space from the hello_network network:

```
$ docker inspect --format '{{json
.NetworkSettings.Networks.hello_network.IPAddress }}' hello
"172.18.0.2"
```

This container will be protected from unauthorized access from any container not running on the correct network. Here's an example from a container running in the default network:

```
# curl -I --connect-timeout 5 http://172.18.0.2:8000/
curl: (28) Connection timed out after 5003 milliseconds
```

However, connecting from a container in the same network is allowed and working as expected:

```
# curl -I http://hello:8000/
HTTP/1.1 200 OK
```

Connecting multiple networks for one container

It can be useful to have a few specific containers available on more than one network; proxies, internal services, and other similar services can face different networking configurations. A single Docker container can connect multiple Docker networks. Take this simple HTTP service listening on port 8000 and launch it on the default bridged network:

```
$ docker run -ti --rm --name hello hello
```

This service is now available to any other container on the default network:

```
# curl -I http://172.17.0.2:8000/
HTTP/1.1 200 OK
```

However, we'd like it to be also available on the *hello_network* Docker network. Let's connect them to the host:

```
$ docker network connect hello_network hello
```

The container now has a new network interface in the `hello_network` subnet:

```
$ docker exec -it hello ip addr
[...]
116: eth0@if117: <BROADCAST,MULTICAST,UP,LOWER_UP> mtu 1500 qdisc
noqueue state UP group default
    link/ether 02:42:ac:11:00:02 brd ff:ff:ff:ff:ff:ff
    inet 172.17.0.2/16 scope global eth0
[...]
118: eth1@if119: <BROADCAST,MULTICAST,UP,LOWER_UP> mtu 1500 qdisc
noqueue state UP group default
    link/ether 02:42:ac:12:00:02 brd ff:ff:ff:ff:ff:ff
    inet 172.18.0.2/16 scope global eth1
[...]
```

This means that it's also available to answer requests from containers on this network!

```
$ curl http://hello:8000
Hello world
```

We'll eventually remove the link to the original network after we're done with it:

```
$ docker network disconnect bridge hello
```

Creating more dynamic containers

We can create better containers than just fixing their usage in advance and executing them. Maybe part of the command is the one to keep (like we always want the OpenVPN binary and options to be executed, no matter what), maybe everything needs to be overridden (that's the toolbox container model, such as a `/bin/bash` command by default, but any other command given in argument can otherwise be executed), or a combination of the two, for a much more dynamic container.

Getting ready

To step through this recipe, you will need a working Docker installation.

How to do it...

To have a fixed command executed by the container, use the ENTRYPOINT instruction. Use an array if the command is followed by arguments to be enforced:

```
FROM debian:stable-slim
RUN apt-get update -y && \
    apt-get install -y apache2 && \
    rm -rf /var/lib/apt/
EXPOSE 80
ENTRYPOINT ["/usr/sbin/apache2ctl", "-D", "FOREGROUND"]
```

To override the whole command at runtime, use the `--entrypoint` option:

```
$ docker run -it --rm --entrypoint /bin/sh httpd
# hostname
585dff032d21
```

To have a command that can be simply overridden with an argument, use the CMD instruction instead of ENTRYPOINT:

```
FROM debian:stable-slim
RUN apt-get update -y && \
    apt-get install -y apache2 && \
    rm -rf /var/lib/apt/
EXPOSE 80
CMD ["/usr/sbin/apache2ctl", "-D", "FOREGROUND"]
```

To override the command, simply give another command as an argument at runtime:

```
$ docker run -it --rm httpd /bin/sh
# hostname
cb1c6a7083ad
```

We can combine both instructions to have a more dynamic container. In this case, we want to obtain a container always executing /usr/sbin/apache2ctl, and by default starting the daemon in foreground, otherwise overridden by any argument at container launch time:

```
FROM debian:stable-slim
RUN apt-get update -y && \
    apt-get install -y apache2 && \
    rm -rf /var/lib/apt/
EXPOSE 80
CMD ["-D", "FOREGROUND"]
ENTRYPOINT ["/usr/sbin/apache2ctl"]
```

If this container is executed as is, nothing changes; apache2ctl gets executed with the -D FOREGROUND option.

However, it becomes a more useful container when giving it arguments, as it dynamically will add them to the apache2ctl command, replacing the original command specified by the CMD instruction:

```
$ docker run -it --rm httpd -v
Server version: Apache/2.4.10 (Debian)
Server built:   Sep 15 2016 20:44:43
```

We can interactively pass /usr/sbin/apache2ctl arguments without the need to override the entrypoint, for example, to propose alternatives Apache configuration files or options.

Auto-configuring dynamic containers

We can't always execute a binary to get what we want. A configuration done dynamically is a very common situation; system paths can be dynamic, users and passwords can be auto-generated, network ports can be contextual, third-party credentials will be different in development and in production, slaves will join their masters, cluster members will find other nodes, and most other similar changing elements will need to adapt at runtime. The trick here is to combine environment variables with the use of a script as an entry point that will be executed no matter what, and behave according to the environment variables, optionally combined with a command from the Dockerfile.

Getting ready

To step through this recipe, you will need a working Docker installation.

How to do it...

Our objective is to create a temporary, dynamic SSH server in a Docker container, with credentials we can't know in advance. So, to make it work as intended, we'll want to execute this container like this:

```
$ docker run -e USER=john -e PASSWORD=s3cur3 sshd
```

Take this simple `Dockerfile` that creates what's necessary to run the Dropbear SSH server on the Alpine Docker image:

```
FROM alpine:latest
RUN apk add --update openssh-sftp-server openssh-client dropbear &&\
    rm -rf /var/cache/apk/*
RUN mkdir /etc/dropbear && touch /var/log/lastlog
COPY entrypoint.sh /
ENTRYPOINT ["/entrypoint.sh"]
CMD ["dropbear", "-RFEmwg", "-p", "22"]
```

When built, this container will start by executing the `entrypoint.sh` script, and then the `dropbear` binary. Here's a sample `entrypoint.sh` that only does simple checks for the `USER` and `PASSWORD` environment variable, creates the required users on the container, sets some permissions, and finally executes the `CMD` instruction from the original Dockerfile:

```
#!/bin/sh

# Checks for USER variable
if [ -z "$USER" ]; then
  echo >&2 'Please set an USER variable (ie.: -e USER=john).'
  exit 1
fi

# Checks for PASSWORD variable
if [ -z "$PASSWORD" ]; then
  echo >&2 'Please set a PASSWORD variable (ie.: -e
PASSWORD=hackme).'
  exit 1
fi

echo "Creating user ${USER}"
adduser -D ${USER} && echo "${USER}:${PASSWORD}" | chpasswd
```

```
echo "Fixing permissions for user ${USER}"
chown -R ${USER}:${USER} /home/${USER}
exec "$@"
```

If this container is executed without any arguments, it errors out, thanks to the check from the entrypoint.sh script:

$ docker run --rm ssh

Please set an USER variable (ie.: -e USER=john).

To properly use this dynamically configured container, use environment variables as required:

$ docker run --rm -h ssh-container -e USER=john -e PASSWORD=s3cur3 -p 22:22 ssh

Creating user john

Password for 'john' changed

Fixing permissions for user john

[1] Nov 29 23:02:02 Not backgrounding

Now try connecting to this container from another terminal or container with proper credentials:

$ ssh john@localhost

[...]

john@localhost's password:

ssh-container:~$ hostname

ssh-container

We're logged in to our SSH container!

Such a dynamic system can be used to give temporary, controlled, and secure SSH access to someone needing, for example, shared volume storage access or similar usages. Shutting down the container just revokes everything and we're done with it.

Better security with unprivileged users

By default, containers execute everything as the root user. Granted that containers are running in an isolated environment, but still, a publicly facing daemon is running as root on a system, and a security breach may give an attacker access to this particular container, and maybe root shell access, giving access at least to the container's Docker overlay network. Would we like to see this issue combined with a 0-day local kernel security breach that would give the attacker access to the Docker host? Probably not. Then, maybe we should keep some of the good old practices and start by executing our daemon as a user other than root.

Getting ready

To step through this recipe, you will need the following:

- ▸ A working Docker installation
- ▸ A sample HTTP server binary (sample code included)

How to do it...

Let's take a simple HTTP server that answers on the port 8000 of the container. Executed through a container, it would look like this, as seen earlier in this book:

```
FROM debian:jessie-slim
COPY src/hello/hello /usr/bin/hello
RUN chmod +x /usr/bin/hello
EXPOSE 8000
ENTRYPOINT ["/usr/bin/hello"]
```

This will work, but things aren't looking that great security-wise; our daemon is, in fact, running as the root user, even though it's running on an unprivileged port:

```
$ ps aux
USER        PID %CPU %MEM    VSZ    RSS TTY       STAT START   TIME
COMMAND
root          1  0.6  0.2  36316   4180 ?         Ssl+ 23:30   0:00
/usr/bin/hello
```

This is suboptimal from a security point of view. Containers are real systems, so they too can have users. Combined with the USER instruction in the Dockerfile, we'll be able to execute commands as an unprivileged user! Here's how an optimized Dockerfile looks, adding a normal user and group for the hello user, and then executing the /usr/bin/hello HTTP server as this new unprivileged user:

```
FROM debian:jessie-slim
COPY src/hello/hello /usr/bin/hello
RUN chmod +x /usr/bin/hello
RUN groupadd -r hello && useradd -r -g hello hello
USER hello
EXPOSE 8000
ENTRYPOINT ["/usr/bin/hello"]
```

Once built and running, the daemon still runs correctly, but as an unprivileged user:

```
$ ps aux
USER        PID %CPU %MEM    VSZ    RSS TTY       STAT START   TIME
COMMAND
hello         1  0.0  0.2  36316   4768 ?         Ssl+ 23:33   0:00
/usr/bin/hello
```

We're now building tougher containers!

Orchestrating with Docker Compose

Launching multiple containers manually can be a hassle, especially when the infrastructure goes increasingly complex. Dependencies, shared variables, and common networking can be easily handled with the orchestration tool named Docker Compose. In a simply YAML file, we can describe what services are needed to run our application (proxy, application, databases, and so on). In this section, we'll show how to create a simple LAMP docker-compose file, then we'll show how we can iterate from that to build some staging and production specific changes.

Getting ready

To step through this recipe, you will need the following:

- ▶ A working Docker installation
- ▶ A working Docker Compose installation

How to do it...

To orchestrate multiple containers together using Docker Compose, let's start with an easy WordPress example. The team at WordPress built a container that auto-configures to some extent through environment variables similar to what we saw earlier in this chapter. If we just apply the documentation shipped with the WordPress Docker container, we end up with the following `docker-compose.yml` at the root of some new directory (it can be a Git repository if needed):

```
version: '2'

services:
  wordpress:
    image: wordpress
    ports:
      - 8080:80
    environment:
      WORDPRESS_DB_PASSWORD: example
  mysql:
    image: mariadb
    environment:
      MYSQL_ROOT_PASSWORD: example
```

This has the great advantage to work out of the box; the latest WordPress and MariaDB images get downloaded, local HTTP port 80 gets redirected on port 8080 on the host, and MySQL stays isolated. The WordPress container takes one environment variable in this case—the MySQL root password, which should match the environment variable from MySQL. We'll see that many more are possible.

Executing Docker Compose will automatically create a Docker network and run the containers:

```
$ docker-compose up
[...]
mysql_1       | 2016-12-01 20:51:14 139820361766848 [Note] mysqld
(mysqld 10.1.19-MariaDB-1~jessie) starting as process 1 ...
[...]
mysql_1       | 2016-12-01 20:51:15 139820361766848 [Note] mysqld:
ready for connections.
[...]
wordpress_1 | [Thu Dec 01 20:51:17.865932 2016] [mpm_prefork:notice]
[pid 1] AH00163: Apache/2.4.10 (Debian) PHP/5.6.28 configured -- resuming
normal operations
wordpress_1 | [Thu Dec 01 20:51:17.865980 2016] [core:notice] [pid
1] AH00094: Command line: 'apache2 -D FOREGROUND'
```

Let's verify we can connect to the WordPress HTTP server locally, on the redirected port `8080`:

```
$ curl -IL http://localhost:8080
HTTP/1.1 302 Found
[...]


HTTP/1.1 200 OK
[...]
```

More information can be seen using the `ps` command:

```
$ docker-compose ps
        Name                    Command              State
Ports
----------------------------------------------------------------
--------------
1basics_mysql_1         docker-entrypoint.sh mysqld      Up
3306/tcp
1basics_wordpress_1     docker-entrypoint.sh apach ...   Up
0.0.0.0:8080->80/tcp
```

Let's ensure the password used for the MySQL root password is really the one provided by the `docker-compose.yml` file, using the `docker-compose exec` command, very similar to the `docker run` command (it takes `docker-compose.yml` names):

```
$ docker-compose exec mysql /usr/bin/mysql -uroot -pexample
[...]

MariaDB [(none)]> show databases;
+--------------------+
| Database           |
+--------------------+
| information_schema |
| mysql              |
| performance_schema |
| wordpress          |
+--------------------+
4 rows in set (0.00 sec)
```

When we're done with our initial Docker Compose environment, let's destroy it; the containers and networks will be removed:

```
$ docker-compose down
```

Extending Docker Compose

Now we know the basics, let's extend the usage a little. We're not happy with the default password and would like to use a better one, so simulate the staging environment. Let's use the overriding feature of Docker Compose for that and create a `docker-compose.staging.yml` file that will simply override the concerned values:

```
version: '2'
services:
  wordpress:
    image: wordpress:4.6
    environment:
      WORDPRESS_DB_PASSWORD: s3cur3
  mysql:
    environment:
      MYSQL_ROOT_PASSWORD: s3cur3
```

The two environment variables `WORDPRESS_DB_PASSWORD` and `MYSQL_ROOT_PASSWORD` will be overridden when `docker-compose` is executed with multiple configuration files taken in order:

```
$ docker-compose -f docker-compose.yml -f docker-compose.staging.yml up
```

Verify that the new password is indeed working for MySQL:

```
$ docker exec -it 1basics_mysql_1 mysql -uroot -ps3cur3
Welcome to the MariaDB monitor.  Commands end with ; or \g.
Your MariaDB connection id is 4
```

We're very easily overriding values with simple YAML files!

Suppose that we now want to include a reverse proxy to the mix, with a slightly earlier version of the Docker image and another MySQL password, to mimic a specific situation we have in production. We can use the excellent dynamic Nginx image from `jwilder/nginx-proxy` to do this job and add a new *proxy* service, sharing port `80` and the local Docker socket as read-only (to dynamically access running containers) on a `docker-compose.production.yml` file:

```
proxy:
  image: jwilder/nginx-proxy
  ports:
    - "80:80"
  volumes:
    - /var/run/docker.sock:/tmp/docker.sock:ro
```

This `nginx-proxy` container needs a variable named `VIRTUAL_HOST` to know what to answer in case of multiple virtual hosts. Let's add it as localhost (or adapt to your local hostname), along with the better password and the WordPress image version:

```
wordpress:
  image: wordpress:4.5
  environment:
    WORDPRESS_DB_PASSWORD: sup3rs3cur3
    VIRTUAL_HOST: localhost
```

Make the password match in the MySQL section as well and we'll be done with our production environment simulation:

```
$ docker-compose -f docker-compose.yml -f docker-
compose.production.yml up
```

Confirm `nginx-proxy` is answering in HTTP/`80` and forwarding a proper HTTP answer from the WordPress container:

```
$ curl -IL http://localhost/
HTTP/1.1 302 Found
Server: nginx/1.11.3
[...]
HTTP/1.1 200 OK
Server: nginx/1.11.3
```

We've seen how, with only a few lines of YAML, we can easily orchestrate containers, how it can be used to handle different cases and environments, and how it can also be successfully extended. This is, however, just a small introduction to what can be done with Docker Compose—it's quite a powerful tool!

See also

- ▸ Nginx-proxy: `https://github.com/jwilder/nginx-proxy`
- ▸ WordPress Docker image: `https://hub.docker.com/_/wordpress/`
- ▸ The Docker Compose documentation: `https://docs.docker.com/compose/`

Linting a Dockerfile

Like any other language, Dockerfiles can and should be linted for updated best practices and code quality checks. Docker is no exception to the rule, and good practices are always moving, getting updates, and might also be a little different between communities. In this section, we'll start with a basic Dockerfile found earlier and end up with a fully double-checked linted file.

Getting ready

To step through this recipe, you will need the following:

- ▸ A working Docker installation
- ▸ An AWS account

How to do it...

Many different linters exist for linting Dockerfiles: Hadolint (`http://hadolint.lukasmartinelli.ch/`) maybe the most used linter, while Project Atomic's `dockerfile_lint` project is perhaps the most complete one (`https://github.com/projectatomic/dockerfile_lint`).

Here's the working Dockerfile from earlier in this book:

```
FROM debian:stable-slim
RUN apt-get update -y \
    && apt-get install -y apache2 \
    && rm -rf /var/lib/apt
ENTRYPOINT ["/usr/sbin/apache2ctl"]
CMD ["-D", "FOREGROUND"]
```

Hadolint

Let's start working with Hadolint, as it's easy to install (prebuilt binaries and Docker images) and use. All rules are explained in Hadolint's wiki (`https://github.com/lukasmartinelli/hadolint/wiki`), and usage is really simple:

```
$ hadolint Dockerfile
```

Alternatively, use the Docker containerized version; it's probably good in CI scripts. Beware of the image size; at the time of writing, the image is 1.7 GB, while the hadolint binary is less than 20 MB:

```
$ docker run --rm -i lukasmartinelli/hadolint < Dockerfile
```

Linting Dockerfiles from this chapter, we'll notice different warnings. Maybe some are false positives, or maybe some rules are just not yet updated to the latest deprecation notices, such as the following:

```
$ hadolint Dockerfile

Dockerfile DL4000 Specify a maintainer of the Dockerfile
```

In fact, this Dockerfile is following Docker 1.13 recommendations, which include to no more include a `maintainer` instruction. However, Hadolint is not yet up to date for this deprecation change, so execute the following to ignore one or more IDs, to still be cool:

```
$ hadolint --ignore DL4000 --ignore <another_ID> Dockerfile
```

Dockerfile_lint

This project lead by the Project Atomic team (`http://www.projectatomic.io/`) is also proposing different checks and strong opinions on how a Dockerfile should be written. These propositions are very often good advice, though.

Execute this to launch `dockerfile_lint` from the official Docker image:

```
$ docker run -it --rm -v $PWD:/root/ projectatomic/dockerfile-lint
dockerfile_lint
```

A certain amount of suggestions will arise (errors, warnings, and info), each with a related reference URL to refer to.

When in doubt, it's often a good move to follow the suggestions and fix the code accordingly.

At the end of this double linting process, our Dockerfile changed a lot, as shown here:

```
FROM debian:stable-slim
LABEL name="apache"
LABEL maintainer="John Doe <john@doe.com>"
```

```
LABEL version=1.0
RUN apt-get update -y \
    && apt-get install -y --no-install-recommends apache2=2.4.10-
10+deb8u7 \
    && apt-get clean \
    && rm -rf /var/lib/apt/lists/*
EXPOSE 80
ENTRYPOINT ["/usr/sbin/apache2ctl"]
CMD ["-D", "FOREGROUND"]
```

We added labels to identify the image, versions, and maintainer, and we fixed a proper version of the apache2 package. So no bad surprise can happen with an untested update (updating the package will need a rebuild of the image), we're cleaning the apt cache more precisely, and we're explicitly exposing a port from the container.

Overall, those changes proposed by the linters helped us a lot in building a much better and stronger container. Their role in CI is crucial; include the linters in your Jenkins, Circle, or Travis CI jobs!

Deploying a private Docker registry with S3 storage

The Docker registry is a central image distribution service. When we *pull* or *push* an image, it's from the Docker registry. It can be commercially hosted (CoreOS Quay `https://quay.io/` is an example, Docker's own `https://hub.docker.com/` is another), or it can be self-hosted (for privacy, speed, bandwidth issues, or company policy). Docker Inc. made it simple for us to deploy it; it's extensively documented and packaged. Amongst the many deployable features, we'll start by simply deploying a single registry ready to be load-balanced, and then we'll switch its backend storage to AWS S3, so disk space will never be an issue again.

Getting ready

To step through this recipe, you will need the following:

- A working Docker installation
- An AWS account with full S3 access

How to do it...

We'll use Docker Compose to work through this recipe. Our objective is to host our own private Docker registry, initially using local storage, then an S3 bucket for infinite space. The registry will be available on `http://localhost:5000`, but feel free to use any other resolvable name or a dedicated server with a locally available name.

To begin with, we need the Docker registry v2 image: `registry:2`. We know from the documentation that port `5000` is exposed by the registry server, so we need to forward it to our host to use it locally. If we are running multiple registries behind a load balancer, it's safe to share a common secret, let's set it to `s3cr3t`.

This is what our initial `docker-compose.yml` file looks like:

```
version: '2'

services:
  registry:
    image: registry:2
    ports:
      - 5000:5000
    environment:
      REGISTRY_HTTP_SECRET: s3cr3t
```

With this simple setup, we already are able to run our own local Docker registry server:

```
$ docker-compose up
```

To upload an image to our private registry, the process is to simply tag the image with the local registry URL and then push it. Execute the following to tag the `ubuntu:16.04` image with `localhost:5000/ubuntu`:

```
$ docker tag ubuntu:16.04 localhost:5000/ubuntu
```

Then, to push the image to the local registry, execute this:

```
$ docker push localhost:5000/ubuntu
```

This Docker image is now stored locally and can be reused without accessing the public network nor the Docker Hub or similar services.

Using an S3 backend

An issue with a highly used local Docker registry is disk space management—it's finite. The good news is that the Docker Registry handles easily an S3 backend (or Swift if we have an internal OpenStack). For the record, Google Cloud and Azure storage are also supported. To enable the S3 backend, only a few variables need to be set in the `docker-compose.yml` file: the AWS region to contact, the keys, and the bucket name.

```
REGISTRY_STORAGE: s3
REGISTRY_STORAGE_S3_REGION: us-east-1
REGISTRY_STORAGE_S3_BUCKET: registry-iacbook
REGISTRY_STORAGE_S3_ACCESSKEY: AKIAXXXXXXXXX
REGISTRY_STORAGE_S3_SECRETKEY: 1234abcde#
```

Destroy (`docker-compose down`) the previous example if you tried it, and start this updated one:

```
$ docker-compose up
```

Now tag again an image locally:

```
$ docker tag ubuntu:16.04 localhost:5000/ubuntu
```

Then, push the image to the local registry:

```
$ docker push localhost:5000/ubuntu
```

Depending on your uplink speed, it will take more or less time for the Registry to sync the layers we push with the AWS S3 backend.

We now have our own local registry with infinite storage!

See also

- ▶ The Docker Registry documentation: `https://docs.docker.com/registry/configuration/`

10
Maintaining Docker Containers

In this chapter, we will cover the following recipes:

- ▶ Testing Docker containers with BATS
- ▶ Test-Driven Development (TDD) with Docker and ServerSpec
- ▶ The workflow for creating automated Docker builds from Git
- ▶ The workflow for connecting the Continuous Integration (CI) system
- ▶ Scanning for vulnerabilities with Quay.io and Docker Cloud
- ▶ Sending Docker logs to AWS CloudWatch Logs
- ▶ Monitoring and getting information out of Docker
- ▶ Debugging containers using sysdig

Introduction

In this chapter, we'll explore some advanced and highly interesting areas that probably most developers today are already used to. Infrastructure code is still code, so it should be no different than software code; the same principle should apply. This means that the Docker code should be testable, the builds automatic, and the CI systems connected to our Git servers so they could continuously apply the tests. In addition to this, security checks should be part of the mandatory release process and the logs easy to access, even if the application is scaled on multiple machines. Also note that containers shouldn't be black boxes, and highly performant debugging tools should be available for us to do our work. The good news is that these topics will be covered in this chapter, because all of this can be done easily.

Testing Docker containers with BATS

BATS (**Bash Automated Testing System**) allows you to have quick and easy tests in a very natural language, without the need of a lot of dependencies. BATS can also grow in complexity as per your requirement. In this section, we'll use Docker with Docker Compose to handle the build and a Makefile to tie the dependencies between the build process and the BATS testing process; this will make it easier to later integrate this process into a CI system.

Getting ready

To step through this recipe, you will need:

- A working Docker installation
- A BATS installation (it's available for all major Linux distributions and Mac OS)

 BATS Version 0.4.0 is used in this chapter.

How to do it...

Let's start with this simple Dockerfile that will install Apache and run it after clearing the cache:

```
FROM debian:stable-slim
LABEL name="apache"
LABEL maintainer="John Doe <john@doe.com>"
LABEL version=1.0
RUN apt-get update -y \
    && apt-get install -y --no-install-recommends apache2=2.4.10-
10+deb8u7 \
    && apt-get clean \
    && rm -rf /var/lib/apt/lists/*
EXPOSE 80
ENTRYPOINT ["/usr/sbin/apache2ctl"]
CMD ["-D", "FOREGROUND"]
```

For convenience, let's create a `docker-compose.yml` file so the image can be built and run easily:

```
version: '2'

services:
  http:
    build: .
    image: demo-httpd
    ports:
      - "80:80"
```

This way, running `docker-compose up` will also build the image if absent. Alternatively, to just build the image, use this code:

```
$ docker-compose build
```

Creating BATS tests

We'll now test two of the main actions this image is supposed to do:

- Install Apache 2.4.10
- Clean the APT cache

Start by creating a `test` folder at the root of our repository that will host the BATS tests:

```
$ mkdir test
```

Our first test is to verify that the installed version of Apache is `2.4.10`, as required. How would we do it manually? We'd probably just execute the following and check the output:

```
$ apache2ctl -v
Server version: Apache/2.4.10 (Debian)
```

This translates in Docker with our image in the following command (`-v` being the command (CMD) for the `apache2ctl ENTRYPOINT` instruction):

```
$ docker run --rm demo-httpd:latest -v
Server version: Apache/2.4.10 (Debian)
```

Basically, now we just have to run `grep` for the correct version:

```
$ docker run --rm demo-httpd:latest -v | grep 2.4.10
Server version: Apache/2.4.10 (Debian)
```

If `grep` is successful, it returns `0`:

```
$ echo $?
0
```

A simple BATS test for a command return code looks like this:

```
@test "test title" {
  run <some command>
  [ $status -eq 0 ]
}
```

We now have everything we need to write our first BATS test in `test/httpd.bats`:

```
@test "Apache version is correct" {
  run docker run --rm demo-httpd:latest -v \| grep 2.4.10
  [ $status -eq 0 ]
}
```

To execute our test, let's launch BATS with the folder containing the tests as arguments:

```
$ bats test
 • Apache version is correct


1 test, 0 failures
```

Good! We're now assured that the correct Apache version is installed.

Let's ensure the APT cache is cleaned after we build the image so we don't waste precious space. Deleting the APT lists means the `/var/lib/apt/lists` folder will become empty, so if you count the files in this folder after this, it should return `0`:

```
$ ls -1 /var/lib/apt/lists | wc -1
```

However, we cannot just send this command to the container like we did for the Apache version; the entry point is `apache2ctl`, and it needs to be overridden by `sh` on the `docker run` command line. Here's the `apt.bats` test file, executing the shell command instead of `apache2ctl`, expecting a successful execution and an output of `0`:

```
@test "apt lists are empty" {
  run docker run --rm --entrypoint="/bin/sh" demo-httpd:latest -c "ls
-1 /var/lib/apt/lists | wc -1"
  [ $status -eq 0 ]
  [ "$output" = "0" ]
}
```

Execute the BATS tests:

```
$ bats test
  apt lists are empty
  Apache version is correct

2 tests, 0 failures
```

Using Makefile to glue it all together

Now this whole process might be a bit tedious in CI, with some additional steps needed before the testing is done (the image needs to be built and made available before it is tested, for example). Let's create a `Makefile` that will take care of the prerequisites for us:

```
test: bats

bats: build
  bats test

build:
  docker-compose build
```

Now when you execute the `make test` command, it will launch the `bats` suite, which itself depends on building the image by `docker-compose`—a much simpler command to integrate in the CI system of your choice:

```
$ make test
docker-compose build
Building http
Step 1 : FROM debian:stable-slim
 ---> d2103c196fde
[...]
Successfully built 1c4f46316f19
bats test
 • apt lists are empty
 • Apache version is correct

2 tests, 0 failures
```

See also

▸   Information on BATS at `https://github.com/sstephenson/bats`

Test-Driven Development (TDD) with Docker and ServerSpec

Docker containers might have a simpler language, but in the end, general concepts remain common and still apply. Testing is good for quality, and writing tests first ensures that we write code that would make a test pass, instead of writing tests after the code is written, which would somehow lead to missed errors. To help us with this, we'll use ServerSpec, based on RSpec, to initiate a TDD workflow along with writing and testing a Docker container. Working like this usually ensures a very high quality of work overall and very sustainable containers.

Getting ready

To step through this recipe, you will need:

▸   A working Docker installation

▸   A working Ruby environment (including Bundler)

How to do it...

Our goal is to create an NGINX container following TDD principles. Before we start to code, let's begin by setting up our environment.

Creating a ServerSpec environment using Bundler

ServerSpec comes as a gem (a Ruby package), and as we'll use Docker APIs, we'll need the `docker-api` gem as well. For ease of deployment, let's create `Gemfile` containing our dependencies inside a `test` group:

```
source 'https://rubygems.org'

group :test do
  gem 'serverspec'
  gem 'docker-api'
end
```

Install these dependencies using Bundler:

```
$ bundle install
Using docker-api 1.33.0
Using serverspec 2.37.2
[...]
Bundle complete! 2 Gemfile dependencies, 18 gems now installed.
```

Now we'll be able to execute `rspec` in our local context using Bundler:

```
$ bundle exec rspec
```

Initializing the tests

Let's start by creating our first Docker Rspec test that will just, for now, initialize the libraries we need and build the Docker image before anything else. It looks like this in spec/Dockerfile_spec.rb:

```
require "serverspec"
require "docker"

describe "Docker NGINX image" do
  before(:all) do
    @image = Docker::Image.build_from_dir('.')

    set :os, family: :debian
    set :backend, :docker
    set :docker_image, @image.id
  end
end
```

TDD – using the Debian Jessie base's Docker image

We now want to use a Debian stable for our project, which happens to be Debian 8 at the moment. To know the current version of a Debian system, just look at the /etc/debian_version file (on Red-Hat-based systems, it's under /etc/redhat_release):

```
$ cat /etc/debian_version
8.6
```

Good! Let's create a definition in ServerSpec, checking for the Debian version through this command:

```
describe "Docker NGINX image" do
[...]
  def debian_version
    command("cat /etc/debian_version").stdout
  end
end
```

Now, the `debian_version` content can be easily queried, for example, by this check:

```
it "installs Debian Jessie" do
  expect(debian_version).to include("8.")
end
```

If this system is running Debian 8, then the test will pass. If the `Dockerfile` is empty, the test will fail:

```
$ bundle exec rspec --color --format documentation
Docker image
  installs Debian Jessie (FAILED - 1)


Failures:

  1) Docker image installs Debian Jessie
     Failure/Error: @image = Docker::Image.build_from_dir('.')
     Docker::Error::ServerError:
       No image was generated. Is your Dockerfile empty?
```

Good! Our test has failed. Let's write the FROM instruction in Dockerfile that will make it pass; this is because the current Debian stable is version 8:

```
FROM debian:stable-slim
```

Save the file and launch the test again:

```
$ bundle exec rspec --color --format documentation
Docker NGINX image
  installs Debian Jessie


Finished in 0.72234 seconds (files took 0.29061 seconds to load)
1 example, 0 failures
```

Good job! Our test has passed, meaning this really is Debian 8.

TDD – installing the NGINX package

Our next objective is to install the `nginx` package. Let's write the Rspec test in `Dockerfile_spec.rb` that will check for this:

```
describe "Docker NGINX image" do
[...]
  describe package('nginx') do
    it { should be_installed }
  end
end
```

Launch the test to be sure it fails:

```
$ bundle exec rspec --color --format documentation
Docker NGINX image
  installs Debian Jessie
  Package "nginx"
    should be installed (FAILED - 1)
```

It's now time to add the instructions to the `Dockerfile` on how to install NGINX:

```
RUN apt-get update -y \
    && apt-get install -y --no-install-recommends nginx=1.6.2-
5+deb8u4 \
    && apt-get clean \
    && rm -rf /var/lib/apt/lists/*
```

Relaunch the tests (it will take some time as it needs to build the image):

```
$ bundle exec rspec --color --format documentation
Docker NGINX image
  installs Debian Jessie
  Package "nginx"
    should be installed


Finished in 51.89 seconds (files took 0.3032 seconds to load)
2 examples, 0 failures
```

We're now sure the `nginx` package is installed.

TDD – running NGINX

Now that we have our image built with NGINX, execute it. Using ServerSpec, we can start a container using the id attribute of the image we built earlier. In the `Dockerfile_spec.rb` file, create and start the container using the image:

```ruby
describe "Docker NGINX image" do
[...]
  describe 'Running the NGINX container' do
    before(:all) do
      @container = Docker::Container.create(
        'Image'      => @image.id
        )
      @container.start
    end
  end
end
```

Using standard ServerSpec checks, verify that an NGINX process is running:

```ruby
describe process("nginx") do
  it { should be_running }
end
```

We can't stop here without cleaning up the container. We need to stop it when we're done with the tests and delete it:

```ruby
after(:all) do
  @container.kill
  @container.delete(:force => true)
end
```

Now we can run the test that will execute the container and fail upon checking for an `nginx` process (we didn't write anything that would launch `nginx`):

```
$ bundle exec rspec --color --format documentation
Docker NGINX image
  installs Debian Jessie
  Package "nginx"
    should be installed
  Running the NGINX container
    Process "nginx"
      should be running (FAILED - 1)
```

Now let's execute /usr/bin/nginx for our container in the foreground, specifically in the Dockerfile:

```
EXPOSE 80
ENTRYPOINT ["/usr/sbin/nginx"]
CMD ["-g", "daemon off;"]
```

Rerun the tests to check whether the nginx process is now running as expected:

```
$ bundle exec rspec --color --format documentation
Docker NGINX image
  installs Debian Jessie
  Package "nginx"
    should be installed
  Running the NGINX container
    Process "nginx"
      should be running


Finished in 1.94 seconds (files took 0.30853 seconds to load)
3 examples, 0 failures
```

To add simplicity when integrating these tests in CI systems, let's create a simple Makefile:

```
test: rspec
rspec:
    bundle exec rspec --color --format documentation
```

Now a simple make test command will launch the ServerSpec tests.

Good job! We've built our first simple Docker container following TDD principles. We can now build more complex and secure containers using this technique.

See also

- ▶ RSpec at http://rspec.info/
- ▶ Docker-api at https://github.com/swipely/docker-api
- ▶ ServerSpec at http://serverspec.org/

The workflow for creating automated Docker builds from Git

Building local containers is a nice thing to do, but what about its wide distribution? We can use the Docker Hub service to store and distribute our containers (or its alternative Quay.io); however, uploading each and every container and version manually will soon be a problem. Consider you need to rebuild dozens of containers in an emergency, because of the existence of another OpenSSL security bug; nobody would want to be the one to upload them one by one, especially with the bad uplink at work. And as we're working with our Docker code using branches and tags, it will be awesome to see the same behavior reflected automatically on the remote Docker registry. This includes two of the Docker Hub (or Quay.io) features: automatically build Docker images upon changes and serve them to the world. We'll do exactly this in this section: create an automated build and distribution pipeline from our code to GitHub to the Docker Hub.

Getting ready

To step through this recipe, you will need:

- A free GitHub account
- A free Docker Hub account
- A Docker project

How to do it...

Our objective is to get a fully working Docker build pipeline. To achieve this, we'll use two free, popular services: GitHub and the Docker Hub. Let's start with the code from the previous section that helped us build an NGINX container; we can alternatively use any other repository on GitHub containing at least a buildable `Dockerfile`. The code needs to actually be on GitHub not just versioned using Git locally. The repository should look like this:

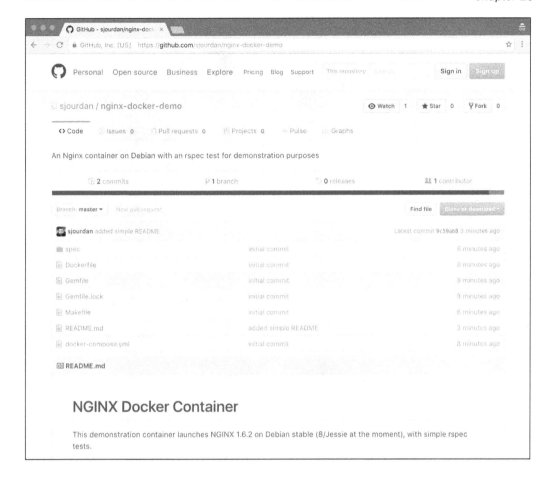

This repository is ready to communicate with other build services.

Creating an automated build on the Docker Hub

The Docker Hub is one of the commercial services from the company that created Docker. It's both a public Docker registry service (with private or public containers, depending on your subscription) and a Docker image build service that can automatically create new images when changes occur in the code. Go to `https://hub.docker.com` and log in or create an account if you don't have any.

Click on **Create Automated Build** in the **Create** menu:

Choose the provider where the infrastructure code is hosted; in our case, it's **GitHub**:

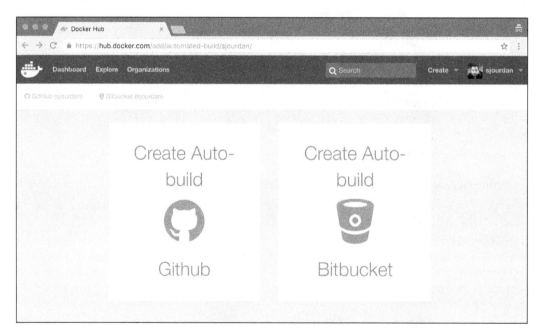

When the synchronization is done, choose the GitHub repository:

Finally, decide on a name for the image (it doesn't have to be the name of the GitHub repository) and the namespace. The namespace could either be your username or an organization if you have one. Write a short description and choose the visibility of the image: private stuff should remain private, while public can stay public. Let's be careful about what we ship:

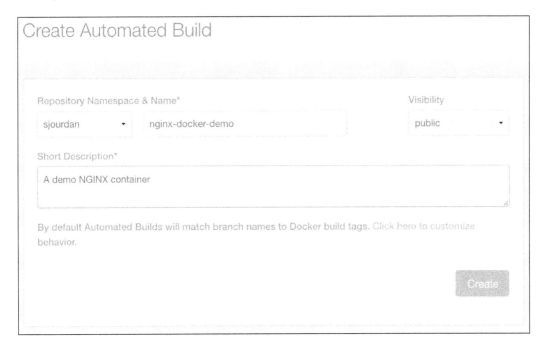

Navigate to **Build Settings** of our Docker Hub's project to trigger an initial build:

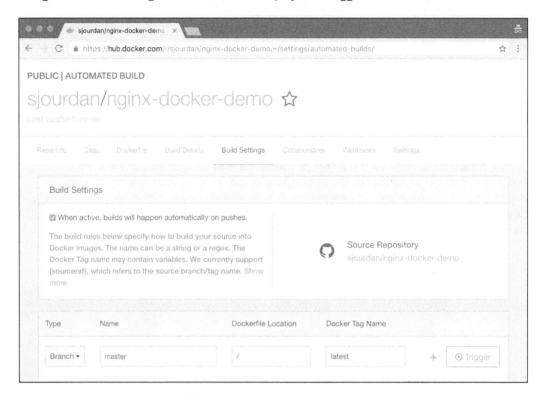

Clicking on the **Trigger** button will create a build. This is done by having `master` as the **Branch** type of our repository; tag the build with the `latest` tag. If, for some reason, the `Dockerfile` of our project wasn't at the root, we could specify it here. This build also allows us to manage different `Dockerfile` for different purposes, such as building the development and production containers differently, among other options.

Once the build is complete (should happen in minutes), navigating to the **Tags** tab will show the available tags (**latest** is the only one we have now) and the size of the image:

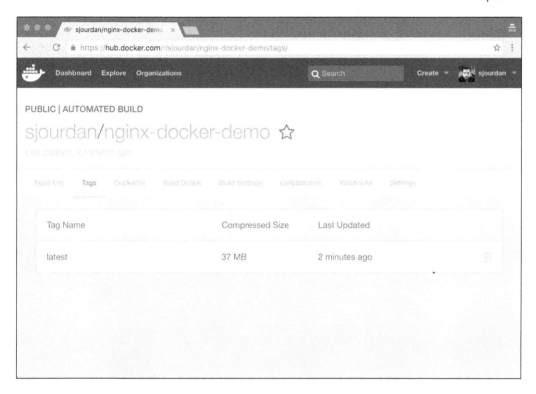

The **Dockerfile** tab shows the content of the `Dockerfile` from which the image has been built, while the **Build Details** tab will list all the builds and their details, including the build output. This is very useful for debugging when things go wrong.

Configuring a GitHub to a Docker Hub-automated build pipeline

Now let's make a modification to the `Dockerfile`, for example, adding a label for the image's name and version:

```
LABEL name="demo-nginx"
LABEL version=1.0
```

Commit and push this change to GitHub:

```
$ git add Dockerfile
$ git commit -m "added some missing labels"
[master f20017b] added some missing labels
 1 file changed, 2 insertions(+)
$ git push
```

What's happening on the Docker Hub? It automatically starts building a new image as soon as it becomes aware of the change on GitHub:

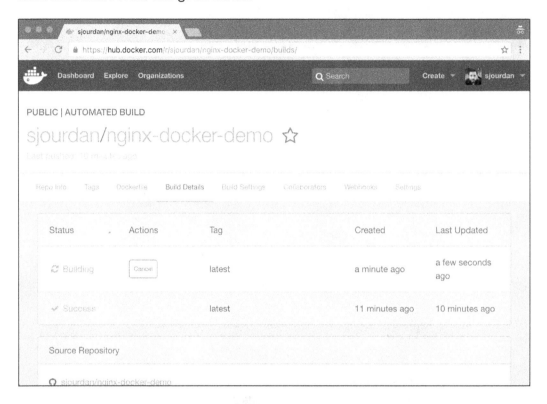

A few seconds later, our newest build is available for everyone to use:

```
$ docker pull sjourdan/nginx-docker-demo
```

Building Docker images using Git tags

As we're happy with this release, we'd like it to be available as a 1.0 tag on the Docker Hub. To do this, we'll need to complete two actions:

- ▸ Configure the Docker Hub to build and tag according to Git tags and not just branches
- ▸ Tag and push our release on Git

For the Docker Hub to build images with the same tags than the ones we set on Git, let's add a new type called **Tag** in the **Build Settings** tab. This will now make the Docker Hub follow the tags we set on Git. It will also build any other tag you may create in the future:

Let's tag our code as `1.0` on Git so we can refer to it later:

```
$ git tag 1.0
$ git push --tags
Total 0 (delta 0), reused 0 (delta 0)
To https://github.com/sjourdan/nginx-docker-demo.git
 * [new tag]         1.0 -> 1.0
```

This just triggered a new build on the Docker Hub, using the tag **1.0**, as we asked to match:

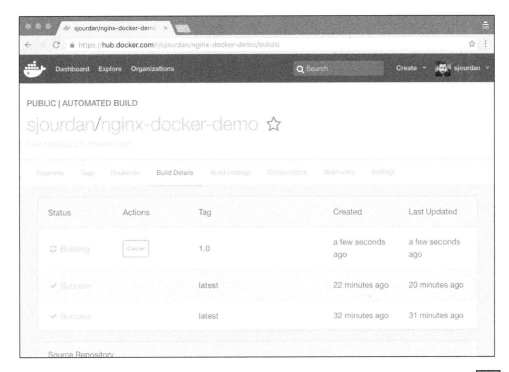

Everyone can now refer to this stable build and use it without fearing a breaking change from the master branch; this branch will always be built with the latest tag:

```
$ docker pull sjourdan/nginx-docker-demo:1.0
```

Even better, from now on, our future Docker projects that need both this container and the stability can simply start with the following line on the `Dockerfile`:

```
FROM sjourdan/nginx-docker-demo:1.0
```

We now have a nice initial workflow for building master and tagged, stable releases of our containers.

The workflow for connecting the Continuous Integration (CI) system

As people working with code and writing tests for it, there's no reason not to see those tests executed in CI. The same way every program has language requirements, ours need to be able to build Docker containers and execute some Ruby code. Being able to fully execute a whole pile of tests automatically, upon any code check-in, is a major quality improvement step. No one can test each and every possibility and regression and special cases from months or maybe years ago. It's true in software code, and it's the same in infrastructure code as well. Let's find an elegant and automated way to execute our infrastructure code tests in CI systematically so this could be another dot connected to the bigger map.

Getting ready

To step through this recipe, you will need:

- A working Docker installation
- A free Travis CI account

How to do it...

We'd like our RSpec integration tests to be executed automatically each time we commit a change on Git. This is the perfect job for a CI system, such as Jenkins, the Circle CI, or the Travis CI. Our only requirement is that the CI platform should build and execute Docker containers and run RSpec tests. Docker support is good with Travis, and it works out of the box. Jenkins would work equally well behind the firewall when properly configured, like most other CI systems. Here's how to configure our CI platform to automatically execute tests on a new commit:

1. Create a free account for the Travis CI or use your own (`https://travis-ci.org/`).

2. Click on the **+** button to add a new GitHub repository:

3. Enable the watching of the repository by Travis:

4. Now add a configuration file for Travis named `.travis.yml` at the root of the repository. This file can contain a lot of information to do many things, but for now, it should simply tell Travis that we need a Ruby environment in a recent Linux distribution running Docker. Also, it should simply execute `make test` for `Makefile`. In our case, this command will execute the RSpec tests:

```
sudo: required
language: ruby
dist: trusty
services:
  - docker
script: make test
```

5. Commit and push this file and it will trigger our first test on Travis:

```
$ git add .travis.yml
$ git commit -m "added travis.yml"
$ git push
```

6. Navigating back to the Travis CI, we can see the tests begin:

7. A few seconds later, the tests pass successfully, assuring us the build is consistent with our expectations. Travis even gives easy access to the output of the commands:

```
271  $ make test                                                    19:87s
272  bundle exec rspec --color --format documentation
273
274  Docker NGINX image
275    installs Debian Jessie
276    Package "nginx"
277      should be installed
278    Running the NGINX container
279      Process "nginx"
280        should be running
281
282  Finished in 19.16 seconds (files took 0.29136 seconds to load)
283  3 examples, 0 failures
284
285
286
287  The command "make test" exited with 0.
288
289  Done. Your build exited with 0.
                                                                    Top ▲
```

We just initiated new steps for integrating automated tests in our workflow. This is getting increasingly important as every project or team grows, and it's getting riskier to ship untested containers into production.

 It's also highly recommended that you include any other test that can be done in this CI system, such as the Docker linters check from earlier in this book. Quality can only go higher: the more the checks, the better. Building quicker tests for a faster feedback loop will then be a new subject.

As with every CI system, the final step after the tests are completed is to package, ship, and deploy the containers. As exciting as this step is, it's also unfortunately far beyond the scope of this book.

Scanning for vulnerabilities with Quay.io and Docker Cloud

One major issue when working with containers is their deprecation and maintenance costs. Too often, containers are built one day, shipped to production because they work, and forgotten there until the next rebuild (which may not happen anytime soon). Libraries are still libraries, and security fixes are pushed every day into distributions package repositories. Sysadmins are used to patch the systems; however, now it's a total anti-pattern to update a running container. Containers need to be rebuilt, exactly like developers are used to rebuilding applications with updated libraries to get rid of bugged code. The exception is that we are lucky enough to have tools that monitor each and every layer of our Docker images and tell us how and when they are vulnerable, allowing us to simply rebuild and redeploy them.

Getting ready

To step through this recipe, you will need:

- A working Docker installation
- A free account at Quay.io and/or a paid account at the Docker Hub

How to do it...

Using the free Quay.io account (by the CoreOS team), push an image to their Docker Registry service after logging in using `docker login`. Here's how to do this using an earlier image from this chapter:

```
$ docker tag sjourdan/nginx-docker-demo:1.0 quay.io/sjourdan/nginx-docker-demo:1.0

$ docker push quay.io/sjourdan/nginx-docker-demo:1.0

The push refers to a repository [quay.io/sjourdan/nginx-docker-demo]

82819c620e5d: Pushed

d07a4f6d2067: Pushed
```

Quay.io has a very nice security feature: as Docker stores passwords in plain text on the local workstation, it's possible to generate an encrypted password from the **settings** tab of your Quay.io account not only for Docker use, but also for Kubernetes, rkt, or Mesos. It's a much better option to use this encrypted password to log in to the service.

After a while, in the **Repository Tags** tab of our image, we'll get a **SECURITY SCAN** summary:

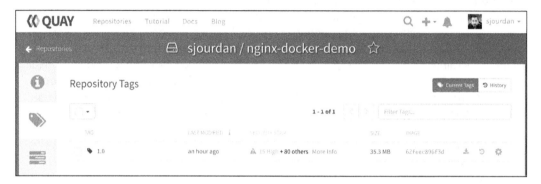

In this example, we have issues to investigate further:

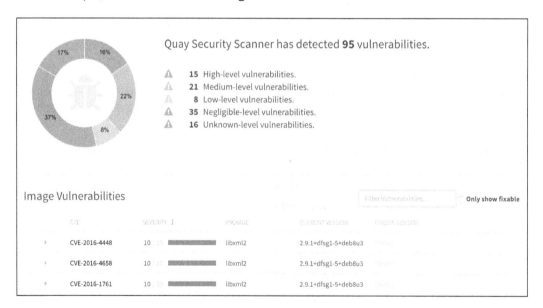

Many vulnerabilities are displayed, but don't be frightened. In fact, none are fixable in our case (click on **Only show fixable** to see what you can do). The reasons are multiple, such as no fix is available currently, the vulnerability doesn't concern the platform we're running on, and so on.

Here's a screenshot of a really vulnerable container and the Quay.io scanner giving helpful advice on the available fixes:

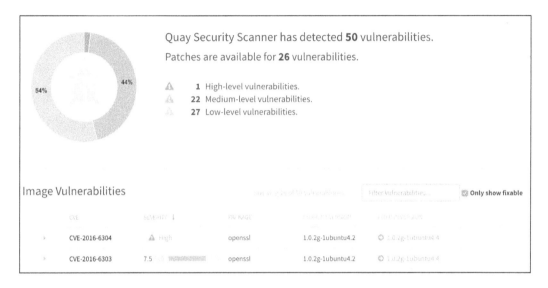

Quay.io Security Scanner will also send reminders by e-mail with a summary of the vulnerabilities found on all the containers it hosts on our account. So we don't have to worry too much about missing out on important security issues.

Using Docker Security Scanning

There's a similar feature on the Docker Hub that uses a paid account, though still in preview at the time of this writing. By default, Docker Security Scanning is not activated, so we have to navigate to the billing tab of the account's interface and tick it to enable it:

Monitor with Docker Security Scanning - available for your private repositories for free while in preview.

From now on, when a new Docker image is created or pushed, the system will scan it quickly and report issues, tag by tag. To access the report summary, just click on the **Tag** tab:

To see details (and the corresponding vulnerabilities), click on the tag number:

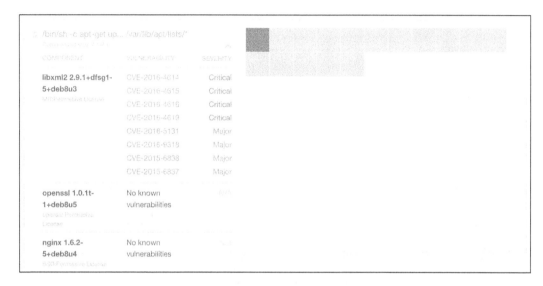

This layer has clear issues! But don't follow this blindly and double-check the said vulnerabilities. All the critical issues in this example only concern Apple platforms and we're running Linux containers.

How it works...

Under the hood, the Quay Security Scanner is based on Clair. Clair is an open source static analysis vulnerability scanner by CoreOS that we can run ourselves or build tools upon. It currently handles Debian, Ubuntu, Alpine, Oracle, and Red Hat security data sources. It gives access to a simple API. Our custom tool can send each Docker image layer we're interested in and get the corresponding vulnerabilities or fixes.

See also

▸ CoreOS Clair at `https://github.com/coreos/clair/`

Sending Docker logs to AWS CloudWatch logs

When we run dozens or hundreds of containers in production, hopefully on a clustered container platform, it soon becomes difficult and tedious to read, search, and process logs—just like it was before when containers with services ran on dozens or hundreds of physical or virtual servers. The problem is that traditional solutions don't work out of the box to handle Docker logs. Luckily, AWS has a nice and easy log-aggregating service, named AWS CloudWatch. Docker has a logging driver just for it. We'll send our Tomcat logs to it right away!

Getting ready

To step through this recipe, you will need:

▸ A working Docker installation

▸ An AWS account

How to do it...

To use AWS CloudWatch Logs, we need at least one **log group**. Use this book's chapter on Terraform code to create a CloudWatch Logs group and a dedicated IAM user, or manually create both.

 As always, with AWS, it's highly recommended that you use a dedicated IAM user for each AWS key pair we'll use. In our case, we can associate the prebuilt IAM policy, named CloudWatchLogsFullAccess, with a new dedicated user in order to be up and running quickly in a secured way.

The Docker daemon needs to run with the AWS credentials in the memory—it's not information we pass to containers, as it's handled by the Docker daemon's log driver. To give the Docker daemon access to the keys we created, let's create an added `systemd` configuration file for the Docker service in `/etc/systemd/system/docker.service.d/aws.conf`:

```
[Service]
Environment="AWS_ACCESS_KEY_ID=AKIAJ..."
Environment="AWS_SECRET_ACCESS_KEY=SW+jdHKd.."
```

Don't forget to reload the `systemd` daemon and restart Docker to apply the changes:

```
$ sudo systemctl daemon-reload
$ sudo systemctl restart docker
```

We're now ready to talk to the AWS APIs through the Docker daemon.

Using the Docker run

Here's a simple way to execute the Tomcat 9 container that uses the `awslogs` driver. Utilize the CloudWatch log group named `docker_logs` on the `us-east-1` data center and automatically create a new stream named `www`:

```
$ sudo docker run -d -p 80:8080 --log-driver="awslogs" --log-opt
awslogs-region="us-east-1" --log-opt awslogs-group="docker_logs" --
log-opt awslogs-stream="www" tomcat:9
```

Navigating over the AWS Console, the new log stream will appear under **Search Log Group**:

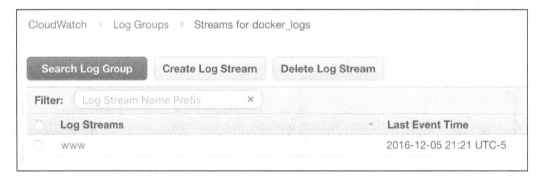

Clicking on the log stream name will give us access to all the output logs from our Tomcat container:

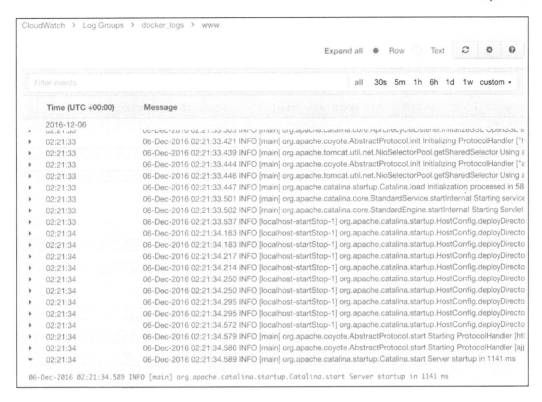

We now have access to unlimited log storage and search features, and the amount of effort we put was very limited!

Using docker-compose

It's also possible to configure the logging driver using Docker Compose. Here's how it works with creating a log stream named `tomcat` under the same log group in `docker-compose.yml`:

```
version: '2'

services:
  tomcat:
    image: tomcat:9
    logging:
      driver: 'awslogs'
      options:
        awslogs-region: 'us-east-1'
        awslogs-group: 'docker_logs'
        awslogs-stream: 'tomcat'
```

Launch the compose as usual:

```
$ sudo docker-compose up
Creating network "ubuntu_default" with the default driver
[...]
tomcat_1   | WARNING: no logs are available with the 'awslogs' log
driver
```

The `tomcat` CloudWatch log stream is now automatically created and the logs flow into it.

Using systemd

Another useful way to launch containers is through the use of systemd. Here's how to create a dynamically named log stream using the systemd unit name (in this case, `tomcat.service`). This is useful on platforms that use multiple instances of the same container to let them all send their logs separately. Here's a working Tomcat systemd service that is running Docker and sending the logs to a dynamically allocated stream name in `/etc/systemd/system/tomcat.service`:

```
[Unit]
Description=Tomcat Container Service
After=docker.service

[Service]
TimeoutStartSec=0
Restart=always
ExecStartPre=/usr/bin/docker pull tomcat:9
ExecStartPre=-/usr/bin/docker kill %n
ExecStartPre=-/usr/bin/docker rm %n
ExecStart=/usr/bin/docker run --rm -p 80:8080 --log-driver=awslogs
--log-opt awslogs-region=us-east-1 --log-opt awslogs-
group=docker_logs --log-opt awslogs-stream=%n --name %n tomcat:9
ExecStop=/usr/bin/docker stop %n

[Install]
WantedBy=multi-user.target
```

Reload systemd and start the `tomcat` unit:

```
$ sudo systemctl daemon-reload
$ sudo systemctl start tomcat
```

Now a third log stream is created with the service name, with the systemd unit logs streaming into it:

Enjoy a centralized and powerful way of storing and accessing logs before you eventually process them!

There's more...

The Docker daemon can stream logs not only to AWS, but also to the more common syslog. This enables a lot of options (such as having traditional `rsyslog` setups and online services compatible with the traditional format). Similarly, it not only sends the logs to `journald`, but also supports the Graylog or Logstash GELF log format. The Fluentd unified logging layer is also supported, while on the platform front, we find support for Splunk and Google Cloud together with AWS CloudWatch logs.

Monitoring and getting information out of Docker

It's often important to get some quick and useful information out of our Docker system when weird problems arise or strange issues start to cripple our performance. What's going on in the system? Is there a container taking up all of the memory? Maybe one minor container just crashed and is eating up all of the CPU. All of this information shouldn't be hard to get, but they are precious for building quality containers. We'll see two tools quite fit for the job: the first one is simply the one shipped with Docker itself, and the second one is a totally different tool by Google named cAdvisor—a web user interface with a lot of useful and easy-to-get information.

Getting ready

To step through this recipe, you will need:

▶ A working Docker installation

How to do it...

There's a few ways to get information out of Docker. We'll explore the first one through the main Docker program.

Using docker stats

To get live metrics about the running containers (CPU, memory, and network), we can use the simple `docker stats` command:

```
$ docker stats

CONTAINER            CPU %               MEM USAGE / LIMIT      MEM %
NET I/O              BLOCK I/O              PIDS

c2904d5b5c89         0.01%               892.9 MB / 8.326 GB    10.72%
258.2 GB / 10.27 GB  374 MB / 0 B         16

0641790f1b30         3.36%               894.4 MB / 8.326 GB    10.74%
258.2 GB / 11.12 GB  419.1 MB / 0 B       16

bc8d85e05be8         112.65%             891.4 MB / 8.326 GB    10.71%
179.6 GB / 536.5 GB  326.6 MB / 0 B       10

a7be664792b3         0.02%               45.37 MB / 8.326 GB    0.54%
17.85 GB / 17.72 GB  18.78 MB / 110.6 kB  18

ab2d4e922949         2.37%               70.34 MB / 8.326 GB    0.84%
83.15 MB / 550 MB    459.7 MB / 143.4 kB  17

08e685124dfd         0.01%               192 MB / 8.326 GB      2.31%
8.76 MB / 42.11 MB   1.499 MB / 14.05 MB  3

5893c5d6f43f         0.74%               546.1 MB / 8.326 GB    6.56%
46.74 MB / 40.22 MB  160.7 MB / 317.9 MB  74

7f21e405bdee         5.23%               8.184 MB / 8.326 GB    0.10%
30.14 GB / 30.28 GB  8.192 kB / 0 B       7
```

It's, however, not overwhelmingly helpful as it's using containers' IDs and not names, and when running many containers, it can start becoming useless because it would be unreadable. So we can use a trick: ask the stats (`docker stats`) of all the running containers (`docker ps`) whose names we extracted using a Go template formatter (`--format`):

```
$ docker stats $(docker ps --format '{{.Names}}')

CONTAINER                 CPU %               MEM USAGE / LIMIT
MEM %                NET I/O              BLOCK I/O             PIDS

sm_streammachine-slave_2  18.34%                889.4 MB / 8.326 GB
10.68%               258.2 GB / 10.27 GB  374 MB / 0 B           16

sm_streammachine-slave_1  28.39%                900.1 MB / 8.326 GB
10.81%               258.2 GB / 11.12 GB  419.1 MB / 0 B         16
```

```
sm_streammachine-master_1     1.89%                     890.4 MB / 8.326 GB
10.69%                179.6 GB / 536.5 GB   326.6 MB / 0 B          10

sm_proxy_1                    0.02%                     45.37 MB / 8.326 GB
0.54%                 17.85 GB / 17.72 GB   18.78 MB / 110.6 kB    18

sm_cadvisor_1                 1.62%                     70.34 MB / 8.326 GB
0.84%                 83.16 MB / 550 MB     459.7 MB / 143.4 kB    17

sm_analytics_1                0.01%                     192 MB / 8.326 GB
2.31%                 8.76 MB / 42.11 MB    1.499 MB / 14.05 MB    3

sm_elasticsearch_1            0.72%                     546.1 MB / 8.326 GB
6.56%                 46.74 MB / 40.22 MB   160.7 MB / 317.9 MB    74

sm_streamer_1                 8.17%                     8.184 MB / 8.326 GB
0.10%                 30.15 GB / 30.29 GB   8.192 kB / 0 B          7
```

Using Google's cAdvisor tool

Google created a nice web tool to see what's going on in machines that run containers: **cAdvisor**. It collects, organizes, and displays metrics about resource usage, container by container, on a given host. Though not interactive, it's still powerful enough, given how easy it is to install and use. To install and use it, simply run the cAdvisor Docker image with volume access to all of the required system information, such as the following:

```
$ sudo docker run \
  --volume=/:/rootfs:ro \
  --volume=/var/run:/var/run:rw \
  --volume=/sys:/sys:ro \
  --volume=/var/lib/docker/:/var/lib/docker:ro \
  --publish=8080:8080 \
  --detach=true \
  --name=cadvisor \
  google/cadvisor:latest
```

Or, if using `docker-compose`:

```
cadvisor:
  volumes:
    - /:/rootfs:ro
    - /var/run:/var/run:rw
    - /sys:/sys:ro
    - /var/lib/docker/:/var/lib/docker:ro
  ports:
    - "8080:8080"
  image: google/cadvisor:latest
  restart: always
```

Navigating to the host's `8080` port (or whatever port you choose to publish) with a web browser will present a web interface where we can navigate and see graphical information about container usage on the host:

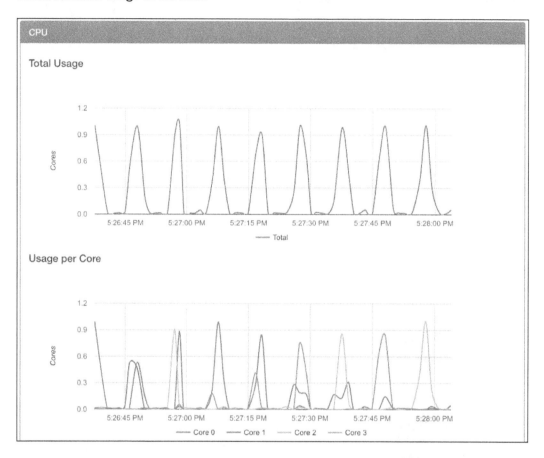

Or, we may have more general gauges giving live indication of resource usage:

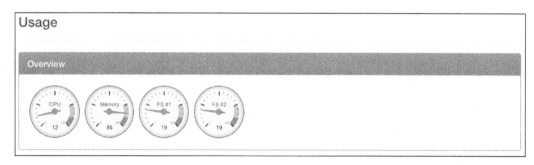

A very useful process table with top-like data from the underlying host is also available with a container-aware context. All of these pieces of data are browsable and they help you gain more in-depth information about a specific container and its content and usage:

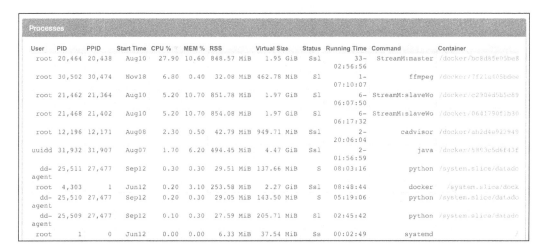

User	PID	PPID	Start Time	CPU %	MEM %	RSS	Virtual Size	Status	Running Time	Command	Container
root	20,464	20,438	Aug10	27.90	10.60	848.57 MiB	1.95 GiB	Ssl	33-02:56:56	StreamM:master	/docker/bc8d65e05be8
root	30,502	30,474	Nov18	6.80	0.40	32.08 MiB	462.78 MiB	Sl	1-07:10:07	ffmpeg	/docker/7f21a405bdee
root	21,462	21,364	Aug10	5.20	10.70	851.78 MiB	1.97 GiB	Sl	6-06:07:50	StreamM:slaveWo	/docker/c2904d5b5c89
root	21,468	21,402	Aug10	5.20	10.70	854.08 MiB	1.97 GiB	Sl	6-06:17:32	StreamM:slaveWo	/docker/0641790f1b30
root	12,196	12,171	Aug08	2.30	0.50	42.79 MiB	949.71 MiB	Ssl	2-20:06:04	cadvisor	/docker/ab2d4e922949
uuidd	31,932	31,907	Aug07	1.70	6.20	494.45 MiB	4.47 GiB	Ssl	2-01:56:59	java	/docker/5893c5d6f43f
dd-agent	25,511	27,477	Sep12	0.30	0.30	29.51 MiB	137.66 MiB	S	08:03:16	python	/system.slice/datado
root	4,303	1	Jun12	0.20	3.10	253.58 MiB	2.27 GiB	Ssl	08:48:44	docker	/system.slice/dock
dd-agent	25,510	27,477	Sep12	0.20	0.30	29.05 MiB	143.50 MiB	S	05:19:06	python	/system.slice/datado
dd-agent	25,509	27,477	Sep12	0.10	0.30	27.59 MiB	205.71 MiB	Sl	02:45:42	python	/system.slice/datado
root	1	0	Jun12	0.00	0.00	6.33 MiB	37.54 MiB	Ss	00:02:49	systemd	/

cAdvisor can also be plugged in to many backend storage systems, such as Prometheus, ElasticSearch, InfluxDB, Redis, statsD, and so on.

> If you plan to let cAdvisor run permanently, it is a good idea to restrict access using simple HTTP authentication. This is supported out of the box by cAdvisor using `--http_auth_file /cadvisor.htpasswd --http_auth_realm my_message`.

See also

▶ cAdvisor GitHub at `https://github.com/google/cadvisor`

▶ cAdvisor storage backends at `https://github.com/google/cadvisor/blob/master/docs/storage/README.md`

Debugging containers using sysdig

Sysdig is an awesome tool that can be used for many purposes, including monitoring, logging, process debugging, network analyzing, and exploring a system in depth. Plus, it includes fantastic Linux container support. It's also scriptable and can be fed with recorded real traffic packet captures for offline analysis. It's an incredible tool that each and every person working with containers should at least know the basics of, and as infrastructure developers used to working with code, we know how important debugging tools are. This is no different with sysdig, and we'll now discover some of its fantastic features related to containers.

Getting ready

To step through this recipe, you will need:

- A working Docker installation
- Sysdig installed and running on the host

How to do it...

Installing sysdig is easy on most platforms, including CoreOS (`http://www.sysdig.org/install/`). However, if you're in a hurry, here's a one liner that will do the job of installing Sysdig on your Linux host. We'd probably choose a better way to deploy it programmatically though, such as Ansible or Chef, through a Docker container or not:

```
$ curl -s
https://s3.amazonaws.com/download.draios.com/stable/install-sysdig |
sudo bash
```

Here's how to get an htop-like view of all the running containers on the system:

```
$ sudo csysdig --view=containers
```

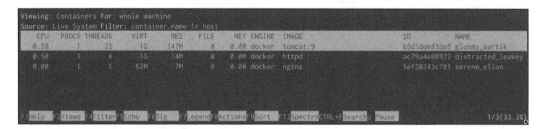

Navigating to the **F2/Views** menu helps you enter many different options to see what's running, from processes to syslog to open files and even the Kubernetes, Marathon, or Mesos integration. Want to see which container is draining all of the IO? You're at the right place:

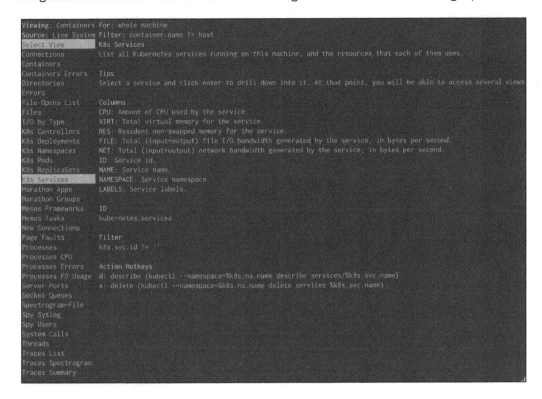

Here's an example of a Tomcat container with a view of all the local and remote connections, IPs, ports, protocols, bandwidth, IOs, and the corresponding commands—terribly useful to find suspicious behavior:

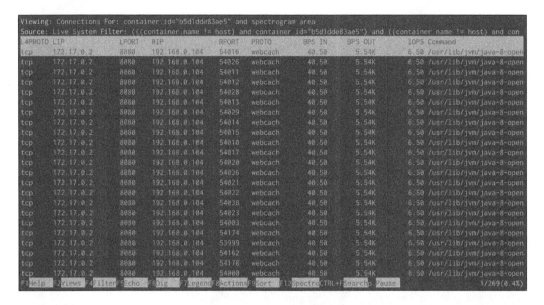

Another useful tool is `F5/Echo`, grabbing what's transiting on this container: (un)encrypted content, logs, output, and more. This is also very useful to maybe catch something wrong with a container acting weird:

```
Viewing: I/O activity For: container.id=b5d1dde83ae5
Source: Live System Filter: (container.name != host) and container.id=b5d1dde83ae5

192.168.0.104 - - [06/Dec/2016:23:56:50 +0000] "GET / HTTP/1.0" 200 11236
192.168.0.104 - - [06/Dec/2016:23:56:50 +0000] "GET / HTTP/1.0" 200 11236
192.168.0.104 - - [06/Dec/2016:23:56:50 +0000] "GET / HTTP/1.0" 200 11236
192.168.0.104 - - [06/Dec/2016:23:56:50 +0000] "GET / HTTP/1.0" 200 11236
192.168.0.104 - - [06/Dec/2016:23:56:50 +0000] "GET / HTTP/1.0" 200 11236
192.168.0.104 - - [06/Dec/2016:23:56:50 +0000] "GET / HTTP/1.0" 200 11236
192.168.0.104 - - [06/Dec/2016:23:56:50 +0000] "GET / HTTP/1.0" 200 11236
192.168.0.104 - - [06/Dec/2016:23:56:50 +0000] "GET / HTTP/1.0" 200 11236
192.168.0.104 - - [06/Dec/2016:23:56:50 +0000] "GET / HTTP/1.0" 200 11236
192.168.0.104 - - [06/Dec/2016:23:56:50 +0000] "GET / HTTP/1.0" 200 11236
192.168.0.104 - - [06/Dec/2016:23:56:50 +0000] "GET / HTTP/1.0" 200 11236
192.168.0.104 - - [06/Dec/2016:23:56:50 +0000] "GET / HTTP/1.0" 200 11236
192.168.0.104 - - [06/Dec/2016:23:56:50 +0000] "GET / HTTP/1.0" 200 11236
192.168.0.104 - - [06/Dec/2016:23:56:50 +0000] "GET / HTTP/1.0" 200 11236
192.168.0.104 - - [06/Dec/2016:23:56:50 +0000] "GET / HTTP/1.0" 200 11236
192.168.0.104 - - [06/Dec/2016:23:56:50 +0000] "GET / HTTP/1.0" 200 11236
192.168.0.104 - - [06/Dec/2016:23:56:50 +0000] "GET / HTTP/1.0" 200 11236
192.168.0.104 - - [06/Dec/2016:23:56:50 +0000] "GET / HTTP/1.0" 200 11236
192.168.0.104 - - [06/Dec/2016:23:56:50 +0000] "GET / HTTP/1.0" 200 11236
19
F1Help  F2View As CTRL+FSearch  Pause BakBack  c Clear CTRL+GGoto                    0/2(0.0%)
```

Another very powerful tool from sysdig is `F6`/`Dig`. This basically offers nothing less than a full-fledged `strace` for a container; imagine the debugging power it has:

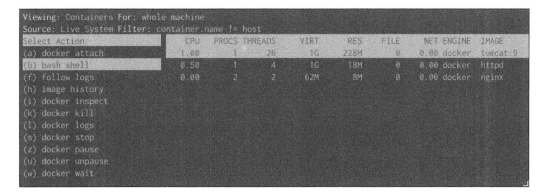

The `F8`/`Actions` feature is a full Docker command integration tool available right from inside sysdig. Select a container and we'll be able to enter it, read logs, see its image history, kill it, and more:

Those commands are also always available right from the main interface: want to gain a shell on this selected container? Just type `b`.

These are just a few of the many powerful things we can do with Sysdig using Docker containers.

See also

- ▸ More general sysdig usage examples at `http://www.sysdig.org/wiki/sysdig-examples/`

Index